Voyage Through the Past Century

Voyage Through the Past Century

Rolf Knight

NEW STAR BOOKS • VANCOUVER • 2013

NEW STAR BOOKS LTD.

107 – 3477 Commercial Street | Vancouver, BC V5N 4E8   CANADA
1574 Gulf Road, #1517 | Point Roberts, WA 98281   USA
www.NewStarBooks.com | info@NewStarBooks.com

The publisher acknowledges the financial support of the Canada Council for the Arts, the Government of Canada through the Canada Book Fund, the British Columbia Arts Council, and the Government of British Columbia through the Book Publishing Tax Credit.

Cataloguing information for this book is available from Library and Archives Canada, www.collectionscanada.gc.ca.

Cover design by Oliver McPartlin
Printed on 100% post-consumer recycled paper.
Printed and bound in Canada by Imprimerie Gauvin, Gatineau, QC
First printing, April 2013

Contents

To the past librarians of the Vancouver Public Library who acquired and retained the books which educated me about the world.

A Reflective Introduction

While this book is an autobiography I have attempted to write it with some degree of anthropological engagement, at least to the extent that there is as much discussion of places and other people over a forty-six year span than there is about my own doings. This account runs from the early 1940s to 1988. The latter date stems from a discussion I had with historian Keith Ralston who mentioned a British Tory cabinet minister of the 1930s who wrote an autobiography entitled *Old Men Forget*. It seemed to me an apt warning; I was then fifty-two years old and somehow didn't think I'd live much longer or retain the acuity of memory that I then still had. Fortunately I did write this account then because after a stroke shortly before my 70th birthday it would have been impossible for me to remember what I once did.

This story covers a period of great change in the world but during which my own role was mainly that of an observer. Occasionally I have alluded to some of my changing viewpoints over time, but usually I present events as I understood them as they happened. The year 1988 wasn't the end of my writing career. I published two books in the 1990s and wrote three unpublished works after the year 2000. However, most of the reminiscences presented here still ring true to me today, twenty-four years later.

There have been some fundamental social changes in the world over the last quarter century during which an entire generation has grown into adulthood. We have witnessed the worldwide destruction of socialism and communism, the goal of so many political activists for more than a century — now gone except for the unrealistic hopes of a few. This victory/defeat has had an impact on many facets of life throughout the world, some of which are only now becoming evident.

In North America the steady shift to the right is seemingly all-encompassing and unstoppable. However, we might remember the explosive emergence of quite radical re-analyses and a massive opposition to the state in America during the 1960s. That emerged from a background in which a broad-based McCarthyism held sway almost everywhere. Witnessing that change was both amazing and heartening for a Canadian to experience. Could something like that develop again? I would hope so but doubt that it ever will.

Whereas Canada once seemed capable of maintaining an independent stance in the world, since the end of the Trudeau era our nation has progressively become a Quisling-led bum boy to the Americans. The provision of oil and other resources, the emergence of unchecked free trade, the provision of Canadian soldiers for American adventures abroad have become almost automatic for Canadian governments. We are evolving into an unchecked free-enterprise state with potentially devastating consequences for ordinary people in Canada.

One reader's response to an earlier, privately printed edition of this autobiography has been to take offense at my portrayal of school days in East Vancouver during the 1940s, a feeling that I have been insufficiently appreciative of those trying to civilize and educate us. On reconsideration I would only underline what is said here. Fortunately this didn't apply to my time at Britannia High School, which happily had no school spirit whatsoever and which let its students develop in whatever ways they would, a quality which I only later came to appreciate.

This and my earlier books deal with mainly nameless individuals and now generally forgotten undertakings, some of which however still have my personal allegiance. You will have to read this book to discover who and what these are.

There are some major gaps in this account: a general absence of discussion about family relations, a silence about various love affairs and so forth. Such have been the themes for some sagacious books but I do not feel that I have anything useful to add to them and instead discuss my various work experiences and my observations of various parts of the world during the period dealt with.

I have probably given myself more appropriate sentiments and more coherent views than I am in fact entitled to. However the events and locales recorded here remain as I remember them, presented with whatever insight and veracity I possess.

Life histories have a fairly long tradition in anthropology and autobiographies, a much longer one in writing. Nevertheless many academics are convinced of the unreliability if not outright lies contained in such work, to say nothing of their derogation of the alleged self-seeking they see hidden in them. However I have found life histories to often be at least as cogent as many more scholarly works. But if you detest such accounts then you shouldn't be reading this book.

In retrospect it would seem that writing was the single endeavor which I ever found to be truly fulfilling and through which I ever contributed anything worthwhile.

Finally, I have not fundamentally changed what I believed about the world and the forces in it. I am still a socialist and will remain so regardless of the worldwide defeats, treachery and retreats imposed by the forces of reaction. So be it.

Rolf Knight
Vancouver
February 2012

ONE

Waiting for the Morning Boat

Allison's Camp and Musketeer Mine

My early memories are like a batch of old photos which have gotten stuck away in a suitcase without rhyme or reason. Some are faded while others are still vibrantly clear. What some of them mean are a puzzle to me.

Images are what I remember most vividly. Of the work trains loaded with logs which came straight through the middle of the camp, past the bunkhouses and past the cookhouse where we lived, heading for the log spill a half mile away. It's a disconnected collage but individual scenes are still clear enough. Allison's camp on Cumshewa Inlet in the then far distant Queen Charlotte Islands during the first year of the Second World War. A railway logging camp with about a hundred men, two women and one child. We lived there for a year when I was between the ages of four and five and my first memories are rooted there.

Mainly they are non-verbal. Smells — of fresh-cut cedar and oil and salty tidal beach. Sounds. The ting-tang of a saw-filer working. It is amazing what comes flooding back if you allow memory free reign.

The cookhouse with our sleeping room in the back was anchored to the edge of the railway grade and built on pilings out over the mud-sand beach. I'd wake up in my cot in the morning, rub the sleep out

The author, in a photo taken at Musketeer Mine in 1941.

of my eyes and blink out over the water of the bay. "What kind of rain clouds today?" Looking up the channel I'd see cloud formations rolling along and the sea either calm or choppy or disappearing in a wind blown curtain of rain and mist. Occasionally there might even be sunshine. Yawning and stretching I surveyed the new day through the window. If the tide was in an edge of the sea lapped a few feet below the floorboards of the room. What more could you want to wake up to — wind, forest, sea and a steam locomotive huffing past the front door.

There were Ali and Phyllis, my father and mother — he was the cook and she was the lunchman — and me. There was Bruno the baker and a couple of elderly men who worked in the cookhouse. We'd sit down and eat together after the camp crew had been fed. After breakfast I'd be buttoned up in a rain slicker, stuck into gumboots and sent out to play. "Remember now," was the daily repeated warning, "Stay off the tracks. Before you cross them look both ways first and if you even see a train stay well away from the tracks till it's passed . . . Like I showed you. Stay away from the water except for the beach. You know where. Don't wander into the forest. And above all, stay away from any machinery. It doesn't matter if it's working or not."

I wasn't sure what "machinery" constituted, really. Donkey engines, certainly. But what about rail switches? The actual logging and yard-ing operations were a dozen miles up the track and I never came in contact with any of that. But there was enough work going on around camp.

"Alright. Now where are you going to go and what are you going to do?" Phyllis would ask. Naturally I wouldn't have the slightest idea.

"Oh, I'll just go down to the beach and collect some shells." That seemed to be a satisfactory answer no matter where I went.

I'd wander along the shore, one stretch of beach about as uninteresting as the next. All those fascinating things you find washed up on the shore or scrabbling around in tidal pools aren't so interesting if you have no one to show them to. I might wander around the bunkhouses and tag along after the bull cook as he cleaned up and got the stove wood in. Maybe there was somebody laid up with a minor injury or who'd quit or been fired and was waiting for the boat to take him out. The yearling deer which had attached itself to the cookhouse towered above me and was too skittish to play with. Though I'm not sure I really knew it, I was lonely. Living in camps seemed to be the normal way of things but it was just not quite right that there were never any other children around.

It must have been a terrible life for my parents. Both of them worked from morning till night, seven days a week. They might get a break for an hour or two in the afternoon on the rare day when everything went smoothly. But for the first time in their lives they were earning enough to save toward buying a house in town. Naturally I didn't then understand what their lives had been and what had brought them here.

A kid in a logging camp was something of a novelty. You were like a mascot, almost as smart as a dog in some ways. Some men would watch out for you but others would give you a bite of plug tobacco which they said was licorice. Very funny. The crew ranged from teenagers to guys who had their own families and kids stashed away in town or on a farm somewhere. Some loggers might talk to me after work or, if a couple of them were in a good mood, might even toss me up in a blanket. That's how I got my collar bone broken; being tossed up in the air and landing on the edge of a steel cot

The break didn't heal properly so finally Phyllis took me down to a doctor in Vancouver and I wound up staying with a couple who had a small farm in North Burnaby. They were friends from the time my parents had washed gold in the Cariboo. My mother hurried back to Allison's camp and I stayed behind, feeling totally abandoned. It must have been hard for her to make that decision but I suppose she was afraid of what else might happen to me around a logging camp. Luckily, most children are both adaptable and as tough as nails.

I came to enjoy having other kids around to play with. But that didn't last very long because a few months later my parents were fired from Allison's and we moved to an old bunkhouse on Beach Avenue, then an out-of-the-way enclave on the city's industrial waterfront.

The Beach Avenue coolie cabins. That would be in early 1941. Our place was on the second floor, second room from the alley. An external wooden walkway connected the string of rooms and I'd sit there beside our open door, back propped against the siding, watching the activity down below around the woodsheds and along the street. Watching people coming and going or following the patterns etched by shifting beams of spring sun and cloud on the small workshops and spidery wharves of False Creek.

I don't know how my parents felt about the place. For them the Beach Avenue cabins probably were just a continuation of the hand-to-mouth existence they had lived during the ten previous years. But I liked it. It was the first place where I felt at home amid our unpredictable comings and goings.

When I was growing up many of our friends were single men who worked in the camps or couples who had emigrated to Canada during the same period my parents had. People who had ridden the freights, camp workers, Peace River homesteaders, prospectors, seamen and jacks of all trades. They were the only kin we had.

Grace Turnbull and her three kids lived next door to us and I'd mosey back and forth during the course of the day. Ebe Koeppen and Hilda would drop by and Ebe might put me on his shoulders as we all went down to Sunset Beach, a wild grassy stretch a few blocks away where you could bring dogs, make fires and have picnics. Hans Stiegelbauer would drop by occasionally when he was in town from one of his prospecting trips. He looked awfully wizened but must have had more stamina than it appeared. Once in a while he would pull some stunt which would make Ali shake his head and mutter, "Hans has really gotten bushed now." But it was all part of the family.

We left Beach Avenue to go up to Musketeer Mine. It was dark, I had a toothache and was howling at having to leave our home. Phyllis was flustered. But there was nothing for it.

Musketeer Mine was on the west coast of Vancouver Island, a mining camp of about sixty men. We took the CPR ferry over to Victoria and waited there to catch the *Maquinna* for her weekly run up the west coast of the Island. At Tofino we waited overnight and the next day boarded a chartered fishing boat up to the head of Bedwell Sound, where the beach depot for a number of fly-by-night mines was located. The last stretch was by truck over a twisting track up the Urus river. By the time we left Musketeer that road had long since been washed out and they had gone back to using a string of pack horses to bring in the supplies.

My more or less continuous memories begin in Musketeer Mine. In one of the snapshots I see Patsy and me together, me sitting on a blasted stump with my gumboots on, looking . . . it's difficult to say how. Cheerfully bewildered? She was my best friend there. That may be too sentimental — but I did like her better than a lot of people I knew.

A boy and his dog amid the unspoiled nature of the Pacific west coast? No! It wasn't idyllic at all. Actually, there weren't many places I could go as a five and six year old. The surrounding forest was like a jungle — it is a rain forest jungle. Dark, impenetrable, forbidding. "Never go out of sight of the buildings. Do you understand that ?" Phyllis intoned. Going down the road a half mile one came to a log bridge across the Urus River. Occasionally, when they had a few hours off, my parents would take me down to the sandy river shore on the other side of the bridge but that was definitely taboo if I was alone. Wandering along the seashore is one thing but patrolling the banks of a rushing river is quite another.

My range was a series of work sites, gangue spills and open areas between the cookhouse and the bunkhouses. I remember once "helping" a couple of carpenters by hammering nails into neatly mortised bunks they'd almost finished building. The rest of the crew watched me do it and thought it was a big joke but that kind of helping out got me banned from wherever men were working. They didn't want me tagging along and getting in the way anyway.

Any scrapes I got into as a kid in those camps? Nothing out of the ordinary. Phyllis had a story about how a miner brought me back after he'd found me playing with sticks of waterlogged dynamite I'd found in an old shack. But I don't remember that. Any normal kid will fall out of trees and crack his bones and get himself cut wherever he is.

There's a snapshot of me on the gentlest of the pack horses. I still

remember her name, Anny, but I haven't the vaguest idea of what I was
wondering about then. What I must have felt was a puzzlement about
the world common to all children. What did words actually mean ?
How could there be such a thing as a "bottomless lake"? Could trees
talk in some way? Does earth burn if the fire is hot enough ? What was
"Just in a manner of speaking" and what was for real ? What is alive ?
I had a lot of trouble with that and tended to feel that virtually everything was alive in some way, from machinery to grass to moving water.

There was little of the joyous curiosity which is supposed to inhere
in childhood about all of this. But there were no particular fears either.
Young kids are fearless anyway. They're too dumb to know better.

Probably the only question which worried me was, "What did my
parents have to do and why? What could appear out of the blue from
one day to the next and totally change where and how we lived our
lives ?" I'm almost positive I felt that in some way.

Camps were almost exclusively populated by men who came to work
and live in them for stints of a few months at a time. In some of the
more established logging villages some of the senior employees might
have their wives and pre-school-aged children with them. But usually
not.

At Musketeer Mine the superintendent had his wife with him. They
lived in the cookhouse on the old camp site about a mile up the side of
the mountain. She was a former school teacher and occasionally Phyllis took me up there. The superintendent's wife made a stab at teaching
me to read and write and tried to convey the concept of addition and
subtraction with a row of empty beer bottles. The idea of squiggles on
paper standing for sounds and words seemed clear enough but what
a changing array of beer bottles was supposed to signify was beyond
me.

Sometimes at night, in that big loft above the kitchen where we lived,
after the coal oil lamp was snuffed out and my parents were in their
bed by the window and I in the cot beside the chimney, Phyllis might
hold a flashlight and Ali would make hand shadows on the ceiling to
accompany some story he made up. These involved tales which could
have been taken from Till Eulenspiegel and probably were. But I once
overheard my mother whispering to my father when they thought
I was asleep. "There are supposed to be over a million dead since it
began. Oh god in heaven." (They were both confirmed atheists who
would have considered god an inhuman fiend had he existed.) "Is

The crew heading into the cookshack for supper at Musketeer Mine, 1941.

that possible? Are any of them going to be left alive if it goes on ?" Of course I don't remember the exact words but the thrust was memorable enough.

"Ah ... just propaganda. They survived everything all these years. They'll survive now too," Ali said. He meant Phyllis's family who already then had lived through twenty years of struggle against and defeat by reaction in Germany.

I didn't understand any of that then but I could sense that Ali didn't know what to say and had the same fears himself. I now know that they were also worried about what might happen to them in Canada. Whether we would be interned. That and whatever other fears crept up on them there, alone in that camp on the edge of nowhere, with the world they'd known being put to the torch.

For Christmas Phyllis got my father a Remington Remette typewriter. An extraordinary luxury. She sent away for it by mail and it came up to Musketeer Mine by steamer, gas boat and packhorse. I can't imagine what she thought Ali was going to do with a typewriter in camp when he didn't even have time to rest let alone write anything. For years I wasn't allowed to touch the machine. Along with the DeForrest shortwave radio it was "not to play with". That typewriter traveled back and forth from BC Collateral pawn shop more than once in the following years. But it was always redeemed.

Just before Christmas I had a run-in with some kitchen knives and almost lost two fingers. My index finger never did straighten out fully. The first aid man stopped the bleeding and applied a swath of bandages. That was all he could do; anyone seriously injured in camps like this was just out of luck. I moped around with my hand in a sling for a while but we only stayed in Musketeeer Mine a month or two longer. I didn't know where we were going but I was happy to leave.

House of the Mountain Ash

A few weeks before my sixth birthday we settled into a shack on Wall Street, on the waterfront of Vancouver East. Our place looked out over the harbour and across Burrard Inlet to the mountains of the North Shore. The house was guarded by seven mountain ash trees and stood on a street half filled with brushy vacant lots. It's the locale I still think of as my childhood home, what Latin Americans call their *patria chica*.

But when we settled down in Vancouver I at first felt very ill at ease with children and didn't quite know what to make of them. I felt more comfortable around adults — at least those we knew.

The nature of the primary resources industries, the particular immigrant experience and the decade-long depression had created a demographic gap. There were relatively few children in parts of Vancouver East and the Downtown Eastside during the mid 1940s. Along two blocks of a residential street, Wall Street, were some twenty family houses. Only three of them contained school-aged children. Among my parents' closest friends were four single camp workers but also five middle-aged immigrant couples. Most of them childless. Those fourteen adults left three children behind them, including myself. The other two are somewhat younger than me, grew up under different conditions and know almost nothing of what is described here. Nor do they want to know.

I was the child in the lives of a number of men and women: former "partners" and workmates and adoptive uncles and aunts. They filled the bill of relatives very well — better than blood kin, I always felt. Maybe that accounts for the feeling of ongoing obligation.

Though I took it for granted then it is surprising how individuals who moved from one job and locale to another could act like an extended family. But they did. We were part of a larger floating community. Our paths crossed in various places and I later wound up working in a camp alongside someone who had once carried me on his shoulders to an outing in Stanley Park. The core was a number of older immigrants and camp workers — German, Irish, Hungarian and others. Those mundane interpersonal loyalties were a triumph of sorts. They gave me, we gave each other, what stability there was in our lives.

Although I never realized it then, there were times when we were desperately poor. I suppose it's a rather clichéd to say that. Ali worked constantly during those years; he didn't drink, smoke, gamble or really buy anything for himself. But sometimes things were very tight. Each spring Phyllis picked and put up batches of stinging nettle tops as a kind of spinach. They have to be gathered when they are young and tender. You blanch them, cook them with bits of bacon and preserve thirty sealers full to eat with potatoes. There were also mason jars filled with wild loganberry or blackberry preserves. We had a lot of that kind of food while I was a kid. Quite nutritious, I suppose.

A good deal of what we ate came out of the backyard garden my mother tended — fresh vegetables from spring to late fall and sealers of produce in the winter. But Phyllis both disliked cooking and was a terrible cook. Maybe that's not fair. Maybe it was those meatless vegetable stews, a taste for which she'd acquired when a child. Since we didn't have a fridge (a screened cooler stood in the shade at the back of the shack) perishables had to be cooked or preserved in short order. Bacon in the form of smoked slabs was good because it kept. Similarly pickled herring and corned beef. Otherwise, Phyllis didn't believe in spices, they supposedly spoiled the natural taste of food.

"But I don't like the natural taste of beans. I like chili peppers."

"Don't be silly. It's much better this way."

At times when there were only a few dollars left in the food budget Phyllis might buy a hog's head down at the farmer's market. They cost twenty-five cents apiece and were lined up on the counters of the butcher stalls, a row of pig's heads staring vacantly down at you. I'd only look at them out of the corner of my eye.

The first thing you do is singe the remaining bristles off over an open flame and then pop the head into a big kettle to boil. Wood-burning stoves are unbeatable for that sort of thing. Ah, no, wait. First you carve off the jowls with a sharp knife. That gives you a pound or two of fatty bacon which you can fry up as a meat base for gravy or render down for schmaltz. Schmaltz blended with fragments of crisped bacon and fried onion spread over fresh rye bread is quite tasty. Phyllis did have a taste for bread and would go six blocks out of her way, or send me, to get the proper kind, especially a Russian sourdough rye which came in semi-spherical loaves from a tiny neighbourhood bakery.

The rest of the hog's head was used for making head cheese. Head cheese was alright but the trouble was that there was so much of it and it had to be eaten up. If there was such a thing as sin, "wasting food" was a cardinal one. It's certainly nothing to be nostalgic about but this was one of a thousand ways by which people then managed their family budgets on the margins of cities like Vancouver.

My parents had grown up under far more difficult conditions than anything I ever remotely encountered. To them, mine was a relatively safe and secure childhood despite life in logging camps and occasional nettle soup. They had survived the once-normal capitalist conditions which carried away so many of the young and old and poor in working-class Germany during the first decades of the twentieth century.

By the time Phyllis was in her late forties she had worked for thirty years, off and on, starting as a thirteen-year-old girl in a Berlin printing shop. She'd worked in heavy industry as a teenager and had lived through a famine and plague of near medieval proportions during the end of the First World War. As a sixteen-year-old girl, the eldest child at home, she'd dodged army and police patrols to scrounge up contraband food to help feed her family. Ali's childhood experiences were different but comparable.

Both of my parents had come of age in a stormy and near apocalyptic epoch. They had been involved in attempts to build a new life within the shell of the old society. Both had careened around Germany during the early twenties as wandering minstrels, burning the candle at both ends at cultural gabfests while in and out of factory work. Their outlook combined elements of utopian socialism, appeals to spontaneity, and an adulation of nature. This was all mixed with an unsubstantiated belief in a fundamental human decency (at least amongst working people) once the corrupting influences of capitalism and the ruling class were stripped away.

All this seems ludicrous to present-day *philosophes*. But the millennial tradition does appear to be a durable part of the human spirit and arises, again and again, in different historical garbs. However, by the time I could understand any of this my parents had consigned much of it to the storehouse of their youthful dreams.

They had immigrated to a semi-colonial Canada at the end of the 1920s and had spent the greater part of the Hungry Thirties pushed from pillar to post, trying to eke out a living by washing gold, working in camps and resorting to whatever catch-as-catch-can stratagems were feasible. Our shack on Wall Street cost about $600 and was paid for by saving from their work in the two camps. After fourteen years in Canada it was the first place they could call home.

Japan's entry into the war unleashed a panic on the Pacific coast. We returned to Vancouver a month or so before the internment of the Japanese-Canadian population, including the family with two boys my age who lived across the street from us. Although I was used to having individuals I knew come and go it was frightening to witness the way in which a family on your block could be made to just disappear.

Even before that happened I felt that something was afoot that could touch all of us, although I didn't know what. Naturally I didn't discuss that with my parents. They tried to shield me from fears they themselves had by not talking about them. It might have been better if they had — though possibly not. My mother told me years later that she feared that the Japanese-Canadian internment could be the prelude to a wider action in which both she and Ali and others might be interned. I think that was what she was surreptitiously preparing me for when she took me to stay with friends and instructed me to do what they said if anything should happen to her and Ali. Strange. I'd forgotten that.

They remained surprisingly resilient through it all. Except to that tide of anti-German racism — there's no other honest term for it — which swirled around us. I only became fully aware of it when I entered school in Vancouver. Phyllis put on a brave front but by the end of the war she was pretty close to a nervous breakdown.

A Garland of Ghost Dance Songs

Phyllis sang to herself a lot after we moved into our shack on Wall Street and she had some privacy. The repertoire included American pop ballads of the early 1930s but consisted mainly of folk songs and dance tunes from turn of the century to 1920s Berlin. Sometimes there were parodies of "Valencia" and "In a Little Konditorei" and the melodies of street singers of her youth.

> Turnip marmalade, turnip marmalade
> Is the foundation of the state.
> *(Children's ditty, circa 1916)*

But she also knew more than I ever will of Mozart and Bach concertos, song cycles of Smetana and Dvorak, the music of Mendelssohn and Grieg and that of daring new innovators of sixty to eighty years ago. That's just the way a part of the working class once was.

Phyllis remained adamantly anti-militarist. Although that outlook was almost subversive in the 1940s it continued to be a fairly widespread attitude among those who came of age within a Socialist tradition before the Great Patriotic War. There was a Wandervögel song she sang composed during the First World War which I once knew but can only remember fragments of now. You have to hear "Flandern In Not" sung to catch its keening power as a memorial. It is a lament and witness — and not just for the soldiers who fell at the Somme either. I knew that song long before we were forced to memorize "In Flanders Fields" in school.

Another song in a comparable vein was "Hörch Kind Hörch", which allegedly stems from the Thirty Years War, an epoch of religious wars, witch hunts and devastation which left deep folk memories in Germany and later entered the iconography of the left. I don't suppose there is any way to translate the bitterly sardonic quality of it.

"Hörch Kind Hörch" is cast in the form of a lullaby which a peasant mother sings to her child as they try to evade ravaging soldiers during the Thirty Years War. But it is really a damning denunciation of the then contemporary rulers and society. That much even I understood as a child. Of course I had only a child's understanding of what it was all about. In fact, it is only recently that I learned that the "mad Christian" alluded to in the song was Prince Christian of Braunschweig, one of the most notorious witch burners and butchers of that period.

> Listen child listen, how the storm wind blows
> It shakes the very house corners
> When the Braunschweiger stands outside
> He will shake them yet more fiercely.
> Learn to pray my child, fold fine your hands
> So that God will turn the mad Christian from us.

Sleep child sleep, be very still, the years will roll away
Soon the recruiting drum will come to summon you
Follow it my child, listen to your mother's advice
For if you fall in battle no soldier can garrote you.
The peasant must leave behind all his goods and belongings
He pays not with gold but with the cold grave.

I see that I've given you the wrong impression. Actually, my parents steered clear of consciously conveying their outlook to me as a child. What came through was largely unintentional. Besides, I juxtaposed songs like the above with renderings of "You Are My Sunshine", the lessons of comic books, and more typical childish concerns. The other stuff was just part of the background.

Mainly, my parents told me children's stories as a child. That many of them were rather medieval seemed appropriate. For instance, "Schlaraffenland". I always thought that Phyllis had made that up until I saw Brueghel's painting of it. You eat your way through a mountain of porridge to get into a sort of sixteenth century Big Rock Candy Mountain. "Stupid," I thought, because I loathed porridge.

Ali was actually the more accomplished story teller of the two and would provide the pauses and mimicry and asides to throw you off the track as a story unfolded. When I was older he shifted to stories about his endless job hunts throughout western Canada, the places he'd been and the people he'd met. He also told those to any adult willing to listen — which weren't many.

Phyllis gave up telling stories after I was old enough to read but until then she dug out and sometimes reedited versions of fairy tales so that the maxims were opposite of the original. I once saw a Mexican film called Macario, Bruno Traven's reworking of a Grimm's Brothers tale. It reminded me of some of her renderings of traditional stories. Alternately, Phyllis might present a more or less straight forward retelling of Peer Gynt as she had seen it on the stage of Berlin theatres during her youth. When I first saw that play staged, thirty years later, there was hardly a scene which I hadn't heard described.

TWO

Education for Democracy

Hastings School vs. the Children's Republic

I got a shock nosing around the Special Collections of the University of B.C. a few years ago. There in a glass display case featuring archival material of Scandinavian cultural organizations in Vancouver was a picture of the first girl I'd had a crush on. Jeanette was a reserved ten-year-old studying the violin when we were in Grade 4 together. "What is this?" I huffed. "That's only thirty-five years ago. George — what are you doing with a picture of Jeanette Lundquist here? She's no older than me."

It sent me back to look at my grade school class pictures. Forty boys and girls arranged in ranks on the steps of Hastings School, our home room teacher beside us with a trace of a harried smile. There we are in tattered wind breakers and knee-length frocks, home-knit sweaters and beribboned pig tails — smirking, inspecting stockings and cloud gazing. Staring back at me.

Reading, roting and arithmetic, laced with great dollops of tribal mythology and obedience training, were what Hastings School in the forties was all about. The central maxims delivered were few but endlessly repeated. You should be grateful you lived in Canada and were part of the British Empire where your freedom was protected by those who understood it. I don't know how many times we heard the old saw, "Some people mistake Liberty ... [a one second dramatic pause] ... for License." That was proffered with intimations of sageness as if it were a pearl of wisdom cast before us for the first time. If this meaningless claptrap was greeted with glazed eyes the follow up would be, "Those of you who are more mature will understand that better than others."

According to examples given the only meaning one could extract was that what you were required to do was "liberty" while anything that those in authority didn't like but couldn't yet forbid was "license". The same with the supposed distinction between "rights" and "privileges". As far as I can remember no teacher ever mentioned anything which was a right — virtually everything was a privilege it seemed. In point of fact, that may have been a lot closer to the reality of the Canadian legal system than we realized with our childish conceptions of natural justice.

Having a library card was a privilege not a right, going to the movies was a privilege, driving an automobile, should we ever have one, was a privilege. A right to a job or to medical care or to a roof over your head were not rights at all. To claim that was willful misinterpretation or the ignorance of people who didn't understand the English language. "Some people" (meaning our parents as much as us) were constantly

The inevitable class picture: Hastings School, 1942. The author is on the far right of the third row.

"mistaking privileges for rights," it seemed. Vancouver East was an old citadel of the Left in British Columbia.

Many of us balked at saying "sir" if it could possibly be avoided. "Sir" was definitely not the same as "mister". It was servile. That was a bone of contention with some teachers. "Answer 'Yes Sir'," they demanded, aware that something more than mere forgetfulness was involved. For them, good manners above all else meant servility in the face of one's "betters". You would try to use a circumlocution and if compelled to do so might mumble "sur" in the most garbled manner possible. Under compulsion you might honourably acquiesce to a lot of things. But it rankled.

Any dissent was neither a right nor a privilege. It was "troublemaking". Disagreeing with what a teacher said constituted "answering back" and as such was a "disciplinary problem" to be remedied by the strap if necessary. It was a rare day when the vice-principal didn't strap some rambunctious children. There might be up to a half dozen boys waiting outside his office to receive their punishment. Usually it was for fighting in the schoolyard but a simple "No I won't" said to a teacher would suffice for a strapping.

A strapping consisted of up to six strokes with a leather razor strap on the palm of each hand. If it struck your wrist it raised welts. During Grades 5 and 6 I got a number of strappings. It wasn't anything to be ashamed of unless you cried. It wasn't the actual pain which rankled; that was no worse than any number of bruises acquired through normal rough housing. It was the indignity, that you were forced to submit to strangers.

There were also a few out-and-out bullies among the teachers. One of the more notorious of that lot once became enraged when a kid threw a spitball while he, the teacher, was writing on the blackboard. Since no one would confess and no one would squeal our teacher went up one aisle and down the other, applying two vigorous strokes with a metal-edged ruler on the upturned palms of each boy and girl in the class. There were about forty of us. Periodically he would stop and remind everybody that, "Because none of you will take the responsibility of reporting the guilty party, coward that he is, the innocent must suffer with the guilty." We would have been about nine years old at the time and he in his fifties.

I suppose that to present day parents who worry about drugs and the juvenile violence prevalent in some schools, accounts of grade schoolroom authoritarianism in Canada of the 1940s may seem charmingly bucolic. But it wasn't.

A provincial law required that we be given a daily dose of Bible reading and recitation of the Lord's Prayer. Bible reading came immediately after inspection of fingernails for dirt and "personal hygiene". Godliness was next to cleanliness in our school. Either your home room teacher read the text or conscripted students in the class to dish up the morning's offering from the Holy Book. Then came the daily morning prayer. "Class, rise. Quiet now. Bow your heads ... Ready, set, pray!"

> I pray dear lord for Jeez' sake
> Send us this day a chocolate cake.
> And if thou dost have lemon pies
> Dear lord, I'd like the largest size.

(No, no! That's T-Bone Slim's rendering. That wasn't the school version.)

Considering the nature of East End Vancouver there must have been a lot of unbelievers at Hastings School. There must have been others who had their own sacred pie card shuffles. Yet in all the years that we suffered through mornings prayers and Bible readings I was the only one who refused to say prayers or read from that book.

My mother had a healthy caution about allowing authorities of any sort know what we believed. Especially during those times. She had taken her reading of the Spanish Inquisition too much to heart. Bible punching was just a rote in grade school. But she didn't believe in pinning a bullseye on herself or her own. Phyllis counseled me to keep my ideas to myself.

"Just go through the motions if there is no way around it. You don't have to let them know what you're thinking. We don't believe any of that but you don't have to tell them that. Tell them you're a 'protestant' if you have to. Sure. We protest, so you can call yourself a 'protestant'."

I don't remember what brought it to a head but some time in Grade 3 I announced in class that "We don't believe in the Bible or God." Actually I didn't have much of an idea what "we" or I did believe in but I was certain it wasn't this. For a basically shy kid I was rather adamant about it. On that point I didn't care what anybody thought.

After initial disbelief, Miss Hamilton, our teacher, gave me the option of standing silently, head bowed, as the good news was being scattered among thorns and on more fertile ground, or waiting in the hall during the Bible readings and prayer. For awhile I traipsed out of the room and moped around the corridor. That was how I first attracted the attention of the school disciplinarians who thereafter knew to keep an eye on me. So after a few weeks I decided it would be better if I stayed in class and just remained ostentatiously silent throughout the whole business.

It sets you apart. It's an invitation to the scapegoating which is always latent in institutions like schools. With a few exceptions my fellow students were quite supportive and tolerant — certainly more so than some of our teachers. I suppose that a yet more draconian school could have forced me to pray, though not believe.

We didn't pledge allegiance to the flag each morning in school as they do down in the Land of the Free. Actually, a genteel controversy existed about just which flag was supposed to be honoured. The British loyalist element was stolidly behind the Union Jack while others daringly held that the Red Ensign was the flag of Canada, "an independent Dominion linked by bonds of loyalty and tradition to Great Britain, etc., etc." But you were required to stand at attention during renditions of God Save the King in school assemblies.

Noncompliance was more feasible in public events. For instance, the end of the program in movie houses was followed by a film strip of the Royal Family, with and without corgis, and their anthem. The royalists in the audience scrambled to their feet and stood at attention, sometimes trying to block those patrons who rushed for the door before King George's mug appeared on screen. Sometimes I refused to stand up regardless of the surrounding indignation. Sure I was embarrassed. But to me royalty were a symbol of oppression, even though I knew that they were no longer the kingpins of the system. The fact that this Royal family was the figurehead of an amorphous caste system in Canada made it so much the worse. Self respect is a difficult and dogmatic taskmaster among ten- and twelve-year-olds.

Hastings School in the 1940s was an all-white school. In a body of five hundred students there weren't more than a half dozen non-white children. It was an Anglo-Canadian school although there were a considerable number of students from Ukrainian, Yugoslav, Italian and other non-English backgrounds. But what we really were children of the western Canadian working class.

As children we were relatively unconcerned about caste lines and the

The author, circa 1946–'47, on a typical East Vancouver sidewalk of the time.

fine distinctions of ethnic derivations. I don't think I was alone in not knowing what the stereotypes of various ethnic groups were or even what counted as an ethnic or national group. The impetus for racial and ethnic antipathies came from the external social environment and even from certain teachers themselves.

For reasons which are still unclear to me the most viciously maligned ethnic group during the era was not the Japanese or any other non-white population but the Russian Doukhobor pacifist community. The hate mongering directed against the Doukhobors was more vicious than any racism. It carried on and reached its peak only during the following decade, resulting in government actions every bit as odious as the internment of the Japanese-Canadian population. Some news-paper politicians built their reputations on that.

However, in the early and mid 1940s there was the war to engage chauvinist sentiments. The war patriotism whipped up at the time was essentially racist. It had its adherents in school as well as everywhere else. How you were categorized had nothing to do with where you were born, how long you had lived in Canada, what your language and culture was. Hardly anyone would have known that I was of German background if it hadn't been for a few teachers who repeatedly brought it up in class. In retrospect, most of my fellow school children were resistant to that invitation to scapegoating — most but not all.

Mr. Dyson was a veteran of World War I and was always waving the bloody shirt. Now, more than sixty years later, I still loathe that man with a passion I cannot put into words. He was at me from Grade 3 on. It culminated in Grade 5 when I refused to recite "In Flanders Fields" because it was a militarist poem. Dyson dragged me out of the classroom and worked himself into a rage which ended with him actually slugging me and sending me tumbling down a double flight of stairs. It was a year after the war had ended and I was then ten years old.

Armistice Day, November 11, was something I sure didn't look forward to. Phyllis remembered the day with a certain wistfulness as the moment when, in her youth, the killing had stopped. But in school we were bombarded with lessons about the sacrifices and great victory won for civilization and the imperial Raj by Britain and her allies in World War I. Each child was expected to buy and wear a red poppy. Actually, a memorial to the dead seemed a good idea to me. But that whole ritual was a tribute to militarism and to British imperialism, not to peace at all. So I wouldn't wear a poppy either. Again, that didn't bother most of my school mates but it did antagonize a number of my teachers. The thing is that I didn't even purposely set out to antagonize them.

The most beneficial thing about Hastings School was that it taught us to read fairly rapidly. But much of the reading was rather simple-minded and stereotypical. For example, a Grade 5 reader called *Caravans* was built around the adventures of an American family who take a cruise around the world on a luxury liner. It was filled with lots of quaint wogs and local colour and bumptious middle class arrogance. Texts like that were presumably intended to combine improved reading skills with what passed as social studies.

Possibly I'm overdoing this, because few of us were much effected by the maxims contained in school books. We didn't expect them to deal with reality. And it's also true that we paid good money to go to movies which were just as inane, if more violent, than our readers. I read adventure stories by Richard Halliburton and Jack London's *Before Adam* and Edgar Rice Burroughs's *Pellucidar*, dated but typical boy's fare. A little later I was enthralled by *Half Seas Over*, the adventures of a surly ship's engineer, an apostle of Duggins Dew of Kirkintilloch, on a British tramp steamer.

Organized sports at school consisted of drills, softball and soccer. I supposed that there wasn't much more that a teacher could do if he or she had to handle a mob of children temporarily freed from the class room. Somehow I had picked up the attitude that "real men" didn't engage in organized sports. That was a nineteenth century outlook and didn't apply anyway since we were schoolchildren. Probably it was just a rationale, since I was never much good at sports. We did play scrub soccer on Commissioner Street under the arc lights of the over-pass leading down to Terminal Dock. But that was just for fun.

I preferred swimming or rowing leaky skiffs around the harbour or exploring the industrial waterfront of Vancouver East with our bunch. "Guns" was the generic title for our amorphous games which involved hiding, climbing, ambushing and blazing away with homemade arse-nals and cap pistols. "I got ya Jimmy. I got ya fair and square. Hey you guys, I got him. He's dead." Not very pacific! We dug hideouts in vacant lots, clambered over castoff marine industrial gear, paddled around docks, boarded derelict ships and ran along the top of boxcars parked on sidings. That was infinitely more interesting than standing around a ballpark waiting for somebody to hit a fly.

Pot was strictly a boy's game. You drew a rough circle in the school-yard dust and divided it into pie-like segments. Then, standing with at least one toe in your own segment you threw your jackknife into someone else's segment, first indicating what you were aiming at. If the knife stuck so that you could get at least two fingers between the handle and the ground you would draw a straight line (a good deal of arguing ensued here) and add the cut-off portion to your own. You lost your turn when the knife failed to stick in. The size of the players territories would wax and wane, since as each got smaller it became more difficult to hit. A player was out when he could no longer get the toe of his shoe in his remaining territory.

I don't remember any kid ever threatening another with a knife. There wasn't even a concerned parents' group lobbying for the dis-arming of school children. But there was a lot of rock throwing and endless schoolyard fights. These involved posturing and scuffles which resulted in bloody noses, split lips and injured pride. We didn't have any mechanism to deal with bullies but there was a general adhesion to some ground rules for fights. No ganging up, no picking on markedly younger kids, no using boots and no hitting somebody when they were down or had given up. There was usually a good-sized crowd around any fight which developed to see that these standards were maintained — but also to see to it that the combatants didn't back out.

There was a seasonality to many schoolyard games. Games of conkers were limited to fall after the horse chestnuts had dropped from boulevard trees. In winter, the best thing apart from Christmas holidays was the chance to have snowball fights. These ranged from individual duels to battles involving a hundred or more kids, with attendant charges and enthusiastic yelling and screaming. Early spring was for wading gumboot-shod in grass-lined ditches, building series of dams to impound rainwater in mini lakes and then undercutting them so that the cascade carried away one dam after another. Yo-yos appeared in late spring as did marbles. Marble games with constantly disputed rules were spawned around the schoolyard; boys scrabbled around on hands and knees, grinding dirt into their clothes like besotted promoters of soap commercials. Tiger's eye marbles, clear amber ones, marbles with milky opaque and crystal windows, others blood-red or ying-yanged black and mustard yellow. Prize shooters, lucky marbles and so forth.

What about girl's games? There were a few neighbourhood girls who participated in our rambles around the waterfront but I really never knew what distinct games they played. Skipping and hopscotch were strictly girl's games. You could see that some guys were intrigued by all this bopping around and rope swinging and arcane skipping chants. But certainly by Grade 3 we wouldn't have been found dead playing "girl's games".

Although boys and girls played together around their own backyards we rapidly sorted ourselves into antagonistic castes at school, where sex and age divisions were stringently adhered to. The way my wife tells it, the situation was a lot less rigid in the one-room school she went to in rural Manitoba.

Who made up this personal "we" and "us"? Until the end of Grade 3 it was a shifting assortment of acquaintances, one of whom drowned off the log booms below his house. But I didn't have any lasting friendships until I was nine and the Wager family moved into the houseboats below our place. John was a few years older than us and bound for the logging camps after Grade 7, like his dad. Bill was exactly my own age while Fred and Anita were a couple of years younger. They and a couple of cousins living in a nearby houseboat with their grandparents were the core of our gang. Despite arguments and times when we weren't talking to each other we were friends during those crucial late childhood years until I was thirteen. Then the Wagers and everyone else who lived in the houseboats were evicted by the National Harbours Board.

In retrospect it was all remarkably innocent compared to what many other children elsewhere have experienced. At twelve and thirteen we were still children. We were younger for our ages than most kids today yet we would be adults sooner. Children growing up on farms could begin to take on some adult tasks earlier than we could. For instance, when I went to visit the Koeppens on their stump ranch in the Columbia Valley the milk truck which took us up and back from the closest rail station was often driven by a fourteen- or fifteen-year-old doing a man's job. That wasn't possible for us in the city .

I don't remember any feelings of "the sky's the limit" as a kid. People normally learn to fit into whatever possibilities there are — sometimes a lot earlier and more narrowly than is necessary. There is one wondrous quality though, of youth more than of childhood. There seems to be time enough for everything. You don't yet realize that there isn't time enough or opportunity to do more than a handful of the things you'd like to. But I wouldn't want to be a child again for anything.

Whenever I hear someone mouthing off about "teaching morality in the classroom" I'm reminded of my own golden rule from school days. A while back my memory was jarred by a high school teacher who trod the boards in televised hearings on educational restructuring in British Columbia. Regaling his audience with overripe imitations of John Diefenbaker he informed the unwashed that,

> When we see Prince Philip shouldering his appointed duties we see a life dedicated to the philosophy of Stoicism. When we see an episode of *Kotter* [a hokey Hollywood sitcom about an inner city school in Brooklyn] we see the result of Permissive Humanism. They are the embodiment of two philosophies which have contended for men's minds, whether you know the correct names of these philosophies or not, since the dawn of civilization. It is that simple and that complex.

Stormy applause here from the local Right-to-Stoicism and Antihumanist League. People in this school district rallied to the side of its high school principal when he threatened to strap any student who refused to recite the Lord's Prayer during morning exercises. That is their conception of morality. If they can't win each heart and mind they'll settle for force to compel conformity. Ignorance may not be bliss but it demands mass adherence if its celebrants are to feel secure. In essence, they want to force others to become just as mean spirited and narrow minded as they themselves are. The kind of schooling they paint in such glowing terms we had. It was rotten. It is not surprising that rotten people find it appealing.

Archive: Education for Democracy

The years between twelve and fourteen are never very easy. The worst time of my life were those three years spent at an institution called Templeton Junior High School. It proceeded on the assumption that its role was to "prepare students for life" (i.e., wage work) in the adult world. There was little expectation that we would go on to anything other than vocational schools; to apprenticeships, if we applied ourselves; and to unskilled work if not. If there were students who didn't fit that pattern Templeton was happy to let either the high schools or the reform schools worry about them.

Templeton was the nadir of mindless regimentation. It was almost as if the school authorities were afraid that this collection of fifteen hundred inmates which they had penned up might at some point overcome their alienation and rebel against what they were being prepared for. Visions of us running amok in riotous disorder. Stringent disciplinary measures had to be maintained.

Passes were an obsession at Templeton. Passes and permits were required every time you turned around. Each student received an identity card which he or she had to carry when in school and show on request to anyone "in authority". The classroom teacher had to fill in your name, identity number, reason for being outside of the classroom, time of issuance and expected time of return. Phenomenal, the amount of class time all this took up.

"Loitering" in the corridors was forbidden. There were only a few places you could legitimately be in school. You could be in class, you could be in a lunch room or in a detention room under supervision of a teacher or you could be "walking the circuit". The last may require a little explanation.

"Walking the circuit" meant shuffling around the perimeter corridor of the school in a counterclockwise direction during lunch hour. Picture it: some five or six hundred kids aged twelve to fifteen stumbling along twilight dim corridors in a set pattern during mid day. The school was built along the lines of a Japanese factory of the 1920s; a sawtoothed roof in the center of the building allowed a dingy natural light to filter through grimed glass into the inner bowels of the plant. Keep moving, no stopping permitted! From time to time teachers of the appropriate sex would check the boys' and girls' washrooms to see that they were being used for the intended purposes and had not been invaded by cliques of loiterers.

The school was rife with monitors. Monitors were students who volunteered to join a kind of student police force supervised by certain teachers. On observing some infraction of the endless rules, monitors issued "tickets" which after being processed by a kangaroo court resulted in "demerits" and "detentions" for the accused. You were supposed to go to a "monitor court" to defend yourself against the charges before a panel of head monitors who determined the "sentence" for the infraction. They were overseen by a wispy twist of a man who got his rocks off by acting like the Red Queen. Ah, the thrill of authority.

There was a "student government" which rubber stamped all this borstal school rigmarole. It was "representative government in action", as the school principal never tired of informing us. "Education for democracy", "an apprenticeship in citizenship" were the claims made about this system. There are an awful lot of quotation marks here but the school was real enough.

Some teachers did occasionally mouth the maxim to "think for yourself" but that was clearly not meant to be taken seriously and woe to you if you did. You were supposed to accept whatever maundering inanities were being dished out by whoever stood in front of you in class. It was a stultifying process. Most junior high school students don't want to buck whatever they decipher the current tide of opinion to be; teenagers are usually gluttons for conformity among their peers. But it hardly does credit to an educational system that it seeks to deepen this taste for conformism.

In class, you were supposed to learn your lesson and nothing else. If you were caught reading other than the assigned text you were "wasting time". Various ploys were used to shame adolescents found "daydreaming". When you had completed "your work" you were supposed to sit silently until everyone else was finished. Just shut down your mind until the next lesson was trundled out.

The subjects taught defy description. English consisted mainly of drills, a grammarian's view of proper usage and an attempt to root out and deaden the ear to the vitality of the living language itself. Literature was comprised of dollops of glop like Sir Walter Scott's "The Lady of the Lake". But History and Social Studies was where mythology really came into its own. History was mainly the kings and queens of England, their reigns and "contributions" — but definitely not their looting and enslavement of nations, including their own. Then on to the major royal houses of the continent. That counted as World History.

For Canadian History teachers served up a few colourful habitants and jolly voyageurs, made a cursory pass at Captain Vancouver, mentioned Colonel Moody of the Royal Engineers, saluted Governor Douglas of the Hudson's Bay Company, and let it go at that. The rest of the planet entered in tangentially, or not at all, according to how it was part of or had opposed the British Empire in its task of spreading civilization. You may think that Brecht's *A Worker Reads History* is merely a Marxist caricature of what traditional school history was. But we were taught exactly that nonsense.

I don't envy teachers their lot. The school was a mutually destructive system and must have been especially demoralizing for any teacher who wanted to provide some intellectual stimulus. Any lesson which dared a wider imagination, on how the brain functions, let's say, was held to be totally beyond our comprehension. Science was a melange of repetitious and often misconstrued memory work: drawing arrows to indicate water-to-land and land-to-water convection currents, Lamarckian views of evolution, or teleological interpretations of natural phenomena were alive and well in the class rooms of Templeton JHS. "Nature abhors a vacuum" — except in our school.

Central to Templeton's claim to providing "practical education" was its Industrial Arts program. In the woodworking shop you turned out useless dust catchers while in electrical shop you wired and rewired bells and lights in various circuits for equally impractical purposes. Hammering out an iron door latch heated on a coal forge in the metal shop was about the most satisfying and very handy if the eighteenth century should ever return.

A primary goal of this training was to prepare us to become reliable hands. Absenteeism was a cardinal sin, regardless of what you did or didn't learn. Doing what you were told, learning what you were told, not talking back and learning to accept regimentation — those were as important lessons as any other education which might be imparted to us. That outlook has made a comeback throughout North America today and is touted as an educational breakthrough.

Getting to work on time was a central lesson which the school attempted to inculcate. If you were a few minutes late in the morning you were barred from entering the classroom until you'd made the trek to the school office. There you would wait for another twenty minutes as the vice principal harangued other latecomers about their excuses. All explanations and reasons tendered by students were always "excuses". After receiving an allotment of detentions you were given a pass which admitted you to your classroom.

It is to our great discredit that we put up with all this prison mentality, this parish pump authoritarianism which pervaded school life, and did little more than grumble about it amongst ourselves. My main solution was to stay away from school as much as possible. I'd get there just before classes started, leave at the crack of noon and go for long walks, and be off the school grounds five minutes after the last class.

Public schools allegedly had a responsibility for molding the character of their students. But most teachers were hopelessly provincial compared to our parents and their friends. Many of us came from backgrounds which were far more cosmopolitan and knowledgeable than our teachers did. But that didn't really provide an effective defense. At most, some parents might console their children with the view that schooling was something that had to be gotten through and not to take the lessons too literally or too much to heart.

I didn't have any clear idea of what the world was like, what were realistic possibilities and what pipe dreams. But I did have a dull foreboding about what might be in the offing. Teachers regaled us endlessly with the refrain, "You don't know how lucky you are. These school days will be the happiest days of your lives when you look back on them." ("Oh Jeez, what if they are even half right?") "You don't have any responsibilities. You have two months off a year, you come in at 9 in the morning and you're out at 3:30. Do you know how many of your fathers have jobs with hours like that? None!"

Apparently, preparing us for work and our place in society required saturating us with the most baleful imprecations of what the future held in store. Strange that these Cassandras didn't think that all this gloom might evoke some rebellion against the fate which supposedly awaited us. Possibly they were only boosting their own egos by making other jobs seem even worse by comparison.

I had no idea of just how liberating, sometimes interesting, and generally bearable work could be. What a tremendous relief it was to find, in my first jobs, that they were all more rewarding and freer than school ever was. At first I feared that the dire predictions of what the world of work entailed might still catch up with me. But in thirty years I had only one job as deadening as life at Templeton.

My Own Map of the Interior

During the late 1940s I spent part of my summers in camp. That is, I visited my father in construction camps he was working in. The first was dike rebuilding project at Deroche in the Fraser Valley. I stayed in one of the crew tents and on afternoons when Ali could take some time off we drove around the surrounding region and visited the places where he had jungled up, or the crumbling remains of relief project camps. This was accompanied by reminiscences of who he had been with when riding the rods or how they had gotten together the ingredients for a mulligan stew in some little town we now passed through. Accounts of the Hungry Thirties, accounts of events which had happened in the distant past, a decade or more earlier.

Another time I stayed with him at Elk Falls camp near Campbell River. The hydro project was winding down so there was plenty of room in the bunkhouses. I'd waltz over to the cookhouse for meals and choose what I wanted — which never included vegetable stews. It seems remarkable now, that camp managers would allow the kids of their employees to stay in a work camp. But those were times when bosses didn't yet make a fetish of boasting that there was nary a free lunch to be had from their multi-million-dollar projects.

When Ali could get away we would mosey around the nearby coal mining town of Cumberland. He had a real knack for striking up conversations with people, a trait I always envied. We might nose around the old coaling berths at Union Bay or the ships' bone yard at Fanny Bay. Interlaced in these outings were snippets of local history as Ali had heard it.

We also made a couple of trips through the interior of B.C. to visit some of his old haunts in the Cariboo and the Bridge River country. There were then only a quarter million people scattered throughout the province outside of Vancouver and the southwestern corner of B.C. Many communities could only be reached by ship or rail. The road network was sketchy and many regions in the province were quite isolated from each other. That's what stretched everything out, made everything seem larger and helped maintain the distinctive regions. The massive road building program of the following decade opened up the interior regions and changed them irrevocably. But in the late 1940s there were few tourists, no Disneyland heritage sites and no "No trespassing" signs. We met local people using local roads or occasionally someone else surveying the haunts of their youth.

The Cariboo had changed very little from what it was in the 1930s and much of the infrastructure was from the turn of the century. On the backland roads you passed squared log ranch buildings and actual ghost towns. They were the earmarks of bypassed resource regions. The Cariboo had been a depressed area for the better part of two generations but it was beautiful.

Lytton, Lillooet, Hundred Mile House, Clinton were still villages dominated by western American frontier architecture of the 1890s. Cache Creek, now a mile-long strip of gas stations, motels and Kentucky Fried Pizza Huts, consisted of one general store. On the benches above the Thompson River were mile upon mile of crumbling wooden flumes and a smattering of stunted apple scrub which bespoke of abandoned orchards returned to sage brush. In the dry mountains west of Lillooet, where the Yalakom enters the Bridge River, my parents had first tried their hand at placer mining. The Moha Road wound up alongside the Yalakom to where Canadian veterans of the Great War had been lured into "ranching" on allotments in the West Cariboo block, most already long since abandoned. All this was grist for Ali's stories.

We headed down backland tracks and bumped along plank roads running over cribbing gouged around the side of cliffs. Our 1928 Essex wheezed up grades and every so often we pulled over to roadside streams to fill the radiator which had boiled over. We crawled along at twenty miles an hour making a hundred miles in a day, constantly stopping to sort through something or other of interest. Once we climbed up to a plateau high above Spence's Bridge where one of the many small mine camps Ali had worked in had stood. Below Lillooet we nosed through runnels of stone which looked like megalithic barrows but were the tailings of placer mining done eighty years earlier. And always the stories of people who had been there before us. Tales of native born and immigrant, with and without names, but with some fragment of a story which linked them to a particular place in Ali's memory. He might even provide dialogue, real or imagined, to flesh out the accounts. They were sometimes nostalgic but also included reminiscences of narrow-minded dolts and two-bit exploiters.

Ali recreated the world he'd been part of as an immigrant migrant worker during the depth of the Depression. He didn't allude to his fears or more personal feelings much — either what they had been or were then. Men didn't talk about that, certainly not with their own children. So that part of it was left for me to guess about when I was older. But he did repopulate the countryside with the people he had known, guys he had worked and traveled with. Details of where they had looked for a job, what the pay and conditions were, who had been washing gold on which bar and what happened to bring them there. None of that, none of what was our own history, was ever mentioned or thought to be of any importance in school.

It is now impossible to convey the meaning which the remnants of the settlement era had for some of us. Possibly the underlying appeal was the aura of expansiveness. That is ironic, considering that most of these artifacts were the remains of settlements and undertakings which had, in one sense, failed or had been worked out and abandoned. But to my eyes these locales were the witnesses of a seemingly more open society.

Those summer visits and trips were usually the high point of my year. We got on very well together, my father and I, while we were traveling around or working in camp together. Unfortunately it wasn't that way when we were at home.

During the half dozen years after the end of the war my parents were in a pretty constant state of dispute with each other — and probably with fate. I don't remember that being the case earlier. Maybe it was the realization that their lives were never going to be significantly better or much different, ever. Maybe it was only what was described as "change of life".

Ali was in the camps or working deep sea much of the time. When he was home there were long periods when the two of them were barely speaking to each other. The fights were always about the most inconsequential things. My father was fundamentally a quick-tempered and effusive person while Phyllis changed a great deal and became ultra-cautious and withdrawn. In many ways they weren't suited to each other. I only realized that much later but it may have become evident to them then.

Who can say what kept the two of them together for almost forty years. Maybe it was the sense of mutual dependence, the sense of being in it together, whatever the quarrels might be. That and a respect for one another. That may seem contradictory but the marriage rested on a loyalty built up through the many difficulties they'd gone through together. Respect and loyalty are emotions at least as strong as love.

But something self destructive had taken hold of Phyllis. Her former resilience gave out and she only wanted some security and to be left alone. "I've had enough of roughing it." She wouldn't come along on the jaunts which Ali tried to promote. "You two go on your own," she'd say, with a touch of being left out. It got so that Phyllis would hardly depart from her accustomed tracks in the city or through Stanley Park. It was sad to watch but also galling.

The worst of it was that Ali was still remarkably vital. I saw his last wrestling match at Exhibition Gardens when he was forty-eight years of age. Ali still wanted to see new places, meet new people and go wherever the path took him. He must have felt trapped. That was what those other fights were really about. Ali worked his life away in jobs he hated in order to support a family which really gave little back to him.

At the time I thought that Phyllis would remain what she had become until her last days. But in her mid fifties, after a series of strokes which no one expected she would survive, she snapped out of her apathy and did her best to enjoy every day as it came. Indeed, she became more calm and philosophic. Gradually, over the course of years, Phyllis overcame most of the physical incapacities engendered by the stroke. But by then it was too late for much of what she and Ali could have enjoyed a decade earlier. I took it as a lesson.

THREE

A Kind of Apprenticeship

On the Gulf Wing

The *Gulf Wing* was a small coastal passenger-freight boat which ran into the outports and logging camps of the lower B.C. coast. She was a converted World War II sub chaser with a beam of about twenty feet and a little over a hundred feet in length, the last serviceable ship of the Gulf Lines, an outfit started up a few years previously which had stepped into the coastal runs abandoned by the larger shipping companies. It was 1950, I was fourteen and my father used some of his contacts to get me the job. I was the mess boy, baggage handler and general go'fer. It was my first job.

At the time you had to have an Unemployment Insurance Book to get a job, a cholera-yellow passport-like document obtained from the Unemployment Insurance Commission. To obtain it you had to be at least sixteen. So I waltzed into the Commission offices, set back my birth date a couple of years, swore to the accuracy of the information tendered and got my passbook. It was still that kind of a world here.

The Gulf Lines was an outfit which would contract to carry anything anywhere within its range of operations if they thought they could possibly make some money at it. If a traveling circus had approached them to carry an elephant up to Halfmoon Bay or somewhere I don't doubt the manager would have considered it. "How big an elephant is it? Ever have it shipped before? Hey Mike. Look up what the coastal tariffs on elephants are."

Once the CPR boat which normally carried freight into Powell River was out of service with engine trouble and the *Gulf Wing* briefly took over the run. We arrived in the middle of the night with our cramped hold stuffed with groceries and the fore deck loaded with cases of bread. What with the wind and spray the bread was beginning to disintegrate by the time we got to Powell River. Every crew member other than the engineer and the cook was rousted out and pressed into service transferring the freight from the deck to the dock by hand. You didn't even ask about overtime.

The *Gulf Wing* was the last of the three ships which the company had had. They had already run one on the rocks and the *Gulf Mariner*, a converted mine layer, moldered away at dockside in Vancouver awaiting the improbable hope that the company could come up with the money to install a fire sprinkler system to meet tightened maritime safety regulations. We made one long and two short runs up the coast each week. As a passenger ship the *Gulf Wing* was alright for day runs but our longest trip was a thirty-hour trip up to the head of Bute Inlet. We could squeeze forty or so people into the lounge but on the longer runs it began to take on a sardine can quality.

Once a week we laid over at Blubber Bay or Vananda, a quarry town on Texada Island. Vananda on a Saturday night, its handful of stores and cafes brightly lit, the local bootleggers operating at full tilt and just about every car, truck and jalopy on the island gunning up and down the road like demented extras in a B-grade California hot-rod movie. On Sunday mornings a clutch of bored-out-of-their-skulls Lolitas would ostentatiously loiter around the dockside, amenable to flirtation and more, one hoped. There were enough of my fellow crew members eager to oblige. I wish I'd been one of them.

As the messboy I had to deal with some passengers as they sobered up and slipped into a hangover on their way back to camp after a spree in town. I wasn't husky for my age, no fighter really, but I had a temper and wasn't willing to take any guff from drunks. An inauspicious combination. A passenger would bad mouth me and I'd answer back in like coin. I kept a short crowbar under the lunch counter for any eventuality. Luckily, a couple of the older deckhands kept an eye out for me. One big Finn intervened once when some logger was about ready to settle my hash. "Ah kid, you're just young and stupid. You'll learn," said my shipmate after I'd begun to breathe normally again.

On another trip a haggard-looking woman in her indiscernible middle age came aboard at Vancouver. She was desperate to talk to somebody and I happened to be handy. She had met her husband while he was stationed in London during the previous war; he'd returned to marry her and had then rushed back to an upcoast logging camp. His new wife was coming out to join him as a surprise. She hadn't been outside Greater London in her life but had now made the trans-Atlantic crossing by ship, come cross Canada by train and was now bound for an isolated float camp half way up Bute Inlet.

"What's it like up there? Is the village pretty? Do they have shops or do you have to go over to the next town for that?" she asks me.

"Jeez" I thought. "Well, it's really what they call a 'float camp' here. Men only live there while they're working. In fact, wives don't usually go along to those camps."

This place was one of the grimmest operations I'd ever seen, a few shacks on some half-waterlogged rafts cabled to a rock wall in just about the most desolate stretch of Bute Inlet. Miles of cliffside without a beach or a place to walk. Maybe a couple dozen men in the crew who would be out on the timber limits or booming ground all day. To top it off, the most bloodthirsty flies I've ever seen lived around the head of Bute Inlet. You wouldn't be tied up there five minutes before these metallic green flies the size of wasps would come buzzing out of the bush, head straight for you and without any further ado bite a little cube out of any exposed flesh.

We're still in the more populated part of the Gulf, passing Sechelt, when she asks hopefully, "Is it like that?" By the time we turn up into Bute Inlet the woman isn't saying anything and is wearing a dazed expression. The afternoon of the next day we glide up to this float camp, blowing the whistle to shake out anyone around. Apart from two guys everybody is out in the bush. Eyes wide with disbelief. "This can't ... there must be a mistake. I can't get off here ... at the wrong ..." she stammers. But it's the right camp and her husband does work there. Surprise!

The skipper pokes his head out of the wheelhouse, wanting to get underway, but doesn't want to get involved in this scene. "It's not as bad as it seems at first. I grew up in places like this," I say to her. But that's not really true and she isn't listening anyway. Finally she debarks and we get underway. I expected to see her on board the next trip back to town but I never saw her again. So I can't provide any character development.

The ship's cook was an easy-going guy in his mid twenties who actually listened to what his fourteen-year-old helper had to say. As I remember, I was then reading For Whom the Bell Tolls and Homage to Catalonia. I'd peel the day's potatoes after breakfast, sitting in the glory hole behind the tiny galley in the stern of the ship. If I piled two bags of spuds one on top of the other I could sit looking out a port hole at whatever came into view and carry out a running conversation with the cook through the open hatch as he clanked around the stove.

In the galley you were on the go from early in the morning till eight at night. We were supposed to accumulate two days off a week but there was always some reason why they didn't actually materialize. The crew quarters consisted of six bunks for eight men in a tiny compartment ahead of the engine room. Talk about muzzle loaders. You'd crawl out of your bunk in the morning and somebody from the previous watch would crawl in behind you.

I worked on the *Gulf Wing* two summer months and earned $35 for what seemed to be a sixty-hour work week. That was a pretty rotten wage even for those times but I enjoyed the job. Sure I knew I was being exploited but what could you do? If you didn't like it you could quit. The Gulf Lines were on the skids and a few years later went broke.

It was the end of an era when almost everyone along the BC coast trundled back and forth from canneries and logging camps, sawmills and small fishing ports, to and from Vancouver by boat. I thought it would go on forever. If I'd understood that it was all ending I might have hung around longer. But probably not. Because I had grown up amidst all of this and was anxious to get away to wherever the important happenings, whatever they might be, were supposedly taking place.

In 1982 there was just one company operating a tiny freighter running from Vancouver to Bella Bella which also took a handful of passengers. That was all that was left of the working coastal passenger fleet. I wanted to make that trip with my wife but it cost something like $600 and was booked up solid, winter and summer, for almost two years in advance. Obviously I'm not the only one who has nostalgic feelings about coastal shipping.

Here's To You My Rambling Boy

When I was fifteen I landed a job with the BC Forest Service on a trail crew operating out of Kamloops which built some of the first roadside campsites in the province. There were a half dozen similar crews around the interior, constituting a cross between the Civilian Conservation Corps and the Relief Camps of the past. We were treated to a surfeit of statements of high purpose, long hours and abysmal pay, $75 a month, all found. For that we put in a forty-four- to fifty-hour work week under conditions most camp workers wouldn't have tolerated.

The funds had been scrounged up from various accounts in the BC Forest Service, which had an infrastructure of depots and work gangs scattered throughout the province. We were listed as a reserve fire fighting unit but the only blaze we ever fought was when one of our own slash fires got away from us and into the trees and we had to call in the regular fire fighting unit to put it out. Which we never did live down.

It's difficult to truly describe the work we did because the crux of it was the language of the body. It was all manual labour using simple hand tools, work which is usually described as unskilled by those who don't know what is entailed. "Ditch digging", as the contemporary phrase had it.

You can describe the externals of such work but that is a long way removed from how your body learns to do the job effectively and without tiring. It's the difference between working well and working your guts out. It's learning the right rhythms and balances, and those are different for everyone. It's how a pickaxe should feel in your hands, the heft you should have. Bring the pickaxe head up to just behind your shoulder, your right hand slips up the handle checking the backstroke with a minimum of effort. There's a momentary balance and then the pick curves down through a short swinging blow as you bend forward — just the right amount — and your hand slides down the handle in a smooth motion to add force to the stroke. The motion of arms, hands, back, shoulders in coordination, all of which you are only vaguely aware of.

If you're healthy and not too tired and aren't being pushed, work like this can be quite satisfying. I was never an athlete so I know that feeling only through manual work, the feeling that your body is functioning in harmony with itself. You pick and mattock and shovel out the dirt. Standing in a waist-deep trench on a summer's day, sweating and feeling the cool damp of the fresh earth, you feel good. Relaxed, a little light-headed maybe. Although hacking away at hardpan will soon give you a headache unless you have someone to spell you off.

Most of our work was like that. Brushing out tent sites and cutting trails, splitting mountains of fire wood, building rock fireplaces and simple wooden structures. Some of it was plain bull work, as when we pulled two-man crosscut saws. Two guys about a year older than me but with some woods experience did most of the falling. But considering the axes, machetes, brushhooks and assorted other instruments of wood butchery we swung around we were fairly responsible and there were no serious accidents — mainly because we didn't have any power tools to contend with.

The trouble with kids on their first jobs is that they still have a feeling that somebody is looking out for them. I did. In real jobs older workers kept their eyes on kids working around them and set them straight about avoiding jackpots they could get themselves into. But as a teenager you have a tendency to feel that if you are given a job to do then it must be alright. Seasoned workers know better and try to make their own estimation of what's safe and what's not.

It was heavy work, especially since we were still adolescents and didn't have our full strength. Although all the tools and techniques we used were totally anachronistic we did get a lot accomplished. At the end of each day you could see what your individual or combined efforts had achieved. That's pretty rare in most jobs. The undertaking seemed to be clearly worthwhile and many of us made a special effort to see that the various tasks were properly done. I doubt whether any of us would have felt that if we'd been working for a contractor trying to make a buck from us.

But the Forest Service took advantage of our youthful feelings of commitment. The supervisors could be pretty exploitative. I once figured out that we'd built six campsites that summer at a cost of about $10,000 for labour and materials. And still they chiseled us out of our days off. Whenever we were scheduled complete a campsite the foreman would con us into working into the night to finish the tasks left undone. That caused a lot of grumbling amongst us but nothing more. Every time we moved to the next work site, breaking camp and setting up again was always done on Sunday, supposedly our day off.

A well built tent camp, as you used to find all over BC, can be quite comfortable. But you have to spend the time and have the materials to make it that way — to build a wooden floor and frame and door. You have to put up a fly and have a good wood or oil heater for each tent. By comparison our camps were just thrown together.

The grub wasn't too bad. The cook whipped up meals which were better than most of us ate at home. But it was a long ways removed from what was acceptable in logging camps. Ham — boiled, fried and cold. Potatoes and beans and endless bully beef stews. Also "CPR strawberries", sometimes known as stewed prunes.

Though we were all young we weren't really 'kids" as that term is understood today. Most of us came from working-class or farm families and all of us had worked before. I was fifteen but most of the crew were a year or two older. However, the most adept guy amongst us was a fourteen-year-old who came from a stump ranch and had already worked with his father in their gyppo logging operation. We alternated on the various jobs, everyone pulled their own weight but pitched in to help each other without too much ever being said. It was a good bunch.

Initially there were doubts about whether anyone (i.e., anyone "desirable") would use the roadside campsites we were building. There were fears among the small town citizenry and moteliers that "tramps" and other disreputable elements would be attracted to the campsites. There also were businessmen frothing at the mouth about "make-work projects" and "government boondoggles". They wanted the pay and working conditions on jobs like ours to be below those offered by the meanest, most rapacious Keremeos entrepreneur.

As it turned out, the campsites were an overwhelming success. They were too successful. Within a few years the tourist industrialists began laying vociferous siege to their Social Credit government which then began setting fees at rates which made competition by private park operators profitable. The public campsites were allowed to take on a parking lot atmosphere and in general wound up as the very antithesis of what had made them appealing in the first place.

The following spring I was determined to get a job which paid real wages. My parents weren't eager for me to get a job in the construction camps since they feared I'd get hooked on the big money and would drop out of school. I wasn't anxious to ask Ali to help me get a job either. The province was wracked by a mini-recession and strikes in the resource industries but the Pacific Great Eastern Railway was hiring men to work on their section gangs. So, not knowing the score, I signed on. I took the boat up to Squamish where the main rail depot was located, was given a couple of blankets and a train ticket and sent up the line to work on a section at the north end of Lac La Hache in the Cariboo. The whole PGE operation, from its rolling stock and track to its working conditions, had changed very little from the 1920s.

The work gangs which laid new track were composed mainly of recent working-class immigrants from Europe. But the section gangs, the track maintenance crews, were drawn largely from the marginal sectors of the regional labour force. It was seen as a job of last resort and I was soon to learn why. The wage rate was about a dollar per hour and conditions in the section houses were abominable. At Lac La Hache eight men were housed in a filthy two-room shack with no electricity and with drinking water packed from the lake. The morning I arrived the men were trying to cook their breakfast and heat wash water on a single airtight heater. There were no beds; a collection of torn mattresses lay on the bare floor, filling one room of the shack. "Oh my god. What have I walked into here?"

The section boss set me to work on an easy task, throwing down rail ties from a flat car and stacking them in piles. What a job. I was dead tired from the trip up there and after about four hours I was totally exhausted.

"Can I stick it out?"

"No. Admit it, you made a mistake. Are you going to live like this?"

"What are my friends going to say if I come back in a few days? They'll say I can't take it."

"What do you care? You don't see any of them up here do you?"

"If these guys working here can do it so can I."

"No you can't !"

"Think of something else, think about sex," I said to myself. But even that didn't help.

My arms and hands were going numb and I started dropping the ties. Just before noon I headed up to the section house, hoisted my pack sack and duffle bag and stumbled down the track. I told the straw boss that I was quitting and he nodded knowingly without saying a word. At that moment my only concern was to get the half mile up the track and around the bend, out of sight of the crew, so I could collapse and rest.

Over time I came to realize that in situations like this, when you are faced with a really rotten job, you just don't do it. It never pays to stick it out.

I staggered down the tracks till I hit the Cariboo Road, then just a two-lane gravel track looping across the rolling parklands and curling around the edges of side hills. There I struck a road building camp. It was supper time and I was beyond shyness. So I trudged over to the cook shack and told the cook what my situation was. He dished up a tremendous meal and the camp boss let me bunk down in one of the crew tents overnight. I slept clear through till next morning. After a huge breakfast I was sent off with a bundle of sandwiches. That wasn't so unusual then. Ali did that for men on the tramp when he cooked in road camps.

Since I still had eight or ten dollars left I decided to hitchhike around the interior and look for work. It was a beautiful, warm spring that year. Local people traveling what were then still mainly backland roads picked me up and were normally quite supportive. I was beginning to think that this migratory search for work wasn't so bad after all. Of course, I also knew that if nothing came of it I had a home and regular meals to return to. My major worry was being picked up by the BC Provincial Police and arrested for vagrancy or whatever else they wanted to extract from their law books.

The highway building projects which were to change the face of the interior were getting into gear. You couldn't drive thirty miles without running in to some bridge-building or tunnel-drilling or highway-widening work. All this blasting and earth moving with heavy equipment clanking around was rather exciting. I don't remember if I had any contradictory feelings about it then or not. At the time the main problem was that road building was about the only employment around and they didn't hire kids my age.

I did get one job offer. Near Ashcroft a man and his wife driving an old truck picked me up and asked if I was looking for work.

"I sure am. Do you know of any?".

"As a matter of fact I need a man for the green chain." They ran a two-by-four sawmill up in the hills. "Four dollars a day and board. You interested?" That was about a third of the union wage at the time.

"All right", I says, because I was getting desperate.

There was an Indian faller from the coast who'd been recruited the same way and we got to talking while bouncing along in the back of the truck. He gets to telling me about what you have to watch out for in operations like this: not to do anything unless you know it's safe, and to get your pay in cash before you leave if you possibly can. As we are about to leave the main road I decided I'd head back to Kamloops to look for work. The sawmill owner threatened to break my head and roared off in a swirl of dust and curses.

There were no jobs of any kind available in Kamloops. I spent two nights sleeping out in Riverside Park. Down to the price of coffee and donuts I sat in an old Chinese cafe trying to get up the nerve to order a meal and afterwards offering to wash dishes to pay for it. But in the end I chickened out. At the BC Forest Service depot I got an off-the-cuff sermon on Responsibility from the head guru behind the camp-site program. He didn't even ask me if I was hungry.

On the way out of Kamloops a guy who turned out to be in charge of the rock crusher at a road camp near Savona gave me a ride. "Any kid that's got the gumption to run around looking for work is good enough to work for me. I'm gonna put you on the crusher and if you work out I'll see if I can get you on as a swamper somewhere." Wow — a job. Real pay, camp meals! I could already see myself greasing up and learning to run a cat. Counting unhatched chickens. The camp superintendent wouldn't sign me on because it was company policy not to hire anyone under eighteen.

So I decided to head back to Vancouver and take my medicine. It took another two days to hitch back home. I was tired, hungry and chastened enough to ask Ali if he could help me get a job in Kitimat.

You'd be mistaken if you've gotten the impression that I somehow felt degraded by these job hunts. Quite the contrary. I took pride in doing what so many men before me had done. If I had wound up selling hot dogs or doing some other kind of "boy's job" in the city, that would have been degrading. Although I wouldn't have put it in those terms, I felt that migratory workers were to be emulated. It may be hard to believe about an alienated sixteen-year-old but that pride was a source of strength. Today, I understand somewhat better that it was making a virtue of a necessity.

No Blue Suede Shoes

High school didn't bother me, possibly because after the first year I wasn't around much. What with coming back from work late in fall, leaving early in spring and taking various self declared leaves in between I didn't put in more than half the school year. I learned what there was to learn anyway. I had money. It wasn't the worst of times.

Britannia was an old school betwixt and between eras. Its five hundred students were working-class children from a variety of ethnic backgrounds. Despite the reminiscences of later respectability mongers who now try to boost their Alma Mater into the typical dreary high school, Britannia was different. It had virtually no school spirit. At the time I didn't realize how healthy that was and how lucky we were.

Ironically, at a reunion of ex-Britannia students held in 1982, its real nature was swept under the rug in the attempts of assorted notables to conjure up a portrait copped from old Andy Hardy movies. It was humorous to hear Dave Barrett, the former NDP Premier, eulogize the school as a formative force in his youth. "Britannia was small but we had a lot of school spirit. Nobody was frozen out," intoned the Beggar King of Coquitlam to the attendant cornpone gobblers. "It was as good as any other school." What pathetic boosterism. It totally misconstrues what was valuable — that Britannia students did not , in general, participate in the high school culture of the 1950s. Most of our social lives took place away from and outside the context of high school. In retrospect, that is far preferable to the petty social hierarchies which others recount, in disgust or pleasure, from their own high school days.

The school left its students to their own devices, to their own neighbourhood friends, elders and work mates. One could, and most did, opt out of that demeaning drivel which passes for social life among many high school students. We pursued more individual interests and more diverse drivel.

The only similarity between my own experience and the usual accounts of teenage travails of that time are those which deal with the misdirected and usually frustrated sexual gropings of the era. An unambiguous lustfulness began in junior high school and continued, mainly unfulfilled, longer than seems possible today. Sexual arousal came in an overwhelming rush and with it endless embarrassments, overcompensations and awkwardness. I doubt that more than a corporal's guard of my class mates had actually engaged in sexual intercourse until their late teens, despite their desires and energetic lies. It might be of interest but others have described all that better than I can.

I worked in camps part of each year throughout high school and had more friends drawn from work than from school. The influences of that outside world were more important than anything taught at Britannia. My main school was the Carnegie Library at Hastings and Main, from which I dug Steinbeck novels and dusty volumes about what were then already obscure events. I was a voracious if unguided reader with a fascination with what might generously be described as social history. There was a phase when I read everything I could lay my hands on about Mexico, another when I was immersed in the recent history of Spain and the Spanish Civil War. At about the same time I read everything I could find about the Industrial Workers of the World and the early American socialist movement.

Most of that had been expurgated from public discussion; probably that was part of its appeal to me. But few people my own age were interested in past struggles which had taken place in our own backyards or around the world. They "didn't believe in it." And they were intelligent and quick witted individuals in other matters. Jim MacFarlan was the one active shit disturber around Britannia, the only one I remember who had the audacity to get up and walk out of one of the rambling panegyrics on British Imperialism delivered by Lt.-Colonel (Rtd.) Yeo, the principal and general satrap of Britannia High.

It is also true that I usually didn't know much about who was sitting beside me in class, what they believed or what they knew. There must have been a wealth of experience in our collective backgrounds — children born in the mid to late 1930s, sons and daughters of immigrants, children of failed farm families, individuals from almost every kind of working-class background in Western Canada. There were undoubtedly others thinking along their own lines but we rarely shared our views.

I came within an ace of dropping out of high school during my final year. Students normally received their high school diplomas by completing requirements throughout the course of the year. But I'd left school three months early to work at Kitimat. Late in May I got a frantic letter from Phyllis telling me that the vice-principal of Britannia had informed her that my graduation was being revoked.

"Yeo, you vindictive bastard. I'll show you." I fired off a telegram to the Department of Education telling them that I was now resident in the soon-to-be town of Kitimat "where I was attempting to further my education etc. etc. And what were the procedures for sitting the provincial exams here?" Kitimat was still a camp with no families, no school and no kids. I didn't say that I was working there.

Amazingly, Victoria set up an examination centre in Kitimat for me alone and arranged to have the United Church minister in Kitimaat Indian village come over by fishboat to administer the four days' worth of exams. He was a young guy who was rather horrified by what he saw. The trouble was that I had forgotten much of what I'd learned and didn't have textbooks with me to brush up on what had been taught during the months I'd been absent. Besides that I was working twelve hours a day, seven days a week on the night shift at the time. Bleary-eyed, I tried to remember what I'd known of algebra and chemical formulas as a stream of twenty-ton Euclids rumbled by.

The result was that while I got my high school diploma the grades were very marginal and I had to defend them when I later tried to enter the University of British Columbia. The dean of admissions decided to let me have a shot at college until I flunked out. Students from similar backgrounds and with similar grades wouldn't be allowed into BC universities today: clearly not university material.

Cut-Rate Icarus

Ali had been down to Mexico a number of times as a seaman and was enthused about the country and its people. So, in December of 1952, with a year of high school Spanish under my belt and a full sixteen years old, I decided that I was going to see Mexico for myself. The earnings from my first stint at Kitimat would cover that. I'd read everything I could get my hands on about Mexico. The plan was to take off a month from school starting with the Christmas break, but if I liked Mexico I intended to stay as long as my money lasted. I had no qualms about anything.

> Cuautla, Adelita.
> The land of Diego Rivera.
> *Si hoy bebo tequila, Mañana tomo jerez!*

While I'd gotten a passport in my own name I also needed a notarized letter verifying parental permission to travel alone. Ali was working in the camps again and the problem was to convince my mother to give me written permission. I talked her into it by appealing to what she had done as a girl my age, which in fact was a good deal more daring. The clincher was, "Besides, it's my own money." Finally, somewhat to my surprise, Phyllis said okay.

But at the border post at Blaine I was taken off the bus by the US Immigration Service and hauled over the coals, the first of many hassles with that outfit. They kept me there and grilled me for the better part of four hours. "Are you running away?" "Where did a kid like you get a passport anyway?" "I wouldn't let a kid of mine travel to Mexico on his own," opined one border guard. (I was going to say that if I was a kid of his I wouldn't have the imagination or initiative to go to Mexico but instead bit my tongue and answered politely.) The immigration officer in charge grumbled about this and that and generally acted as if the purity of Utah and the protection of America rested on his shoulders. Why is it that immigration officials everywhere in the world seem to be the most smug and arrogant pricks to be found in their respective countries?

Mainly it boiled down to them thinking that I was sneaking into the land of bilk and money to snatch a job out of the mouths of Americans. "Why would I do that? I can get a decent job without coming to the States ... Sir! I just want a transit visa to get to the Mexican border." That ruffled their feathers and I had to sit around another couple of hours until the Chief Immigration Officer of Blaine station arranged a Board of Inquiry to decide my case. It consisted of him and three other honchos around the place.

I'm sworn in to testify, a sixteen-year-old facing four army surplus St. Peters guarding the borders of heaven on earth. The Chief tells me that I'm under no legal obligation to participate in this inquiry but that if I don't they will take that into account. I figured that was it and I'd have to return to Canada and try another border post.

They quiz me again about my papers, where I got my money and where I figure on crossing into Mexico. They still had me pegged as hot to become an assistant *lavaplatos* in Los Angeles or something. As it happened, this was just a couple of weeks before the McCarren-Walter Immigration Control Act was to come into effect, one of the more odious pieces of McCarthyist legislation which virtually gave the 'Migra carte blanche powers to exclude anyone not to their liking. It even gave them powers to deport naturalized American citizens without trial if they were suspected of having been engaged in some act, word or thought prejudicial to Cold War Americanism. There was a whole mess of new regulations and an expanded list of prohibited categories of entrants into the land of the free.

The Chief asks, "Do you now or have you ever belonged to the Federation of Labour Youth?" That was a minuscule Communist Party outfit which I doubt that one in a thousand Canadians had ever heard of.

"No Sir. But . . . ah . . ."

"Yes. Speak up." They lean forward and their ears perk up.

"I did belong to a labour union, Sir! On my last job." It was a passing flippancy accompanied with eyeball rolling on my part.

"Don't you act smart with us or I'll terminate this inquiry right now." ("En boca cerrada no entran moscas.") He was quicker on the uptake than I'd expected.

Finally they gave me a one-week transit visa which had to be turned in at the US border station at Nogales before crossing into Mexico. Whether I would be allowed to pass back through the States after the new immigration act was in force was left up to those on the other end to worry about. That was fine with me.

Down the Pacific Highway and into Portland, where I stop off and try to find the old loggers district I've read about in Archie Binns and Stewart Holbrook but which had passed away a generation before. Through the mountains and down into the Napa Valley where — "Jesus, it's spring." Down the coast to Angeltown and then east across the Mojave into Tuscon where a hot December sun is ripening the oranges. Despite everything, parts of America are beautiful.

If you thought that after this build-up you'd at least see Mexico through the eyes of a sixteen-year-old romantic then you're out of luck. I got to Nogales, a dusty little border town, on Christmas eve and crossed over to the Mexico side only to find that the train I'd planned to travel down the coast on didn't leave for another two days. All of a sudden I got lonely.

"You can't turn back now. What are people back home going to say after you told them that you are going to Mexico?"

Repuesta: "This is supposed to be exciting but it's no fun this way. Who says I have to please somebody else anyway?".

"It's supposed to be an adventure. There's supposed to be some difficulty in it. What sort of a seaman are you going to be if you are even afraid to go to Mexico on your own ?"

"I'm not afraid, I'm lonely. And I am going to visit my friend in LA," an increasingly stubborn ego answered back. There was a guy I'd worked with in Kitimat who was spending the winter visiting his sister in Los Angeles. It didn't strike me as unusual that I could find somebody from the camps a thousand miles from home. So I returned to LA, stayed with some other friends, made the rounds of the city and waltzed into the US Immigration Service about a week after my transit visa had expired and after the McCarran-Walter Act was in force. The desk officer was so dumbfounded that he gave me an extension of forty-eight hours to get back over the Canadian border or face arrest. That was alright too. I'd had enough of the US of A.

After coming back from the States I still had some money burning a hole in my pocket. Down at the Rex Cinema, locale of childhood matinees, I happened to see Breaking the Sound Barrier. There is a scene in which a minor character is learning to fly in an old Gypsy Moth. He panics on trying to land during his first solo, stalls the plane and is killed in the crash. The sequence is filmed from the cockpit. Although I had never been especially interested in flying, that grabbed me. "Say, that's something. I bet I could learn to fly."

So I trekked out to Vancouver airport, then merely a cluster of small huts and hangars on the south shore of Sea Island, and signed up with the Royal Canadian Flying Club. That outfit was hooked into a government scheme which refunded a third of the cost of the lessons if you got your basic pilot's license.

At sixteen I may have seemed rather young to be flying but the instructors were quite nonchalant about it and treated me like anyone else. I went out to the airport on weekends and took off school days to take lessons. I didn't tell my parents what I was doing — it was going to be a surprise, to show what I could do on my own, I suppose. It never crossed my mind that their feelings would be hurt. That's typical of the teenager I was.

Fleet Canucks were the planes we learned on. Wood and canvas two-seaters with a stick control, without a radio and with almost no instruments. When I say there were almost no instruments, I mean — well, for instance, the air speed indicator is important because at landing it's critical to come in as slow as possible yet keep your air speed above the stalling range. If you're at a thousand feet altitude or more a stall is no great consequence with these light planes. But a stall while landing can easily lead to a crash. The air speed indicator on the Fleet Canucks was merely a strip of thin spring steel on a calibrated arch attached to the wing strut on the pilot's side. Air rushing past the indicator was supposed to bend the indicator back to give you the speed reading — if it wasn't stuck and if you could make it out through the rain and grime. Usually you just looked at how fast the ground was coming up at you to estimate your landing speed.

They were a great trainer though, almost foolproof. With its over-head wing and light engine a Fleet Canuck would level out almost on its own once you had the nose down and had the plane straightened out. They also had a tremendous glide ratio and with a bit of finesse you could have landed on one of the grassy fields on Lulu Island without power.

The instructors weren't for dragging things out. They went through what we were going to do that day and cautioned you about whatever mistakes you'd made previously. They ran through the drill again once when we were in the air and then handed the ship over to you. The first few hours you are at the controls the plane yaws, pitches, rolls and side slips spasmodically. But the instructional policy was maximum hands-on practice as soon as possible. It worked well. It was basic stuff. Flying by the seat of your pants, getting the feel of the stick when the ship's ready to pull up at take-off, getting the feel of a properly made turn, getting the look of glide angles on landing, and so forth. It comes easy at that age.

Actually, flying was easier than learning how to drive. The only procedure that was somewhat tricky was landing. It takes some experience to estimate how fast the ground is coming up at you, what kind of glide angle to set in order to get into the space you have to land in. When you're about fifteen feet above the ground you cut the engine way back and level out so that the plane sinks down. You've got to have a certain amount of momentum or she'll just pancake in, which is murder on the undercarriage. Alternately, if you come down too steeply you'll have to pull up and the aircraft may float when you cut the engine. That was the only time the instructors lost their cool. "Cut back the throttle! Bring her up! You're flying the nose into the ground!" A jolt of excitement there.

I soloed after ten hours, which was about the average. Jesus what a feeling, that first time you are up on your own. The instructor takes you through the basic landing drill one more time without hinting that you are going to solo. Then, as you are about to take off for the third time he unbuckles, steps out of the plane and says "Okay, it's all yours. Just do exactly like you've been doing and you'll be fine. Give yourself lots of room on approach to land. Now wait till I get away before you rev her up."

You are sitting on the grassy landing strip at forty-five degrees to the control tower and then move the plane into take-off position. Keep your eyes glued on the tower to catch the green light they'll flash you as clearance to take off. There it is. Push the throttle full in, hold the stick tight with both hands, we're picking up speed racing down the grassy strip. The tail rises off the ground and at forty miles an hour you can feel the nose wanting to lift. You hold her down a bit longer — there is definitely a feel to it — then at the right moment you give a slight pull back on the stick and the plane leaps into the air.

You set the nose into the correct climb angle, not too steep now. The engine roars, all sixty-five horsepower. You're climbing to a thousand feet. "I DID IT! Woo-hee!" You look over to where the instructor would normally be sitting — empty. You are up there on your own and singing at the top of your lungs. The solo is only a mundane ten-minute circuit around the airport before you land and it's over before you know it. But it's one hell of an experience.

There was more instruction after soloing but mainly I practiced take-off and landing and various other manoeuvres over Delta farmlands. Emergency landings was a real bugbear with the instructors. You'd take the plane up to about three thousand feet and the instructor would cut the engine, kick the rudder pedal, bring the stick back and over so the ship would go into a stall and then a spin. He'd then hand the controls back to you. You were supposed to bring the ship out of the spin within five hundred feet. Then, simulating an engine failure, you set the plane into a glide path for some grass field you'd picked for an emergency landing and descend in a zig zag pattern. The idea was to develop a habit of how to handle a stall and to give you confidence so you wouldn't panic if the engine cut out.

In these drills you were always supposed to push in the throttle and pull up before you got to five hundred feet above the ground. But once when I was up on my own I picked a long pasture with cows grazing on it and glided down to a hundred feet to watch them kick their heels and galomp away in all directions. Sixteen-year-olds can be responsible under certain conditions but when they get tired of being that they can quickly return to being sixteen-year-olds.

My last flight was a trip from Sea Island to Chilliwack. You can drive it now in an hour on the freeway, which is about the time it took me to fly there and land. Those Fleet Canucks only did about eighty miles an hour. I detoured through a no-go area to pass over Sumas Mountain. I'd looked up at that mountain so many times when going out to visit Koeppen's stump ranch behind Cultus Lake as a kid that I had to fly over it. Between fighting the updrafts and downdrafts I surveyed the upper Fraser Valley, the abandoned interurban line that brought us up from Vancouver snaking along the edge of the mountains on the other side of the valley, Sardis, where we'd wait for the milk truck, Vedder Mountain where I'd gotten myself lost as a kid.

Shortly after my seventeenth birthday I had gotten my license, had left school and was back in Kitimat again. Learning to fly took about six weeks and cost me three hundred dollars. I've often spent ten times that amount without ever knowing where it went. Even though I had no desire to fly afterward it was one of the best uses I ever made of my money.

Ah well, adolescent triumphs. Everyone has their own. But how did I manage it all then? More energy? Greater opportunities? Jobs in camps, trips abroad and minor adventures were intermixed with reading extensively, lusting after girls, going on mountain climbing trips and often feeling bored.

None of it was really planned. Most of what I did stemmed from spur-of-the-moment decisions and opportunities. What job you might get and where was unpredictable. What problems and possibilities one might find at work or while traveling were equally unforeseeable. I usually didn't even talk over these decisions with anyone before launching into them. I was willing enough to listen to advice as long as I wasn't required to follow it.

Kitimat

Money

During 1952 and 1953 the Kitimat project was the biggest construction undertaking to hit BC in over a generation. It involved work in three widely separated sites, the largest of which was Kitimat, where a huge aluminum smelter, port and town were being built at the previously isolated head of Douglas Channel. Kitimat itself was comprised of three separate construction camps. During the height of the project there were rarely less than two thousand men working there, usually on a week-round basis. There was a continual round of coming and going with few men staying more than four months at a stretch. By the time I got there they were clearing the site and laying the foundations for the smelter, which began to rise the following year.

Kitimat Constructors was a consortium of construction companies which somehow had gotten a cost-plus contract from Alcan and were assured a percentage of the construction costs as profit if the work was finished on schedule. "The more cost the more plus," as the old saying goes. That accounts for the lavish use of men and equipment and the eighty-four-hour work weeks. Getting off the boat you were greeted by a sign which read "Welcome To Kitimat", and in smaller letters, "May your stay be pleasant and profitable. Private property. No trespassing." I worked there for two months in 1952 and some five months in 1953.

Signs on the main dock welcoming workers to Kitimat.

It was a one hundred percent unionized site. The housing, food and pay were tops. You could earn three times as much in Kitimat as you could working in the city although your life in camp consisted of working, eating and sleeping. I was going to say "and nobody ever killed themselves working" but that's not true. In fact there are always men killed and maimed in construction projects like that.

Men and machines swirled about in a constant, twenty-four-hour-a-day, seven-day-a-week frenzy. "Harnessing the rivers", "moving mountains", "taming the Volga" and so forth. I've got to admit that I was hooked on the drama of megaprojects. But of course the main thing was the big money to be made. Although I was all for environmental conservation elsewhere, it didn't seem to enter into my thinking about Kitimat. I feel differently about those kinds of projects now.

The Kitimat river, a gravelly oversized stream, was an incredibly productive salmon river. One used to hear stories from oldtimers about how the Fraser had once teemed with salmon runs so thick that in places you could spear fish with a pitch fork. I never believed it. But the Kitimat river was pretty close to that. From a log footbridge you could see salmon by the thousands, clutches of them every few feet, pointing upstream and hovering in the water, twisting upriver a bit and then stopping again.

The people living in Kitimaat Indian village across the channel must have hated us and what we were doing. I didn't think much about that either but I would have hated it if it had been my home, because we just tore the head of the inlet apart. When the project was finished a supremely ugly smelter and a deadening company town stood on what had been an isolated rainforest delta.

Midsummer's Eve, 1952

A Norwegian, an affable giant of a guy, worked on the night shift of the cookhouse with me during the first year. He'd only been in Canada a short while and was homesick and depressed by life in Kitimat. We got to talking about where he had been the previous midsummer's eve — camping with his girlfriend in the mountains of Norway. Although it was already early July we decided that we should honour the arrival of summer by cracking some of our newly bottled wine.

I don't remember whose idea it had been to do some brewing but we had gallons of homemade wine stashed away. "That's not going to be near ready yet. It'll be yeasty fruit juice," says Max, the chief cook and perpetual killjoy.

"Haven't ya heard of spring wine?"

So, one by one, we trek over to the bunkhouse and sneak back with bottles of indeed yeasty but already quite potent wine. First a libation to Midsummer's Eve. "Hail, and Welcome the Sun."

But as more bottles appear the celebration loses its high purpose. From sampling the wine we got into tasting everyone's batch. By the time the day shift came on we were draped around the mess hall in various states of good cheer.

Who else was on that crew? There was Art, a punch-drunk old boxer in his late forties. His face had been mashed up and his brains scrambled in too many fights and although he was a friendly guy you often couldn't make out what he was getting at because his speech was badly slurred. Art did watercolours in his time off, usually not very good copies of French impressionist paintings. It's too bad that neither he nor anyone else twigged to the possibilities of painting what was going on around us.

I've already mentioned Max, a grousy Dutchman who'd been working in camps since the 1930s. He knew Ali from various places they'd worked together and he had once helped smuggle my father back to

Vancouver in his steamer cabin when Ali was stuck, flat broke, at some wharf somewhere. It comes to me that I was taking a correspondence course that summer which included an English translation of a Euripides play. To my surprise it turned out that Max, a true misanthropist, was an enthusiast of the classics. Without benefit of drink he launched into recitations of Catullus or god knows what interspersed with gloomy predictions of what camp work would entail.

There was also a young French Canadian and a recent Italian immigrant on the crew who I have difficulty keeping straight. They were both homesick and feeling that they'd fallen off the end of the world. And there was the sandwich man. Luckily we didn't see too much of him because he hated "DPs" — "displaced persons", a phrase that became part of the language in the years after World War II, and which meant something akin to "Bohunk" in the vernacular no matter where they were from and regardless of whether they had arrived last week or had been in Canada for the last forty years.

Kitimat was teeming with men from throughout Canada and with recent European immigrants. They were all typically referred to as "DPs".). Italian, Yugoslav, German and almost every immigrant from Europe encountered that to one degree or another. It was incumbent upon immigrants to volunteer that Canada was "the greatest country on earth" rather than respond to the freefloating racism in the manner it deserved. It was infuriating to see.

My best friend was also on that night shift crew. Mike Tarrida had been in the country for about two years by then, most of it spent working in camps. He wanted it understood that he was a Catalan and not a Spaniard. Miguel was in his mid thirties but had already lived through more than a full lifetime of experiences and tribulations before arriving in Canada. Normally he claimed, "I don't know nothing from nothing." That was a response intended to shortcircuit the maunderings of those who took upon themselves to educate the "DPs" about the world.

Mike had been born and raised in Barcelona and was a living part of that city's revolutionary heritage. Both he and his father had been arrested and worked-over by the police during the repression which followed the 1934 miners rising in Asturias. Mike made satiric jibes at his own youthful ideals but he was one of those who were once known as an *obrero conciente*.

Miguel could recite long passages of Frederico Garcia Lorca by

The Delta King, *an actual sternwheeler brought in 1953 to provide temporary housing for Alcan workers.*

heart. There were a couple of Lorca's poems in an anthology I had packed along and I couldn't see they were all that great. Literary criticism while scrubbing pots on the night shift in the Kitimat cookhouse. Mike quotes a long passage from the "Romanza de la Guardia Civil" which contains a phrase "Con calaveras plumbas", referring to the Spanish Civil Guard, the three-cornered-hat gang.

"What does it say, translate," directs Professor Tarrida.

"Ah . . . with lead something other. 'With lead heads'."

"The bone in the head. What is the word in English?" Miguel asks.

"Skull. With leaden skulls. That's more or less the same as what I said."

"No . . . Lead skulls so thick that no ideas, no feelings can enter their heads. What else. What else has heads of lead?"

"I don't know. All sorts of things," say I, unpoetically.

"The bullets in the guns they carry. Their skulls are like bullets, the bullets are their heads — the Guardia Civil."

"Ah come on Mike, that's not all in that little phrase."

Tarrida raises his eyebrows and throws up his hands in a characteristic gesture. "You are a student. And you are reading Lorca. You must hear the soul of this poetry."

My own enthusiasm may have resurrected some of Miguel's own youthful feelings but he felt impelled to temper his tales with accounts of sometimes bitter absurdity as a cautionary measure. I heard of Casas Viejas from a man who remembered the rage with which the citizens of Barcelona learned of the fate of a group of Andalusian peasant anarchists who attempted to set up a village republic only to be massacred by the Guardia Civil. There were reminiscences of names and incidents which had entered Spanish working-class folk memory in the generation long prelude to the civil war. Also accounts of El Campesino and Sabater and their raids into Spain after the collapse of the Republic.

Miguel himself had been no older than me when he had fought with a Confederacion Nacional del Trabajo militia unit on the Aragon front. When Franco's army swept into Catalonia in late 1938, Miguel along with some three hundred thousand other men, women and children fled up the coast for their lives. While the French government grudgingly accepted most of them, the French military and police treated the Republican refugees as criminals and interned most of them in prison camps, where many indeed died. Miguel was a veteran of a defeated revolutionary army, the inheritor of a mulifaceted socialist heritage, an internee in a prison camp established by the democratic government of France by the time he was nineteen.

Two years later France had fallen and the Vichy regime, with the support of a wide sector of the French population, joined itself to the Axis war effort. Miguel and other able bodied Spaniards in the internment camps were given the choice of serving in labour battalions building German military installations in France or being returned to Spain where they faced certain imprisonment and possible execution. There were then as many political prisoners in Spain as there were in German concentration camps. So Miguel allowed himself to be conscripted into a labour battalion. The French Left was indifferent about the matter at first but within a year such work was seen as "collaborating with the enemy". Makar Potrebenko, a survivor of both the Russian revolution and Polish fascism in the occupied Ukraine, understood those complexities when we talked about Tarrida's story a generation later. The impossible and absurd choices which people face in situations like this.

An old friend of Tarrida's was also working in Kitimat. Jose was also Catalan. With his swarthy complexion and minimal English Jose was at times the butt of racist mouthings-off. He felt that no one who hadn't experienced the events they had lived through could understand them. For that matter, he figured that most people who had lived through those times hadn't understood what was going on even as it was going on around them. At the time I thought that Jose was just being cynical. I could understand why he felt the way he did but that as a general conclusion it was ridiculous. Now, I'm inclined to agree with him.

Shortly after I left the cookhouse and got a real job. A "real job" meant working outside, building or wrecking something. The job I got didn't even pay as much as I earned in the kitchen because while the wage rate was higher we didn't get as much overtime. Everyone wanted as much overtime as possible because the more you earned the quicker you could get a stake together and get out.

The smelter site was situated on a deltaic bog and was being built up of sand and gravel trucked in from a nearby sandhill and dredged up out of the inlet. A slurry of sand and water was pumped in from the sea bottom and spewed over the site. As each layer was drained and consolidated an endless string of trucks, ten-ton Macks and twenty-ton Euclids and even heavier belly dumps, humped and bumped through a perpetual haze of dust or a mist of mud to deposit their loads. Cats and graders clanked and shuffled about, draglines whizzed their flying shuttles out into boggy sinks, scooping out muck. This went on for most of the day and night. The first crews of cement and ironworkers were at work and by the time I left a framework of steel girders for the smelter itself had begun to rise.

All hiring was supposedly done out of union halls or the Kitimat Constructors office in Vancouver. That was the way it actually did work for the skilled trades but for unskilled labour there was usually a way to shift over without leaving camp. I wanted to learn how to operate heavy construction equipment, it didn't matter what kind, so I hoped to land a job as a swamper on one of the rigs. But I never did. I always wound up on some unskilled job in all the camps I was in.

I wound up on a labour gang engaged in cleaning out the drainage channels and clearing the debris from around the sluice gates. There were chewed up remnants of logs and roots which had somehow been pumped through the pipeline which had to be removed.

You worked on your own most of time, prying out the debris and manhandling it to where a truck and front end loader could get at it. The bigger pieces were winched out by cable. During the course of a day I might drift over to where another guy was doing the same job but most of them on that gang were recent Yugoslav or Italian immigrants not much interested in conversation. So sometimes I'd be out there in the afternoon rain singing or talking to myself as the truck came along. "Talking to yerself now eh? Time to catch the boat out when ya start that kid."

There was one incident involving that floating pipeline I remember vividly. I almost drowned while trying to swim out to it. The pipeline was only a hundred and fifty yards off shore and I was then a strong swimmer but about two thirds of the way out my arms went numb. No strength, like rubber. ("Don't panic, speed up and get the blood circulating! . . . I can't . . . Roll on your back and kick your legs! . . . Ah, this works.") But after another thirty yards my legs went numb too. ("This can't be . . . Don't think, just kick! Kick, legs, Kick! Help, I'm sinking. I can't drown here. Oh no.")

I wasn't twenty yards from the pipeline but didn't think I'd make it. I was scared yet at the same time couldn't believe that this was happening to me. By flexing my body I somehow managed to wriggle the last distance and fortunately found a strut to hang on to. After I had my arms out of the water for a few minutes enough strength returned so that I could pull myself up on to the pontoons. Shivering and yelling I finally attracted the attention of a guy working on the dock. He rounded up a rowboat and came out and got me. "Of all the God damn fucking stupid stunts. Where the fucking hell do you think you are — English Bay?" I didn't care what he said, I was just thankful to be alive.

By the end of five months I'd saved more than two thousand dollars, which was a hell of a lot of money then, and it was burning a hole in my pocket. I left Kitimat without anything definite in mind except making good use of my money. I wasn't going to blow my stake on a spree. Then that two thousand in my pocket would have bought a couple of acres of overgrown farmland with an old shack on it around Fort Langley. But I wasn't going to waste my hard-earned money buying land. Only a few years earlier Ebe Koeppen had offered to give me a couple of acres split off from the homestead he was selling up in the Columbia Valley. Using my money wisely for me meant going on a trip.

It was twenty-five years before I saw Kitimat again. I had gone up to Terrace in the mid 1970s to see about a teaching job. Since I was in the neighbourhood I decided to zip down and see how Kitimat had turned out. There had been a bitter strike the year before in which a small army of Mounties had arrested some two hundred strikers in a scene which could have been taken from the organizing drives of the 1930s. The dastardly Alcan workers had refused to accept a wage rollback by the federal Anti-Inflation Board. They were cited for contempt of court and arrested for striking. That may have contributed to the oppressive aura of the place.

I didn't recognize anything. The only thing which looked familiar was the old dock beyond the edge of town and the view down Douglas Channel. Just before leaving I found the overgrown foundations of one of the bunkhouses I'd lived in. Work camps had their faults but they were certainly less deadening than the kind of "stable industrial community" which Kitimat had become.

FIVE

Berlin Diary

Shipping Out

After coming down from Kitimat the first plan — i.e., pipe dream — was to buy an old fishing boat in California and cruise down the coast of Mexico and Central America with a friend of mine from camp. But he backed out. So instead I steamed off to Berlin, which was going to be just a stop on the way to Spain.

I suppose there must have been some cheaper and slower way I could have gotten to Europe. But it took me two weeks of solid traveling to get from Vancouver to Berlin. Across the northern States by bus, through former mine towns like Butte, over rolling short grass prairies and past Minnesota woodlots. A day spent wandering around Chicago and visiting the still functioning IWW headquarters on North Halstead. Then eastward and back across the border into a blue-lawed Toronto Sunday and on to Quebec City, where the ship I'd booked passage on was laying.

The *Arosa Kulm* was one of the oldest passenger ships still operating on the North Atlantic crossing. Passenger ships were then being replaced by air travel but these boats carried the last waves of European working-class immigrants to Canada. The fare for dormitory class, Quebec City to Bremerhaven, bunk and board for almost seven days and nights, was one hundred and fifty dollars. There was the

Olympic Line and the Home Line and the outfit which ran the *Arosa Kulm*. She was about six thousand tons, built in the 1920s, and on the lower decks red-leaded rust flaked off the iron work like orange snow. The obligatory witticism was that she was the flagship of the Swiss merchant navy because the company head offices were in Zürich. She was registered in Panama, naturally.

Dormitory accommodations were as spartan as any camp I ever lived in but it was a good way to meet your fellow travelers. Since it was the last run of the season the ship was only quarter booked and we had plenty of room. Dormitory class was far preferable to traveling by luxury liner because of the better class of people one met on the *Arosa Kulm*.

It wasn't boring, the days didn't drag. It was great. We sat around on deck when it wasn't too cold or stormy and lounged around the *Bierstube* when it was. There were enough interesting people to talk and listen to. I got to know two guys well enough so that I later visited them in their industrial towns in the Ruhr. In addition, sitting at our third-class table was Diamond Jenness and his wife. Although I wasn't interested in anthropology at the time, I'd read part of his monumentally boring Indians of Canada . He must have recently retired from the National Museum of Canada. Hopefully when I was an anthropologist I never appeared to others the way he did.

About a day west of Land's End we see the first British trawlers dipping and diving over the high swells, like a scene out of Grierson's Drifters . We pass up the English Channel and the next afternoon approach the estuary of Bremerhaven. The sea just seemed to merge into the land. ("Jesus, it's a swamp.") We dock and are quickly processed through immigration and customs. None of the problems I'd been anticipating arise, so I could dispense with the sundry impractical schemes I'd mulled over in case of trouble with Immigration officials, such as leaving the ship as a crewman. A bunch of us troop down to the boat train and soon are lurching through the night. By the time I got to Braunschweig I was on my own and early in the morning, before dawn, I got to the airport and flew into Berlin

East Berlin had become the capitol of the German Democratic Republic while West Berlin continued to be administered by the three western occupying powers. Although the Berlin Blockade had ended some five years earlier its aura still hung over the city and its connections to the rest of Germany. The "Berlin airlift" had been one of the first campaigns of the cold war and in 1953 I broadly accepted the western accounts of it. It was only after being in Berlin and listening to people that I began to realize how much hype had been involved.

There was however a steady stream of people leaving the GDR for "the west". They were called *Flüchtlinge* (escapees) in the West German press but with a growing connotation of what "DP" meant in Canada. Almost two million such emigrants had left the GDR since the end of the war. It was easy enough to do then; you just went to Berlin and walked across the open border. Despite the claims of both East and West one can't make a blanket evaluation of why people stayed or left or what kind of people they were. In addition, there were seven to eight million true refugees in West Germany, survivors of those German populations which had been driven from their ancestral homelands in eastern Germany and Bohemia at the end of the war by national liberators. The atrocities and cynical chauvinism involved in that process didn't then lead me to re-evaluate my understandings, partly because I couldn't sort out the reality from the propaganda.

Maybe it was because of the battered leather jacket, heavy fisherman's trousers and work boots I wore. It may have been the pack sack I lugged around. But for one reason or another I was often pegged as one of the *Flüchtlinge*. Some of the recently resurrected German burghers looked at me like the respectable citizenry of West Vancouver might look at someone who had just dropped off the freights. But appearing like a refugee was a good mask in public. If I kept my replies short I could even pass as a native speaker of German, although one with an indefinable accent.

In the Stone City

I arrived at Tempelhof on a cold, early November morning. I'd decided that before going to look up any of my relatives I'd wander around Berlin to get some impressions of the city. I knew that it had been devastated during the war and had seen pictures of the effect of saturation bombing eight years earlier. But no newsreel or magazine article, not even Ali's selectively toned down accounts of his visit in 1947, could prepare me for my first morning in Berlin.

I boarded a bus headed into the city without any destination in mind. I'd just ride, look, get off and wander around. I had a feeling of anticipation but I didn't know of what. It turned out to be All Souls Day.

Berlin, 1943. This does not give any true idea of the scale of destruction.

Morning. A weak sun peeked through mist drifting along the streets. Empty, hardly anyone on the streets. Silent. The first person I see on the street is an old woman in a shawl, all in black, hobbling along. It may sound theatrical but that is the way reality is at times.

We were soon into what had once been an apartment district off the southern core of Berlin. That was when I began to get an intimation of what devastation means. Though I didn't know it then this was not one of the most heavily bombed districts. ("My God.") The road detours around islands of consolidated rubble and fragmented scenes appear from and disappear again into the mist. Off to one side a broken, gap-toothed line of what had been brick apartment buildings. Some are just heaps of shored-up rubble behind brick facades. Others are partly patched up, the first two floors inhabited, gutted upper floors visible through windowless sockets. As we get into the core of Berlin there are more signs of life; streetcars and trucks and a pod of people here and there waiting for a trolley.

I get off the bus to wander down one street and up another, past battered tenement buildings and fields of rubble. From time to time gusts of wind blow dust and fragments of plaster and broken brick and tinkling shards of glass down from the upper stories of ruins. These were the artifacts of a war which had ended eight years before and which had already been relegated to history by most North Americans.

Late that afternoon I got to Spandau and headed over to my grandmother's address. She was the only one of that generation left alive — my mother's mother. I had never known any of my relatives and I can't say I had any special feeling of connection to them. Nevertheless. I ring the bell of a battered but more or less intact brownstone apartment building. "Yes, who is it?" A shrunken and suspicious old lady stands at the door.

"Rolf . . . Phyllis's son . . . Your grandson."

"Oh, my dear. I never thought I would see you again," followed by crying. The first thing she wanted know after hearing that my parents were alright was, "My god, you're not here as part of the American army are you?" And she began to belabor me with warnings about the dangers of sex and the threat of war preparations, in about that order.

Right or wrong, I couldn't take much of that. In fact, my grandmother rubbed me the wrong way. I was pretty callow. Here was someone who had come of age in the working-class districts of Berlin during the last quarter of the nineteenth century. Did I have the patience to ask her about that world? Of course not.

I went to stay at an uncle's place in a block of workers' flats built in the 1920s on the northernmost outskirts of Spandau. It was a rather impressive complex for its time. You could walk down to the River Havel through a cluster of Laubgarten plots or hike over to a pine forest which abutted the East German frontier. But it was a long streetcar ride from Berlin proper and it was a strained arrangement at my uncle's.

Werner had gone through the hunger and chaos which had decimated the Berlin working class during World War I. As a young construction worker he had briefly been part of the Communist resistance to the Nazi regime and, along with his older brothers Fritz and Kurt, had wound up in one of the early concentration camps during the mid 1930s. Werner had survived that, been released and then conscripted and sent into the invasion of the Soviet Union. There he was captured and held in a prisoner-of-war camp for five years after the end of the war.

Werner had returned from a Soviet POW camp just two years earlier and he didn't want to or couldn't talk about any of it. I doubt whether I would have understood the absurdities involved anyway. He was a physical and nervous wreck. To top it off his wife had inoperable cancer and although they lived together they barely talked to each other. Their sixteen-year-old daughter hovered around, torn between filial duty and the desire to get the hell out of the situation as soon as possible.

It was only in the previous year that food, the basic staples, had been available at prices which most working people could afford. In East Berlin a rationing system was still in effect. The availability of food in West Berlin didn't mean that luxury goods such as coffee, meat, fruit and so forth were generally available to much of the population. Money was the rationing system in effect there. But there were enough potatoes and green vegetables to fill up on. People sometimes ate them in gargantuan quantities, like the first meal I had at Werner's place.

His daughter brought in a heaping bowl of steamed potatoes in their jackets and put it on the table in front of me. "That surely can't be for two people," I thought. No, that was my bowl of potatoes with another one for Werner. Each of us also got a dish of sauce with a fragment of herring in it. Potatoes and Brussels sprouts, cabbage or cauliflower soups; tasty enough but never really complete if you were used to a meat diet. "Do you ... ah ... Do people here always have such big meals?" I asked. That was one of the few times I got a laugh out of Werner. They were all thin as rakes too.

It was a cold winter in Berlin, the kind of cold which seeps through your clothes and saps your body heat. Coal was expensive and few places were ever really heated, neither stores nor public buildings nor apartments. Families bought their weekly supply of fuel from backyard lots by the kilo. Ten kilos of coal briquettes and an armful of kindling wood carted home in a rickety hand cart looking as if they were straight out of a Zille or Baluschek sketch. The same applied in Fritz's place over in East Berlin, and he was a party functionary.

If you were chilled from a day outside you never got warm until you crawled into bed. The only places which were heated, overheated actually, were the small neighbourhood pubs and dives. There you'd find regular customers nursing along a beer or knocking back an occasional schnapps and reading their newspapers or playing cards. I'd often sit in one of these pubs with a drink just to warm up. Everybody thought it was quite humorous that I, a Canadian coming from the lands of ice and snow, should make such a fuss about the cold. How elderly people survived winter I don't know.

Die Unzerstörbare Stadt ("The Indestructible City") was the title of a photo history of Berlin which was making a splash at the time. "Indestructible? Well, they knocked it into pretty small pieces just the

The author and relatives,
Berlin, 1953.

same," quipped my grandmother. Trüb (gloomy) doesn't convey the quality of Berlin in the winter of 1953. "Battered" would be a better word. Yet in some way Berlin was a compelling city to my eyes. No sea, no mountains, spread over a rolling sandy plain astride the Havel and Spree, which by my standards hardly passed muster as rivers. It surprised me that I felt that way.

It was a few weeks before I learned what ruins really are. It was the Hallisches Tor district near Kreuzberg, off the eastern core of Berlin, in what had been one of the older and most densely packed working-class districts in the city. I suppose Stalingrad and Warsaw and the London docks looked like this immediately after the war. Although I'll try to describe it, it was indescribable.

Standing on a station platform of an elevated train on a bright December morning, the sun appearing and disappearing behind puffy clouds scudding across the sky. Shifting patches of shadow and light are dappled on the fields of rubble and the shells of buildings. About four miles to the northeast, looking like a giant Mayan temple mound in the process of being raised, sits Klamottenberg. It's a man-made hill being built of trainloads of blasted brick and stone, smashed plaster and mashed woodwork, the odds and ends of fittings and undoubtedly the incinerated fragments of what were once human beings. It is built of the debris of tens of thousands of bombed-out and razed buildings which are gradually being cleared.

The Hallisches Tor district had been an old tenement area, you could see that from the surviving shells of buildings. Tenements once four or five stories high, twenty or more families to a building, two to three dozen buildings to a block, a hundred blocks to a square mile, I don't know how many square miles. Total and complete devastation. I stood on the elevated train platform and stared out across a plain of broken rubble and ruins.

You couldn't tell how large these bombed-out areas were with any degree of accuracy because there were no streets anymore. They were all filled with rubble where apartment houses had collapsed on each other and burned. It looked as if a huge scythe had been drawn across this area cutting everything down to a hillocked rubble field two to three storeys high. When you rode past these districts at night it seemed that you were traveling through an inner city moor.

Some islands of burned-out tenements still stood, just the outer walls. When you looked more closely you saw they were filled with collapsed wreckage of the upper storeys. Here and there a gully or a block-sized crater showed the exposed façades of burned out buildings. Everything else had collapsed or had been leveled. The surface of this pitted plateau was composed of shattered sections of stone and segments of brick wall, the stub of a chimney, a fragment of a roof, a few structural beams. Surrealistically, a bathtub or a rotting piece of furniture stuck out from the tussocks of grass and even small saplings which grew on top of the rubble.

How can anybody have survived that ? How many did survive in these districts? Close to a hundred thousand civilians died in Berlin during bombings. They were blown apart or crushed to death in collapsing buildings, they died in fires or were asphyxiated or maimed so badly that they finally succumbed. Carpet bombing, incendiary bombs, thousand-plane raids against what became virtually undefended targets, and finally the massive Soviet artillery barrages in the battle of Berlin.

It was Allied policy to concentrate their saturation bombing raids on the most densely packed areas of the large cities, so it was mainly working class areas which were hit. Not even the factory districts seem to have been as intensively bombed or been as totally destroyed as this. Those who died in these ruins were overwhelmingly members of the Berlin working class: some three quarters of them were women, children and old men.. They were a people who, in point of fact, had been among the first victims of the Nazis. They were members of a class who in general had dared more and done more in the earlier fight against fascism than had those who bombed them.

What makes me angry is not only the fate of those German working people. There were millions of others in Europe who suffered equally. I wouldn't presume to judge whether it is more horrible to die in an incendiary bomb fire, by a bullet or in a gas chamber. What makes me so bitter is that those who claim to speak for the victims of fascism are often only slanderers fostering their own brands of national chauvinism. Many of those who died in the ruins of Berlin were double victims, defeated by the Nazis, killed in the bombings and then maligned by other triumphant chauvinists proclaiming their moral superiority.

That's how I feel now. But at the time it was just mindboggling. It was impossible to comprehend what these ruins, that war, meant in human terms.

I returned to the Hallisches Tor later with the intent of going through the area. The district was uninhabited but a few lanes, like canyons, had been cleared through the rubble. Work crews were digging out and stacking brick to be used in new construction elsewhere. I had intended to climb across the rubble field despite the signs which warned "Danger / Entrance Forbidden". But when I got there the heart just went out of me.

"Rolf is going out to look at ruins again," said my aunt sardonically. "Ach — you can't know what ruins are. We've already cleared up the worst of them." She, a woman in her early fifties, actually was working part-time to clean bricks taken from the rubble of East Berlin. That was Fritz's wife.

Biograph: Shadows of Lost Ancestors

Sophie Kohanek was the last person in my mother's generation still living in Berlin. When I knew her Sophie was in her mid-fifties; she looked older but acted much younger. She and her son lived in Siemensstadt, a district of deadening efficiency flats clustered around the plants of the Siemens company. Klaus was a musician by avocation and electrotechnician by dint of having to earn a living. I felt, for the first time, that I'd finally found some lost kin.

Sophie was a *Wandervogel* still, a sedate hippie with graying hair and a fetish about vegetarianism. Her pantheistic outlook might have been at home in California. There were musical instruments, potted plants and home-made health food stashed around their tiny apartment. That's where I wound up staying much of the time I was in Berlin. I'd roll out my sleeping bag on the floor after an evening of lute and mandolin music and talk.

Presenting fragments of people's lives always distorts things. The times they were a part of, the contradictions, real and apparent, which make sense in the round may seem ludicrous or unbelievable in brief vignettes. One has to rely upon the intuitive capabilities of the reader.

Sophie was of Polish extraction but there was little trace of that background. The Berlin working class at one time had been a melting pot drawing in and incorporating people from throughout Central Europe. Sophie's husband had been a trade union functionary in the early 1930s, had survived years in a concentration camp and had been released sometime before the beginning of the war. In Berlin again, he managed to make contact with a remnant of an underground network. To the Nazi regime (as to any state anywhere) this counted as "treason" and "subversion". Sophie herself didn't know what role he had played and years later she still wondered whether it had made any sense. He had a pistol which he gave to Sophie to hide for him; that in itself was an offense punishable by death. After the war he was one of those who took off to live in the GDR, leaving his old wife and son behind. Without a score card it's often difficult to know who the real heroes and heroines were.

Sophie and Klaus had lived in a nearby apartment block during the war and had come through it physically unscathed. Klaus just managed to escape being dragooned into serving as a munitions passer on the flak batteries around the city, which at the end were being manned partly by fourteen- and fifteen-year-old boys and even girls.

The Battle for Berlin took place during the final month of the war in Europe. It was a totally pointless battle which turned the city into a funeral pyre for the Nazi regime and in the process cost additional hundreds of thousands of Russian and German lives. In order to prevent "capitulation" the *Sicherheitsdienst* or SD, the regime's intelligence agency, combed the city for any man still capable of carrying a rifle and hung "deserters" and "defeat mongers" from lamp posts. Luckily there were no major battles around Siemensstadt but there was scattered sniping at advancing Soviet patrols, either by those who felt they had nothing left to lose or by youthful zealots hopped up on Valhalla and willing to take everyone else with them. Sophie was largely apolitical and her unadorned account of those last few days had a certain authenticity for me.

She had told me this story from the last days of the war. There had been sniping from an apartment building across from where she and her son were hiding, lying flat against the floor and pressed up against an inner wall. Right below them was a Red Army patrol. "The officer yelled, 'Up there, up there. Fire on those windows up there.'" She heard one of the soldiers answer "I can't fire sir. There's a woman in the way." Sophie understood Russian as well as Polish.

Considering the brutality engendered on all sides in that war, Sophie's experience was probably atypical. Certainly it was anecdotal. Yet it was the most important thing she remembered of those final, horrendous weeks. It said something to her about the tenacity of human decency which ultimately might be more important than the policies implemented by governments.

Sophie earned a living doing housework and Klaus worked in a factory. I wandered around the city during a cold but sunny winter. I rarely consulted a map because knowing where I was going would spoil the surprise. For instance, it finally struck me that there actually was a zoo in the centre of the city near the Bahnhof Zoo. So I trudged down there and after a few minutes came smack up against a couple of caribou mooching around beside a full-scale replica of a Haida longhouse. "What are you doing here?" I asked them, half expecting a reply from fellow British Columbians. I'd have been amazed to know that Bella Coola carvers and dancers contracted by the Berlin Ethnographic Museum had wintered over in that town during the 1880s.

Sophie, Klaus and I wanted to make one trip to the Spree Wald, a lake and forest district to the southeast of the city which had been a favorite locale for nature outings since the nineteenth century. But it was in the GDR now, and out of bounds. Sophie taught me what little I ever knew about the guitar and also taught me the words to "Die Warshavianka". In effect, she was the only true kinsman I met in Berlin.

Two of my mother's brothers were living in East Berlin. Fritz's family had been killed in the wartime bombings but he had married again and his second wife came equipped with a teenage daughter. Under the circumstances it seemed only proper to bring along food when I visited people. But Fritz wouldn't allow it, feeling it was a reflection on the living standard in East Berlin.

"Listen Fritz, that's the way we do it in Canada. We bring something along if we're going to a meal or are going to stay with friends." That was an exaggeration but wasn't untrue amongst our circle of friends. "It's like . . . sharing."

"Now, Nephew Rolf. You are a stranger here. I understand that. But I wiped Litze's, your mother's, nose before she went to school . . ."

"Ah well, if that's the way you're going to be about it then . . ." I say, stuck for a fitting reply.

"There is no way you can imagine what we went through, what happened here in Germany. But one thing you have to understand when you come to us — we are not going to weaken the economy of the DDR by so much as one penny for those who want to strangle us. I know very well you are going down to those money changers and getting sixteen of our marks for your American dollar. That is twelve marks stolen from our economy for every dollar you exchange."

"Oh Fritz," his wife interjects in an exasperated tone.

"Yes, that's what it is. Stealing," says Fritz. "So I don't want you to bring anything else along, except your honorable self [making a sarcastic bow], who is always welcome." That's the sort of rhetoric you'd get from him at the drop of a hat. Later on the exchanges got somewhat hotter as he tried to extend avuncular discipline over a recently acquired nephew.

"There's something wrong with that boy. Always restless, never can sit down, has to be on the go somewhere, nowhere." And so on and so forth.

("What the hell are you talking about Fritz? Just what were you doing when you were only a year or two older than me.") Unfortunately I just thought that and didn't say it. I'd glare at him though. Glare, glare. But he hardly noticed it.

Fritz was something of a household tyrant but even I had to recognize that he had been through it all. Although he was only fifty-five years old and looked younger, he had already lived through a number of historic epochs, from the heterodox socialist working-class culture of pre-

World War I Berlin to the trenches of Flanders and through the drawn out and repeatedly defeated revolutionary struggles against German reaction, of which Nazism was initially just one strand. During the Wiemar era Fritz had had numerous close calls, being beaten almost to death once by SA storm troopers and another time by the police. He had lived an underground existence and survived a long stint in Sachsenhausen concentration camp in the 1930s. During the Second World War he had served in a forced labour battalion and had witnessed the destruction of fascism but also the deaths of his own family and most of his comrades. He was an active participant in attempting to build a socialist state in the remnant of central Germany under aegis of a Russian occupying power (which Fritz necessarily saw as the "Socialist Motherland".) All the twists and turns, contradictions, illusions and compromises which that quarter century entailed.

Maybe he was right. Maybe there is no way of understanding it from a distance. But I think that many of the visions of his youth hadn't survived in him. They had been burned out.

Actually, Fritz didn't have much time to spend with relatives. We went on a couple of long walks through what remained of the old sections of East Berlin. One overcast January day we walked around some of the sites of a distant past. He had actually been a clandestine member of the original Spartacus faction and part of the patchwork of revolutionary soldiers' committees in the final months of the First World War. In January of 1919 he was with the Spartacist rising in Berlin. We walked past the bombed-out shell of a railway station, Stettiner Bannhof, where, thirty-five years earlier, Fritz and his detachment had held out, hoping for reinforcements which never came, and then dispersing underground as best they could. Come to think of it, that may have been during the Independent Socialist rising in March of that same year, however impossible that may seem to politically tidy minds.

Fritz had also been involved in opposing the Kapp putsch in 1920. It is described in popular history books as a comic-opera exercise, yet no other working class in Europe managed to stop a powerful military coup through a combination of armed resistance and a general strike. Even before I'd met Fritz I'd heard my father talk of his part in all that. Despite our quarrels I held Fritz in a certain awe.

His wife let a lot pass with an occasional quizzical remark. It was her daughter, Fritz's stepdaughter, who was chaffing at the bit. I don't think he ever had her measure. In a way she was an inheritor of what the past struggles had been about, although both she and Fritz might have disputed that.

While Lotte was a member of the Free German Youth, the Communist Party's youth organization, she chafed under its hand-me-down maxims and prudery. On the surface she might have been mistaken for one of those "alienated youth" which Neues Deutschland pontificated about. In fact she wasn't alienated at all and she didn't have the slightest desire to "go west". But she was fed up with the rigidities of the system and especially with authorities who thought they had a right to stick their noses under or into every bed.

Lotte was just completing her trade school training and was apprenticing as a machinist. I was somewhat put off by this mere girl doing what I'd never been able to do. But Lotte took it as a given since a good half of her apprentice group were women. "That's only surprising to someone from a capitalist society," she said smugly. I don't know how much gender equality there was in the GDR but it touches on an bit of historical irony. The Saturday Evening Post and similar journals of the time pilloried "communist totalitarianism" by reporting that women in countries like the GDR had to work in factories and in other jobs "like men" and that their children were enrolled in state-run nurseries while they did so. Monstrous.

Lotte and I once toured Stalin-Allee, a showpiece housing project which was then much in the news. It was supposed to be an example of the city beautiful which only socialism could or would build. But it was a slice of Victorian wedding cake monumentalism; facades of gleaming white plaster over brick, decorative columns and an architecture vaguely reminiscent of Moscow university. What the thinking behind the Stalin-Allee was I never learned because it was quite atypical of the rebuilding going on in East Berlin at the time. Mainly they were restoring those buildings which could be preserved or were putting up the kinds of functional apartment blocks common to cities everywhere today. Some projects, like the subway station-cum-underground shopping complex at Alexanderplatz, showed that there were architects in the GDR who could come up with exciting and modern designs.

Lotte had been on the margins of the Stalin-Allee demonstrations during the previous spring. While she supported the demands of the construction workers she felt things had gotten out of hand. It had started as a more or less spontaneous strike by bricklayers refusing higher work quotas set by a zealous bureaucracy. On the second day the bricklayers were joined by most of the other construction workers on the project and that in turn evolved into a more general protest demonstration. There was scattered rioting in Berlin which spread to other cities in the GDR, and the paramilitary police and even units of the Soviet army were sent in to suppress it. That had been on June 17, 1953, some six months earlier. Stalin had just died.

While one could travel back and forth between East and West Berlin without hindrance, I wanted to travel around the GDR itself. That was another matter. For that you needed a visa. So I wandered down to the Police Presidium, a fortress-like building near Alexanderplatz. After much showing of papers I'm directed to the visa section.

The government official in charge was a friendly, rather tired-looking young woman. I figured her for twenty. We get to talking and I'm becoming expansive about having "come all the way from the woodcutter camps of the forests of Canada." Laying it on thick in other words. I'm beginning to wonder if I could date her. "Would you be interested in showing me something of the city from a Berliner's eyes and practicing your English or correcting my German?" I think that was the line I was going to use.

She was really quite appealing, kind of wistful, for an official at the East Berlin police headquarters during the height of the cold war. I was an odd sort of fish to come swimming in there in those years, a bumptious seventeen-year-old Canadian without any particular purpose or official connections and speaking an ungrammatical German with a Berlin dialect I was trying to accentuate.

It turns out she's not empowered to grant visas in cases like mine and I have to go to another office. There's a handshake and a smile and I trundle off to see some higher muckamuck.

"You damn fool," I say to myself as I'm already going down the corridor. "Why didn't you ask her for a date?

"No, that's ridiculous — she's a government official and she's older than me too."

"So how old could she be? That's just an excuse, because as usual you were too scared to ask her out. Do you have to be handed everything on a plate? Go back now and say something like —"

"No. It's too late now."

"Well, it's no wonder you're always alone."

I could hitchhike around BC looking for work, ship in an out of work camps, flit across frontiers manned by American or East German border guards without qualms, but I was too shy to ask a girl for a date.

The senior official in charge of travel visas turned out to be an archetypal bureaucrat such as one finds in immigration offices in all corners of the known world. Indeterminately middle-aged, deaf and dumb to anything that isn't in his sheaf of regulations and convinced that he is the first line of defence against foreign infiltration. "Just what are doing here anyway? What purpose do you have in coming to our country?" You know the type.

I tell him that I want to visit some of the places where my father had grown up to see what they looked like. That I was here now but didn't know if I'd ever be back. Nothing particularly convincing but also nothing contrived. The whole thing sounded suspicious to him, naturally.

"We know that elements in the West recruit and try to smuggle young delinquents into our country to stir up troubles. We are not going to let it happen again. Of that you can be sure."

"Are you saying that I'm a juvenile delinquent — or what?" I answer, with a touch of anger.

So that was that. No visa for me. Still, nobody said anything about being in East Berlin and I continued to come and go as I pleased.

By the end of February I had run out of money and had to return to Canada. I flew to New York, bused back to Vancouver and got home a few days before my eighteenth birthday, broke, not particularly happy to be home again, feeling I hadn't done whatever it was I was going to do on my trip to Europe, and unenthused about having to work in the camps again. But less that two weeks later I was on the skeleton crew reopening the La Joie construction camp on the Bridge River.

Apart from Klaus Kohanek I never heard from any of my relatives again. Over the following years I occasionally met or listened to intellectuals from the German Democratic Republic and was repeatedly amazed at how indistinguishable they are from their counterparts among the North American bourgeoisie. So maybe Lotte was not the inheritor of the struggles waged by people like Fritz.

SIX

Bridge River Tales

Archive: Of a Mine Valley

In the depths of a wintry March I went up to the Bridge River country to work at La Joie camp near Goldbridge and stayed there a full six months. Somehow, floating in and out of the camps, and trips to Berlin and back, didn't seem especially discontinuous.

The way into the Bridge River was to take a Union steamship to Squamish and then the Pacific Great Eastern train up to Shalalth, a thrice-a-week run with four passenger coaches behind an aging steam locomotive. From there you rode the Neal Evans "stage" over the mountains and followed the Bridge River up to the mines. There was no direct road link to the outside. Although the region was less than two hundred miles from Vancouver it involved a major trip, and many families living in Bralorne hadn't been out of the valley in years.

I had heard stories of the Bridge River Country since my earliest childhood, tales of prospecting and shambling mine towns and abandoned workings. A phenomenal number of people we knew had passed through that small, isolated mountain district at one time or another. Leo Paulcer and Hans Stiegelbauer and Ali had been through there many times during their periodic job searches. The country around the camp wasn't empty.

With beginnings at the end of the last century, the mines reached their apogee during the 1930s when the region was widely and mistakenly known as a kind of Shangri-la where jobs were available in the dozen or so mini gold mines sporadically in operation. By the 1950s only Bralorne and Pioneer mines still remained, both of them archetypal company mine towns. The area had settled into the senescence which overtakes most mining districts after an initial halcyon boom period.

The Bridge River valley is a forty-mile-long cleft twisting between the eastern flanks of the Coast Mountains. Here and there it is bordered by narrow benches and small flats. The region is in the dry belt and is clothed with open pine forests and natural grass meadows. Cadwallader Creek, the main gold bearing tributary, joins the Bridge River at Goldbridge. It's a narrow, raging stream which rushes down from a high mountain saddle cutting deep gorges as it goes. Scattered hamlets and abandoned mine camps — Pioneer Extension, Fish Lake, Paymaster and others — were threaded alongside a one-and-a-half-lane gravel road which hugged the cliff sides, trundled over timber cribbing, careened around spurs, leapt from ledge to ledge and switchbacked up and down mountainsides.

That high in the mountains winter hangs on a long time. You get a false spring in May; warm winds melt the snow, the willows redden and seem ready to burst into bud, new grass appears and the road turns into a corrugated series of potholes, until a cold snap puts you back into winter. But when spring does arrive its explosive. A mountain spring is like no other season anywhere on earth.

The La Joie project was part of a hydro generating complex built a few years earlier. We were then in the process of heightening and strengthening the rock fill reserve dam. It was the best camp I ever worked in, mainly because of the region. After settling in I had the strange sensation of returning to a place I'd known as a child, though I'd never been in the Bridge River before. Ebe Koeppen was up there too. That's the way it went if you worked in camps a while, you were always crossing paths with people you knew from elsewhere. Ebe was also one of my adoptive relatives and I could remember him carrying me on his shoulders at some picnic or other when I was a young child.

At first I worked night shift in the cookhouse and had most of the day free to myself. But by the time spring rolled around I was working on the warehouse gang. The camp was comprised mainly of truck drivers, heavy equipment operators and mechanics and not much in

Goldbridge camp, Bridge River, 1959.

the way of general labour. What we did mainly was to unload supply trucks and then, shortly after, load the same stuff from the warehouse into our own truck and deliver it around the worksite. It was fairly leisurely work with neither much brain nor brawn required. The only thing I loathed was handling sacks of cement. It wasn't exhausting work but for some reason the feel of cement dust over paper sacks effected me like chalk screeching on a blackboard. There's not much to tell of in that kind of job but it was an easygoing crew to work with.

Sometimes three or four of us would be sent up to Gun Lake to wait for a charter flight bringing in repair parts for heavy equipment. We'd become very conscientious and make sure to be there waiting for the plane, usually a half hour or more early so we could get a quick swim — pilfered pleasures always being the sweetest. Since we only worked eight hours a day and had Sundays off one could explore the valley. It was a good place for getting to know people outside of camp.

Minto was a ghost town about a half dozen miles down the valley. It wasn't that old but it was typical of the frontier mine towns throughout western North America in the late nineteenth century. Ali had briefly gotten a job there during the late 1930s. The leads petered out and the town was largely deserted in 1942, at which time it became an internment camp for a couple of hundred Japanese Canadians. By 1954 it was a ghost town again.

Wayside and Congress were two derelict camps on the way to Gold-bridge, collections of mouldering bunkhouses and rusting machinery smack beside the main and only road through the valley. Wayside had some personal significance. It was one of those fly-by-night opera-tions in which the promoter was always scratching around to rustle up funds, its stock sold on the strength of "promising new assays". Ali had cooked there too in the 1930s and had gotten part of his last paycheque in Wayside stock on a take-it-or-leave-it basis. Just when I was born the mine hit a pocket of gold ore and the stock went up enough so that it paid the hospital bills for my delivery. People's Capitalism at work.

The road leaps the river below Goldbridge and deposits you on an alluvial flat. Off to one side is a place once marked on large-scale land maps as Haylmore. It consisted of a tumbled down mill shed half washed away by Cadwallader Creek, a large cabin and its single res-ident, Will Haylmore. He had been in the Bridge River valley since the first years of the century and was a local notable once known to hundreds if not thousands of people throughout the interior. Hayl-more was in his mid seventies when I met him and continued to live in his one cabin town until he died almost twenty years later. He was a tall gaunt figure with a shoulder-length mane of white hair and a thin drooping moustache who looked rather like an Edwardian illustration of the knight-errant of La Mancha.

Haylmore had left England at the end of the previous century but his heart was still in the England of the old Queen. That was the real England to him. The walls of his cabin, a long rambling structure with a huge main hall and a homemade solarium, were studded with fading portraits of young men in blazers and of lithographs of neo-gothic bell towers. Threadbare but once elegant India rugs lay on the floor, and a bookshelf sported assorted Morocco-bound volumes intermixed with frayed pamphlets. Haylmore still tended a large garden behind his place and experimented with plants in a crazy-quilt kind of green house he'd built. The approach to the cabin was a mini-Macchu Pichu of rock-walled ledges and raised stone patios. That was the result of his personal make-work project a generation earlier. Long after he was dead this rock work remained as a megalithic memorial.

I heard of Haylmore long before I met him. During the worst of the Hungry Thirties he had laid on a free lunch for itinerant job seekers drifting in and out of the valley. That same long table which stood in his hall had been decked with whatever edibles he'd been able to rustle up. It was only breadline charity but twenty years later one could meet men who remembered it.

A half mile up the road was Goldbridge, one of the few settlements in the valley which was not attached to some mine or another. Its main surviving business was a bustling hotel beer parlour. The graveyard for all the Bridge River mine towns was on the edge of Goldbridge. I was looking for Hans Stiegelbauer's grave. You got no sense of how large the graveyard was until you began walking through it because it was overgrown with tall grasses, poplar and saskatoonberries. Wooden markers and scattered headstones were interspersed through the brush.

Hans had been another of my adoptive uncles, a prospector who became part of our family. He was a wizened little guy, old before his time and always a little odd. Stiegelbauer was from a mountain village in Austria, had survived the First World War and had determined to get out of Europe for good. He was already a prospector when my parents arrived in BC in 1930 and it was he who tried to teach Ali and a bunch of other unemployed the fundamentals of washing placer gold. That was a strategy of desperation which thousands followed into the dollar-a-day gold creeks of the interior during those years.

Sometime near the end of the Second World War Hans set out to

The abandoned laundry in Goldbridge, a ghost town by 1974 when this photo was taken.

prospect around the edges of the Bridge River country. He teamed up with an Indian partner and they decided to winter over in a cabin they had. The long and short of it was that Hans collapsed on the trail and froze to death, or so the BC Provincial Police said. He'd been buried in Goldbridge cemetery. That would have been about a decade before I got there.

I never did find his grave because most of the wooden markers had fallen over and were illegible. But what I did find were the grave markers of others who probably were not unlike Stiegelbauer, if one could extrapolate from the fragments of information remaining. They had come from the four corners of Europe and America and died in this distant mountain valley. "The King of Norway" read one inscription, alluding to a nickname whose pungency was now lost. Others buried here came from Macedonia and Portugal, Maine and Montana, Ashcroft and Port Arthur, some whose lives had spanned much of an era and others who had barely entered into adulthood. "So Hans . . . If it's got to be anywhere this is in better company than most. Adieu."

The road climbs through a series of hairpin turns and steep switchbacks to a series of "flats" — though called that only in local terminology. Scattered along the way are the remains of yet more mine camps reduced to a litter of rusting equipment. The shafts driven into the side of the mountain beckoned adventurous kids so that where on the coast standard parental warnings usually included "Stay off the log booms," in the Bridge River it was "Don't go near the shafts."

Bralorne and Pioneer Mines were still going concerns in 1954. They were mine towns and not camps. Bralorne was not unattractive but it definitely was a company town in the classic mold. It had residential areas graded in desirability and rank, the largest being a compact block with a hundred frame cottages. The whole town, the houses people lived in, the roads, the municipal services and store properties, almost everything, was owned and run by the mining company. Pioneer had only recently gotten out of operating its own company store which local people unregenerately insisted on calling The Company Store.

Pioneer Mine was situated at the top end of the valley in a saddle between two mountains. You entered it through a cleft possibly thirty yards wide which Cadwallader Creek had cut through the rock. As you did you found yourself in a small natural bowl. The crusher sheds and the mill hung on the hillside above the village and enclosed conveyor housings arched over the main street and bunkhouses in the centre of the settlement. No picture of an Appalachian coal camp or of *Night Comes to the Cumberlands* I've seen was quite as stark as Pioneer.

Silicosis was always an "occupational hazard" (as civil servant philosophers had it) among hardrock miners, especially in mines like Pioneer. The powdered rock from drilling and blasting hangs in the air underground despite ventilation and damping and is inhaled. It lodges in the lungs and clogs and cuts the capillaries. Proper mining procedures were supposed to reduce the risk of silicosis but after twenty years of underground work many miners had the first symptoms of the disease. They're constantly short of breath, the heart strains to circulate the poorly oxygenated blood. As the condition advances the victims begin to suck air and cough blood. There's no cure. Men gradually but visibly begin to die. A pair of not-so-old men, haggard and drained, sit on the porch of the company store on a summer day talking, wheezing and sometimes gasping for air. Everyone knows them and what their trouble is. What we can learn to endure is frightening.

The owners of Pioneer Mines were notorious among even the anti-union employers of B.C. Sometime in the early 1940s miners had staged an underground sit down strike there but it had been smashed and the strikers were expelled from the town. The Mine, Mill and Smelterworkers Union had reorganized Pioneer and I figured that there must be some kind of militant labour tradition present there. Maybe there was. If so it was closed to outsiders. The community club at Pioneer put out a nostalgic booklet about the place the year the mine finally folded and everyone was evicted. I suppose the sense of home can come to attach to any place.

On Mountain Roads

Until I got up to the Bridge River I wasn't all that eager to learn how to drive. "When you're older I'll teach you how to drive properly," said Ali, which he then put off indefinitely. So it turned out that I had a pilot's license before I could drive.

"Okay, so you've got a pilot's license. But driving a car isn't like flying a plane. There's traffic and tricks of the road and things to look out for." But I finally held Ali to his promise and I did learn how to drive on those mountain roads.

"The first thing is to learn how to hold the wheel. I taught you that before but you've already forgotten. You're not driving down Broadway here."

"Hmm..."

"So ... Hold the wheel on both sides, a little above the centre. Turn the wheel so, so that you always have two hands on it. If you hit a rock or a patch of ice you don't want the wheel to spin out of your grip just because you haven't got a good hold on it."

"Yeah, yeah. Okay."

"Well listen to what I'm telling you and do it. You let them punks drive around with one hand but you're going to learn how to drive right or not at all. Another thing — never hook your thumbs around the wheel like you're doing now. Keep them up by your fingers, along the top of the wheel. If you hit a really bad hole the wheel can spin out of your hands and you won't be able to grab hold."

"Ah come on Ali. Maybe that was the way to drive when you were first up here but that doesn't happen anymore. Nobody worries about where their thumbs are."

"You think you know it all — but you don't. Do as I tell you and maybe it'll save you an accident. You can see what going over the bank here means. Don't try to be so smart." The three- and four-hundred-foot drops along the side of the road were rather impressive.

"Pump the brakes or you'll burn them out on these steep grades and you won't have them when you need them. Pump and then let them up. They'll seize up on you if you just keep them down."

Then I was supposed to learn to double clutch, revving up the motor in neutral as I shifted down. "Why do I have to learn this? This isn't a five ton truck."

"You're learning how to drive — or not? You're learning to drive not just this car. You don't know what you're going to be driving and where you're going to be driving and what may turn up, so you should have some idea what to do when you need it. Let's say your brakes fail —"

"Oh Jesus. Brakes don't fail on these modern cars." It was a 1948 Dodge.

"Brakes fail! They do, on these cars like any other. On these roads you have to know how to slow down by using the motor, by shifting down. That means double clutching — and fast too, otherwise you'll never get her into a lower gear."

("Oh boy, what next.")

"Alright. Now turn off just beyond that big burned stump up ahead ... Slow down. SLOW DOWN ... GEAR DOWN ... Jesus Christ. How often have I got to tell you. Slow down before you turn."

"I did slow down."

"Slower, go slower on these roads so you can react to what comes up ahead. There could have been anything around that turnoff. See, you're running right through that mud hole. Have some sense! If you hit a patch of ice making a turn at that speed you'll slide right off the road."

"Well it was right in front of me. What else was I going to do."

"Pick your way around a hole like that unless you know what it's like. You should have hit that solid patch to the left, then you'd have been sure of having traction."

"What? What about staying off soft shoulders that you're always yelling about?"

"Use your eyes. You can see that's a rock-solid shoulder. No, don't slow down here. Give her gas. Get a run on that grade before she slows down. Jesus!"

At least once a session would come the startled shout, "Watch out for that hole. Oh ... you're going to break the axle yet."

The road up to Bralorne was corrugated with stretches of washboard which shook a car so violently you thought it would shake the bolts loose. Although the road was constantly graded, trucks would soon rework the surface into a solid chop. You'd experiment with different speeds till you found one in which your car bumped along the tops of the crests with a minimum of jarring. Unfortunately, that speed was usually too fast or too slow for the road conditions and made for some rather spastic driving styles.

There were few road signs to worry about but for some reason I'd taken the "Watch For Rolling Rock" signs literally and at first drove along scanning the cliffs ahead. I didn't know what you were supposed to do if you did see rock rolling down.

"What are you doing?" asks Ali. "Watch for rock on the road. How do you expect to see what's coming down the road if you're gawking up the side of the hill all the time. You just do that in a place like Big Slide or Moha."

"Oh sure. I know that."

"Watch that loose shale. Slow down. What? Never mind if I don't slow down. I know how to drive and you don't." That was his standard

Driving lessons for mountain roads. The author and his father, Bridge River country, 1954.

reply. In the city he was a terrible driver but he could drive up impossible mountain trails and down snow-drifted roads or negotiate tracks running through northern gumbo and muskeg and almost always get through.

On those one-and-a-half-lane roads the general principle was to stay near the centre when you could see ahead and only pull over to your side when approaching a blind curve — of which there were plenty. There were also stretches of one-lane cribbing where the roadway crept around bluffs on narrow ledges formed by embedding a breastwork of logs and timbers into the cliffside. These would have "turnouts", portions of roadway just barely wide enough for two vehicles to sneak by each other. When meeting an oncoming car the informal rules of the road were that the one nearest the turnout had to back up to where you could pass. But trucks had the right of way. The bigger the truck the more right of way it had.

You drove to the conditions of the road and if you weren't too tired and if you weren't in a rush to get to your destination each trip could be a bit of an adventure. I've been describing the main road up to the mines. Once you left that the tracks into the side valleys and plateaus became more rudimentary. It was always more adventurous when you were using somebody else's vehicle because those roads were awfully hard on cars: windshields smashed from flying rock, stoved-in oil pans, tires cut up by sharp shale after a few thousand miles, shocks and steering mechanism which required constant replacement.

"Be prepared to help yourself," was Ali's motto. "There aren't any gas stations you can run to here so you got to remember to have a few things along in case you need them." One was a five-gallon container of gas, which we resorted to regularly because Ali had forgotten to fill up the tank. Then there was putting on and removing tire chains. How I hated them; kneeling in the snow and slush of April and May, hands numb, trying to get the chain to fit around a tire which was patently one size to large for the chains. Finally, after being soaked through, you'd get the chains on exactly straight and hammer down the swivel locks with a tire iron. "Look. Leave the chains on Ali. If you take them off we'll just have to put them on again next trip or the one after that." But no, he didn't believe in that.

The trunk was always half filled with a towing cable, screwdrivers and wrenches, rolls of black electrical tape and lengths of wire, a folding shovel and a jack. There was also an assortment of old water pumps and indeterminate parts which had been replaced because they were worn out. The trouble was that Ali was quite unmechanical. It was only by endless tinkering, lots of cursing and a good deal of luck that he ever repaired anything on the road.

There would also be a tarp and blankets, an axe and a frying pan but rarely any food. "Matches — you've always got to have matches with you. You have to be able to make a fire under any conditions if you need it." That was a basic catechism.

"Road Culture," Tom Brose would have called it. Brose was a wild American Catholic Worker-type and sometime college professor of my later acquaintance who used to hunt out backland roads and swoop around them in a manner calculated to test his guardian angel. Ali and Brose would have gotten on like a house afire. They were a lot alike. Fundamentally, Ali wasn't cautious in what he did, having learned the lesson that one had to be able to catch life on the fly.

SEVEN

Life In the Ice Age

Report From Limbo

While I worked in camps I was still enmeshed, to a degree, in the imperatives of an earlier generation of migrant workers. "The Fifties" as an era hit home to me only after I came down from the Bridge River in late 1954. Like any number of crucial things in my life, how I got involved with university life was sort of accidental. There was no calling which beckoned me and I didn't consider Phyllis's repeated advice to "learn a good trade". I only knew that I didn't want to work in the camps anymore except as a stopgap measure. In retrospect it seems obvious that I hung around university as a way of putting off any decision about "what to do with my life". That's the sort of phrase one used then. Maybe I was expecting a goal to fall from the heavens ... Bop. Eureka!

Until the end of World War II the University of British Columbia had been a provincial university for the regional middle class. The first breach in its clubby ranks was made by the masses of returned war veterans going back to school on veterans benefits. However, even in the early 1950s far less than five per cent of working-class children went to college. As for the children of camp workers, Jim MacFarlan, later the president of the BC Teachers Federation, was the only one I ever met at university. For a long time I didn't know what the hell I was doing there.

Most youths from working-class backgrounds entering university did so with the intent of studying something practical, in the vein of advanced vocational training. I first gravitated to engineering and made it through the initial year of the maths and sciences. But by the end of the first month of the actual engineering program I came to the realization that I was totally hopeless at it. Calculus was beyond comprehension. The moment of truth came in a drafting class. The task was to draw the projections of a machine tool piece standing in the middle of the room. Half way through the two-hour session I'm still sitting there mulling it over without any idea of how it should be done. The penny drops. "This is impossible. I quit."

The conclusion was inescapable. There were just some things that I would never learn to do adequately no matter how hard I tried. Surprisingly, far from being depressing that realization gave me a feeling of liberation. I refused to study something "practical" and instead enrolled in a swath of courses for no other reason than pure interest. Nothing useful could come of any of my studies. Certainly there was no possibility they would ever lead to a job. Thusly assured I could settle down to learn what I wanted as I wanted.

In retrospect, the era was a golden age for obscurantist social science and re-tailored history, a time of endemic amnesia and of systematic distortions, breathtaking in their gall and in their presumption of ignorance among the intended audience. The most eyeball-rolling hokum was peddled as sagacity, fabrications passed off as indisputable facts. Whole fields of inquiry had been silenced by self-imposed taboos and it became bad form even to mention whole classes of events. When a book like Forrest LaViolette's *The Canadian Japanese Canadians in World War II*, published in 1948, arose in class discussion it was sniffily dismissed as unscholarly — meaning that it stuck its nose into a topic which then was expunged. Reading Michael Rogin's *The Intellectuals and McCarthy* a quarter century later even I am amazed at how thoroughly we were gulled.

I presume that the above did not apply to the natural and applied sciences, although even there one had people like Gordon Shrum, chairman of the physics department and all-round satrap of the National Defence sciences. He reveled in being called "Canada's Edward Teller" and was not adverse to indulge in a little witch hunting around the university. However, my purview of the intellectual tenor of the times was more or less limited to the social sciences. Even here there were some real scholars. But often they were little appreciated or even recognized. Wayne Suttles was one. It wasn't until a decade later that I realized he was one of the greatest ethnologists of our generation — just tolerated at the University of BC. And similarly for others in other fields

Ironic as it may seem to those who know anthropology mainly through its exotic side, the discipline appealed to me for exactly the opposite reason. Sociology was awash in metaphysics, and ethnography was a breath of fresh air by comparison. There was still a strong materialist strain in anthropology — especially in the older and then unfashionable works. Anthropolgy was not limited to dissecting the intricacies of patrilateral cross-cousin marriage or pursuing the symbolism of ritual toenail painting among some tribe or another, though god knows there was enough of that around. There were also fine-grained studies of how peoples dealt with the world around them and what their everyday lives were. Ethnographies documented how specific societies meshed social organization and productive techniques, how political power and ideology operated and conflicted in particular cases.

Despite everything, I became enthralled by the university. For three years I just about lived in the bowels of the library. Nothing had led me to suspect that schools might be committed to the pursuit of knowledge, however skewed it was in hindsight. There were courses on no end of fascinating topics and students actually interested in learning about them.

In contrast, the social life of the University of BC actually did approximate caricatures of 1950s collegiana. I don't even want to remember it. There are many people I worked with who I remember in detail but hardly any fellow students from those years who I have more than a hazy recollection of. It all runs together in my mind — sophomoric sophistries, posturings over the latest fashions in sage insights, prim or boorish parties. It was almost as if the high school culture I had escaped while actually at high school had ensnared me in those first years at university.

I was constantly on the search for women as sexual objects. No apologies intended though. If that also led to friendships or love affairs (but certainly not marriage) so much the better. But sex was the main thing. That was a primary reason behind getting a place of my own whenever I had the money. But sexual encounters brought to fruition were dispiritingly infrequent. Maybe I was too hungry or to blind to recognize obvious possibilities. There must have been young women around with similar desires and needs.

I got on well enough with women when we were talking like some of the guys. But just let it turn to sexual interest and it was closing time. Alternately, there were occasions when girls (sometimes women) made what I only later deciphered as the then necessarily staid advances; but with no response on my part. Then I wondered why they were snarky the next time we met. My sexual awkwardness went hand in hand with a self assurance when traipsing around the world, with an unconcern for what was considered acceptable or held to be possible.

Anybody who's crossed paths with Paddy Henderson probably remembers her. We ran together in Ron Dore's class on Modern Japanese History. Paddy was a latter-day version of Agnes Smedley crossed with Bette Midler. She'd declaim Joe Hill's,

> That's the rebel girl, that's the rebel girl
> To the working class she's a precious pearl. *etc., etc.*

Sheesh!

Paddy had grown up not far from the North Vancouver dockyards. It was one of those platonic oil and water friendships between two people of similar backgrounds and the same basic outlook who just rub each other the wrong way. She'd drop the most simplified maxims into a conversation whenever she didn't like the direction it was taking. The fact that she knew better made it doubly annoying. Which is just what she intended. I never would have admitted it then but I had a sneaking admiration of her.

When I first met her Paddy had just come back from a place called Murdochville, a mining town in the eastern Gaspé region which had gone through a very bitter strike. She was sporting a leg in a cast which she said had been broken when she'd jumped out of a back window of the union hall to escape the Quebec Provincial Police. It was still the Quebec of Premier Maurice Duplessis, and Murdochville was a company town which forbade access to outsiders. To get into the place Paddy had to stow away in a hidden space of a delivery truck. That's not the sort of thing which every historian can put on his or her *curriculum vitae*.

God knows what Paddy thought she was doing; she didn't seem to have any better reasons for her decisions than I did. She became interested in Japan, began studying Japanese and the next I heard had gotten herself a scholarship to Tenrikkyo University. After an interlude of study and Buddhist serenity she'd departed from Tenrikkyo U. That was the last I heard of her for many years.

About twenty years later I met Paddy's younger sister on a Vancouver picket line and found out that the wild orientalist was back in BC and was ensconced as a professor of Asian Studies. She had married into a Japanese family and had lived in the scrutable middle-class suburbs of Tokyo. For awhile she'd also appeared in a Japanese soap opera serial where she played "the other woman". She now had a daughter, "Thirteen going on forty, who lectures me when I drink too much and tucks me into bed," Paddy told me with pride and a certain amazement, when we next met.

After a few drinks and some talk of where we had been over the past twenty years Paddy and I got into an argument about professional feminists who cross picket lines and soon were snarling at one another. It's good that you can rely on some things not changing.

I guess there is no point to this, other than a reminiscence about one other student from a working-class background who passed through the University of BC in the fifties and who refused to accept the times we were living in.

Archive: Free Speech, 1955

I.F. Stone called them "The Fearful Fifties". It is difficult to recapture that subliminal feeling of caution which existed. Individuals who were fearless in a great many things, men who were not frightened of purely physical confrontations might still have an amorphous dread of what files were being compiled by some unknown government agency. Few might admit to feeling that way but it was part of the climate of the times. It was instituted in Canada with the quiet smugness so typical of this country. It is only somewhat of an exaggeration to characterize the Louis St-Laurent government which presided over much of the era as a Canadian Vichy regime.

In retrospect, the University of BC was heir to the political fashions of the day. That was partly the contribution made by the newly recruited American and English academics, but *bona fide* Canadian intellects demonstrated that they could clamber onto the bandwagon as fast as anyone else. They dispensed their Cold War scholarship for an entire generation. Even today, much of the substratum of "common knowledge" about events of the twentieth century stems from the wave of historical rewriting carried out by the Cold War academics of the 1950s.

No one admitted that the University of BC was enmeshed in the Cold War. The "excesses" of the McCarthy era were something which Americans engaged in. "We" handled those things with so much more civility and good taste. It worked just as well as Roman circuses. The occasional cautious criticisms of McCarthyism issuing from the Canadian intelligentsia were fig leaves not quite covering compliance to the political dogmas of the time. We didn't need witch hunts to stifle a dissenting indigenous scholarship. The shameful poltroonery of it all.

A classic demonstration of Cold War hysteria arose when a freedom-loving mob of students stopped Tim Buck from giving a talk at the University of BC. Buck was then in his seventies, a frail man who had been a leader of the Communist Party in Canada since the early 1920s. He had been its spokesman during a long period of illegality and had been imprisoned along with other party leaders during the 1930s. He'd witnessed the upsurge of the left during the Depression and had gone along with the twists and turns of party policy during the Stalin era. I wasn't all that enamoured of Tim Buck but whatever one thought of him he was a historic figure of the Canadian left.

The "Canadian Intelligence Service", a homegrown analogue of the John Birch Society and no direct relation to the federal government spy agency created in the 1970s, had been busy preparing for Buck's talk. The auditorium was packed with their student networkers twenty minutes before Buck was supposed to speak. Squads of engineering students had ensconced themselves in the back of the hall and in the balcony and were behaving in their Saturday night wrestling manner.

The Labour Progressive Club on campus had arranged that talk, and Jim MacFarlan opened the meeting with a rendition of O Canada. "Put Canada First" was the theme of Buck's presentation, an appeal for an alliance of Canadian workers and the democratic middle class to keep Canada from becoming a powder monkey for the United States.. It was moderate to a fault and without a trace of any appeal to socialism or class struggle. Nevertheless, a student in the row of seats in front of me leaned over to his buddy and remarked in a mock-horrified tone, "Why, that's Communist talk!" Not everyone was hostile but part of the crowd was a mob which whipped itself into a frenzy. "Shut up," they screamed, and "Take him off", and chanted "Go back to Russia."

Buck tried to say that he was a Canadian, had been a Canadian long before most of their parents had been born. This raised even greater yowls of indignation. It touched a sore point. That someone like Tim Buck would challenge their view of themselves and tell them that they didn't have the patent rights on what being Canadian was.

"What about the slave labour camps?" was a refrain taken up by the mob as their leaders called for an emigré professor who was waiting in the wings for his walk-on bit. He was supposed to "confront" Buck and "look him in the eye", take over the stage and give his own spiel. The stage management of the right has changed little over the intervening half century.

"Yes, I know about political prisoners. I was a political prisoner here in Canada and so were hundreds of others. Here, not somewhere on the other side of the world," Buck answered. That was something of a surprise and the audience stopped to listen for a minute or two, but soon decided it was all a Commie lie. Now apples and other objects came whizzing across the auditorium and onto the stage. Whatever it was they were throwing would have hurt too. One missile hit the lectern and knocked it over.

At that point Jim adjourned the meeting and hustled Buck out of a side door to a waiting car. A gaggle of student intelligences took over the stage, capered about, were cheered by the audience, had nothing to say but congratulated themselves for this exercise in moral vigilance.

The college newspaper came out the next day with an angry account of "McCarthyism on campus" but the Vancouver yellow press chortled about "the limits of free speech". The Dean of Arts pontificated about how "even those viewpoints which are abhorrent to the community at large should have a chance to be heard in a university so that the listeners may learn why they find it abhorrent," blah, blah. He then went on to impose restrictions on the speakers which university clubs could invite on campus. Horning in on the act and playing his role as a character out of Dickens, Student Dean Malcolm McGregor opined that the whole affair was the lamentable consequence of allowing members of the lower orders to intrude their manners into university halls. You could make of that what you pleased.

I don't want to suggest that I escaped being affected by the mindset of the times. Although I was considered to be an injudicious gadfly by many students and professors I was fettered by the isolation and feelings of powerlessness which the era perpetrated. For instance, by the late 1950s the war in Algeria had become what the Vietnam war was to later be. It was clearly an extraordinarily murderous colonial war, with endemic torture, death squads and the emergence of an openly fascist formation in the Secret Army Organization. All that was general knowledge to those who wanted to know. One would think that there would have been some dissent on a university campus, even in deepest Point Grey. Nothing. I myself was outraged by the France's actions in Algeria so there must have been others who felt similarly. Why didn't any of us at least voice some opposition to that war?

In some spheres I was completely gulled by the reigning propaganda. Probably the most glaring example of my misconceptions were those about Israel and the Palestinians. I actually bought that Hollywood image of David and Goliath, of egalitarian *Kibbutzim* and feudal Arab fanaticism. It entailed a willingness to be misled about Israel and its supporters. I then wouldn't have listened to any documentation of Zionist racism and mass murder. I was even considering living on a kibbutz for a year to see what communal life was like and was in correspondence with the Hashomer Hatzair, a left-wing kibbutz federation. I had no inkling of the brutal and chauvinistic state apparatus which both left and right in Israel had created. How could I have been so blind when I knew better in other areas? I now feel I should apologize to the Palestinian people, the living and the dead, and to the other victims of the Israeli regime. Not that it makes an iota of difference.

If the 1950s seem uncannily like the 1980s there were also some important differences. America was then the hegemonic power in the world and its industrial and military supremacy was unchallenged. The Cold War *Gleichschaltung* which ensorceled so many people didn't have to play alongside economic decline, and the rulers of North America could offer some material payoffs in return for people keeping their heads down and their noses to the grindstone. It was a rare period of rising real incomes for working people, if also a diminution of their freedom and their class heritage

It was only by the middle of the decade that television reached into most homes in Canada. One should consider how recent, how unparalleled that then-new vehicle of thought manipulation was. The electronic media ceaselessly dished up a menu fostering mass regression. Pandemic juvenility and Comstockery pervaded everything. In American movies it became tantamount to sacrilege to portray the US president, whether it be Abilene Ike or Boss Pendergast's boy Harry, in person. Like god, the voice of the unseen-but-all-seeing President would drift into a scene and the film hero would stammer his understanding of the message from on high. Absolute and total political servility became the mark of good citizenship. You're mistaken if you believe that a comparable ethos did not prevail in Canada.

The 1950s were probably most terrible for those who had come of age earlier and who had an understanding of the world which they were unwilling to submerge in the know-nothingism of the times. To them it must have seemed that the lights were going out all over North America with little prospect of seeing them relit in their own lifetime. For others, like my own parents, who had witnessed the world they had known eclipsed by the rise of fascism and the replacement of socialist internationalism by national chauvinism, something like that had happened earlier. But to me the mid 1950s were a time of drugged somnambulism.

It wasn't just political reaction which marked the era but also a mind boggling provincialism and conformism. The children of men and women who had once crossed the continent with a dollar in their pockets but with the most audacious visions in their packs, the off-spring of parents who had experienced great hardships but who could still reach out a hand to strangers, their children now worried about where their career plans might take them twenty years down the road. They worried about this and that and about being out of step with whatever the current wisdom was. It was an era of systematically fostered, epidemic Babbittry.

One cannot understand or appreciate the counterculture of the 1960s, however escapist and transitory some of it may have been, without knowing the soul-destroying, mind-numbing vacuity of the previous decade. Quite simply, the so called "youth revolt" of the 1960s — and a lot of its participants were not so young — was a rejection of Cold War doxology and the society it had produced.

Sugar and Fish Oil

The BC Sugar Refinery was a huge old factory on Powell Street. It was there I got my first job in town after deciding to quit the camps. I tramped the streets of industrial Vancouver inquiring at factories, warehouses, canneries and construction sites and hiring offices. "No Help Wanted" signs hung on factory gates and office doors. Anyone who had anything to do with hiring acted as if he were the lord of creation. Finally I got on at the sugar refinery.

"We'll give you a try and see how you work out. You're not very big for the work here. Are you sure you can handle it?"

"Oh sure. I worked a couple of years in construction and I was always able to keep up with anybody. I'm not very big but I'm wiry." What a lie.

It turned out to be the worst, the most mindless and exhausting bull labour I ever did in my life. The plant was straight out of the nineteenth century. I was constantly struggling to hang on from rest break to rest break. In this refinery, then one of the largest plants in Vancouver East, everything was handled, stacked and shifted around by hand. It was the kind of work which gangs of labourers had done from time immemorial. I never saw anything like it in any camp or in any other job before or since.

Much of the Rogers plant was a series of cavernous storage areas ranging over four floors. Light filtered in through grimed-over windows at the front but beyond that a dark twilight prevailed, interspersed with pools of light below hooded lamps. The floors were cramped by pillars and alleyways. Chutes led from one level to another so that gravity could supplement muscle power.

One of my first jobs there was pulling 50-pound sugar sacks off a chute as they came sliding down and piling them on a hand trolley. Pull one, ta-cha, pull two, ta-cha, pull five 50-pound sacks of sugar, twisting them so they drop horizontally across your trolley. When loaded you tilt the trolley back so you've got just the right balance, otherwise you'll be fighting the weight all the way. You swivel out of the way fast as the next guy comes wheeling up, and trot the load down the aisles, around posts, over battered uneven plank floors, down to where the loads are being stacked. Line it up and let the trolley tilt forward. Jerk out the blade and hope the load will come off evenly. Then jog back to the chute so you'll be in your proper turn and the guys you are working with won't complain that you're not pulling your weight. You do that twenty times in an hour, eight full hours a day.

It was not only physically exhausting work, it was soul destroying. There were men who had worked in those jobs at BC Sugar Refinery for eight, ten and more years. "Some guys here complain but I know that this company has put food on the table and a roof over my head since I started here," I was astounded to hear one veteran employee say. Amazement was followed by anger and then desperation.

"You'll get used to it. If all these other guys can stand it so can you," says one voice. "Who wants to get used to it ? To hell with it, go back to the camps," answers another.

"No!"

My last job there was pitching empty raw sugar sacks, wagonload after wagonload of them, up on to a mountain of other such sacks. I was pondering all this and taking a two-minute breather when a couple of supervisors wandered by. Since I was only working twice as hard as on any other job, I was loafing and was fired the next day. I didn't mind being fired from Rogers but I was afraid that all jobs in the city I'd be able to get would be like this.

"Is this the price you have to pay for staying in town? Is this what work in factories is really like? This is like the stories we used to laugh at in camp. No wonder Ali keeps shipping out. Why do people put up with this ? Jeez — what am I going to do?"

But shortly after that I landed a job at Western Fish Oil, a small reduction and processing plant beside LaPointe Pier. It was a family-like affair with about a dozen employees. They bought fish oil and dog-fish liver from canneries up coast and processed it into the ingredients of vitamins, food supplements and cosmetics.

The plant consisted of a herd of storage tanks and a gaggle of pres-surized lines, filtration presses and centrifuges scattered through a cluster of sheds. There was a lot of repainting and simple maintenance work which varied from day to day. That, and clearing the presses and loading rail cars with drums of processed oil. You worked on your own or with a few other guys at a pace which was steady but not hectic. You could talk with your co-workers on the job, though I can't remember what we did talk about. It was a smelly but civilized place to work after Rogers Sugar.

The worst task was emptying out the five-gallon tins of half-rotted dogfish livers which were shipped in from Bella Bella or wherever. They became the primary constituent of some vitamin preparation. Nothing was as foul — a brownish green glop. The smell got on your skin and even though you stripped, took a soapy shower and changed into street clothes after work, when you got home you had to take another bath. I was staying in the basement of my parents' house that summer, which was within walking distance of the plant. Phyllis got into air fresheners in a big way.

The one thing about the fish oil plant which makes me shudder was the lack of industrial safety on the job I did there during the follow-ing winter. I needed money while attending university and the owners were amenable to having me work alone in the plant over the weekends. In addition to being the night watchman I cleared the filter presses. It was quite dangerous, partly because of the lack of some simple safety devices but mainly due to my own stupidity.

A couple of times a night I'd break open these two big presses, about forty iron plates looking like huge waffle irons swathed in canvas through which the raw fish oil was pumped under pressure. Some two or three hundred pounds of wax would accumulate on the can-vas filters which you scraped off before closing up the press. Run-ning underneath was a two-foot-wide trough in which a power augur turned to carry the wax away to a melting pit. Here I was in the middle of the night, leaning over to pry the plates apart and reaching out to scrape off the canvas filters, standing on oil- and wax-soaked planking while, as often as not, the augur turned below me. You were supposed to switch the augur off whenever you worked around the press but that meant a dozen trips across the shop floor every time. So often I just left the augur running. It was just luck that nothing happened. If I'd have slipped into the trough the least that would have happened is that I would have lost a leg.

It's usual to load the responsibility for safety on to workers, espe-cially if they are unorganized. Yet you do these things not because you're lazy or want to live dangerously but because of the pressures of the work. You never should! That would be the first thing I'd teach everyone starting a job.

An Interlude with William Morris

For a couple of years, from spring to early fall, I worked on labour gangs for the Vancouver Parks Board. Part of the summer we'd be in Stanley Park, that thousand-acre wooded peninsula abutting down-town Vancouver. The recurrent jobs included scything grass, cutting back the salmonberry and salal bush, and brushing out the walking trails. Picture it: you're working just off the city core on an early sum-mer morning, amid meadows of tall grass and the smell of new-mown hay or on forest paths with the aroma of cedar in your nostrils. If it was raining that was okay, if it was hot that was fine too.

Working with hand tools can give you a good feeling. There can be a sense of discovery in finding the right rhythms. Scything, for instance. Anyone can scythe or use a brush hook. But to do it well, so that you can lay a stroke exactly where you want, with just the right motion, almost effortlessly — that takes practice and can be quite satisfying.

In scything you're constantly changing the angle of the stroke and your stance in order to cut the swards with just the right slicing motion. The first thing is to keep the blade sharp — really sharp. Stop and resharpen the blade every ten minutes. Tip the crooked shaft so that the scythe blade rests under your outstretched arm. The whetstone which should be in your back pocket comes out, and you hone the edge with long curving sweeps down one side of the blade and back on the other, all in one motion. *Zzr-ree-ing, Zzr-raa-ang, Zzr-ree-ing.*

Now move ahead in a slow shuffle, your arms crooked, your body a quarter turn away from the direction you are scything in, your back bent very slightly forward. Swing from the shoulders, evenly. Your arms should only pull the scythe toward you in the final cutting curve. Don't reach out for the stroke, step into it and keep the blade parallel to the ground. Not too wide a sweep now or it won't cut clean on the outer edge and you'll only have to do it again, which is harder when you've butchered a swath. If the grass isn't wet and if you are working rhythmically you will actually hear the scythe singing.

There were three of us who regularly worked on brushing out the trails: Matti, Steve and me. Sometimes we were joined by a brash ex-high rigger, a spiritual descendant of Tight Line Johnson, who was always knocking off one-liners about "the Important Issues of the Day". I wish I could remember some of them.

Steve was a strange bird, a big guy of about sixty, a Ukrainian immigrant who had landed in the Alberta coal fields during the early 1920s. Class militancy was intermixed with his later fundamentalist religious conversion. Cheerfully apocalyptic, waiting for the Last Days when all exploiters would get their just desserts, Steve was keeping track of their sins in case God missed something. He was a Seventh Day Adventist. From time to time he would begin some account of the skulduggery of the capitalists which you could imagine a long-ago soap-boxer delivering — but then end up with the proposition of how God was testing humanity so that all the scum would come to the top and could then be skimmed off and cast into Hell. Capitalism was literally the work of the devil, according to Steve.

He had lost an arm in a mine accident around Drumheller during the 1930s, had never gotten any compensation and had barely survived a number of years in a Kootenay squatter's shack before coming to Vancouver during the war to get a job in the shipyards. Here he joined the Adventists who had, he claimed, saved not only his soul but his earthly life.

Steve had a wooden stump with a no-nonsense hook coming out of the end. Working on a park trail in the morning mist, his hook jerking as he hacked away at the brush with a machete, Steve could be an intimidating sight. His fulminations would have been a little scary except that he was such a warm and considerate guy to work with.

Steve's off-the-cuff Bible maxims used to drive Matti straight up the wall. Matti might say something like, "Seeing everything you been through you ought to know better than be caught by the Bible thumpers." Or he might launch into his own version of *The Preacher and the Slave.*

> Holy rollers come out on the tout
> They holler, they jump and they shout
> Till they got all yer money in their drum
> Then they say you can go on the bum.
> You will eat, bye and bye
> God'll serve you with hot apple pie
> Work and pray, live on hay
> You'll get ADVENTIST pie in the sky.

I'd laugh but it didn't faze Steve at all. "You fellas shouldn't mock God ... But seeing as you is decent working fellas you got the chance to be saved up to the day you die," he might answer.

Although Matti was only in his fifties he looked a lot older. He was a real Red Finn. He'd been a teenager in one of the small Finnish industrial towns when the civil war broke out in 1918. His family had been part of the left and his elder brother had been a member of the workers militia many of whose members, after the defeat of the revolution, were executed by the Mannerheim White Guardists. Matti had been smuggled out of Finland through Sweden and been gotten to friends in northern Ontario, where he completed his growing up amid the Canadian Finnish diaspora there during the 1920s. He'd been a sawmill worker, miner and migrant worker throughout western Canada during the Depression.

Whatever their limitations, Steve and Matti had a healthy contempt for the official propaganda of the day. In their own ways both of them felt that working people everywhere were or should be comrades — unless they proved themselves to be otherwise. Well, they were of another age, of a generation when many of the most combative working people had emigrated to North America.

We were members of the Vancouver Civic Outside Workers Union, one of the few which had retained its left-wing leadership during the labour purges. The union periodically came under fire from the Canadian Labour Congress, the so-called Canadian House of Labour (which invited the predictable Polly Bergen quip to the effect that "A house is not a home"). But the VCOWU did a good job as a union and had the support of its members. It actively defended the job security and working conditions of its members and we knew it. The fact that there was a real union willing to go to bat for you may have affected on-the-job relationships; there wasn't the backbiting and bickering you often find on jobs where men are powerless. It made for a civilized working environment.

For a while we packed rock for the seawall being built around Stanley Park. The job was under the direction of an old stonemason who had been talked into coming out of retirement just to do this job — a quiet, barrel-chested guy with a tricky heart.

Most of the rock which went into the seawall came from huge boulders along the shoreline. Powder holes were drilled into them and the blasting was highly controlled. *Pang-pfft.* That would drive a crack into the parent rock. The stone mason would come along later with this little hammer — *tap-tap, tunk-tap, tunk-thunk* — to one side and then the other. He'd cock his head and squint at the grain of the rock, figuring where the hidden fault lines, if any, ran. Maybe he'd make a mark here and there. A couple of his helpers would wield the sledge hammer.

"Here, hit it right here." BONK! Nothing.

"Here. Down a bit." ... *Grunk — Crea-ack!* And this huge slab of rock which you'd figure a sledge hammer would just bounce off of splits and is gradually broken down into quarters and sixteenths and finally into usable-sized pieces to be laid along the line of the rising seawall.

About a decade later when I was living in New York people flocked to see Felix Greene's documentary film *China*. It was a visually impressive film but one glorifying the Maoist policy of development through self-reliance and use of indigenous Chinese technology. For many

American viewers this was all intermixed with an anti-technological philosophy which was becoming fashionable. The film's appeal rested on a mixed bag of Third Worldism alloyed with a hankering to rediscover some simple panaceas, particularly those applicable to other people.

One of the most powerful and most remarked upon scenes in that movie was of how the Chinese had organized traditional techniques to quarry stone and slide it down a hillside into junks to build a railway causeway. It lovingly details how this was all accomplished by hand, with ingenious but hardly novel techniques. The movie didn't show the heavy construction equipment which had fallen into disrepair because of the-self reliance policy.

"I'd like my children to see that," said a usually level headed friend of mine, a native New Yorker, naturally. "What the Chinese can do with so little. We would need mountains of money and a fleet of machines to do that. It really opens your eyes to what people can accomplish on their own if they work together," etc., etc.

"Yes, it's impressive. But how do you think the railways and tunnels and buildings and such stuff were built, right here, in this country? And not so long ago. That's not so revolutionary. Bull labour isn't something that should be glorified unless there are no other options." A little Saturday evening soapboxing on my part. "Hell, you can still find men alive who helped string the rails and blast the grades through the mountains of BC, people who built things just as impressive as what we saw in that film, and without much more machinery. 'Cause I knew some of them when I was a kid."

That was totally removed from the world of the people I said it to. They didn't quite disbelieve me but they couldn't picture American working people as having done what these Chinese quarry workers and river hogs were doing. So, despite the foregoing Morrisiana and appreciation of manual labour in 1966, I preached the beauty of machinery doing the work which machines and not men or women should do.

EIGHT

The Bight of Benin

Archive: A Bit of Colonial History

After being at university for three years I was desperate to get away from that life in particular and from North America in general. An exchange student scholarship for Nigeria was announced by the World University Service; I applied and won the competition. One had to pay one's own passage over there and back but I could only afford a one-way ticket.

The coasts of West Africa were once known respectively as the Grain Coast, the Ivory Coast, the Gold Coast and the Slave Coast. Nigeria was a part of the Slave Coast. The devastation wrecked by the slave trade needs no recapitulation. Although the international slave trade had been more or less eliminated by the mid nineteenth century, indigenous slavery continued into the first years of the twentieth century in some regions of West Africa. In 1957 it was possible to find individuals in Nigeria who knew slavery firsthand as children. It was still a living folk memory.

While there had been trading forts of various European powers along the coast since the seventeenth century it was the Royal Niger Company which later consolidated its control over the region around Lagos and laid the foundations for the colony of Nigeria. Colonizing-trading companies were a system of stock jobbing imperialism which the British, Dutch, French and Portuguese empires long used. It required that the company provide its own military and administrative infrastructure over the region it had received monopoly trade rights to. The trouble was that sooner or later these trade companies got into difficulties, had their private armies defeated, were threatened by competing companies under other colonial regimes, or they simply found the costs of the colonial infrastructure to be prohibitive. They then set up a hue-and-cry about defending the flag in order to have their territories incorporated into the colonial system administered by the Imperial government itself.

Nigeria was a late and marginal addition to a British Empire which had far more pressing interests elsewhere. While colonialism is based upon the material interests of the imperial country (i.e., the interests of the ruling classes of those nations) not all colonial histories were the same. Within a widespread and long-lasting imperial system a strict profit-loss balance sheet may not be fundamental in every particular case. Colonial enterprise in Nigeria was profitable primarily to a few trading-shipping companies. That was why throughout the latter half of the nineteenth century there was a continual debate within British capitalist circles as to whether regions like Nigeria should be incorporated into the Empire or not.

The British government took over direct colonial control of the Nigerian coast and then expanded into the interior only near the end of the nineteenth century, in conjunction with the final carving up of Africa among the European colonial powers. The last indigenous states were conquered shortly after 1900 and the present-day boundaries of Nigeria laid out, almost accidentally. Virtually no European plantations, cattle ranches, rubber estates or other forms of land alienation were allowed to emerge. European settlers were excluded by policy and less than 20,000 Europeans, mainly administrators, traders and their families, resided in the country at any time throughout most of its history.

According to a quip made by Kwame Nkrumah a half century later, the then-newly independent Ghanaian government should consider building a monument to the Anopheles mosquito, since European colonists had been dissuaded from settling in West Africa because of malaria. It was a joke which Nigerian students thought was funny. Europeans had had comparable but less jovial feelings about Nigeria in the days before malarial prophylactics. A bit of Kiplingesque doggerel warned,

Beware young man of the Bight of Benin
Where few come out though many go in.

Nigeria was left as a trade colony with the land in the hands of the native peoples. Such profits as were made came from the buying and exporting cocoa, palm and shea nut oil and a limited range of comparable agricultural products grown almost exclusively by native farmers. Nigeria was always marginal in the Imperial scheme of things and was run on a shoestring budget. That may be difficult to appreciate today when Nigeria is the most populous and powerful state in Africa.

Indirect rule was a colonial strategy which reached its apogee in Nigeria. It was a strategy for maintaining a vast, potentially fractious region under some semblance of order on the cheap. As it evolved in Nigeria indirect rule tended to consolidate the political power of indigenous rulers. The system retained a checkerboard of hundreds of greater and lesser native rulers and indigenous political entities in the countryside, each guarding its own local prerogatives. The British colonial regime kept its nose out of day-to-day life. It normally supported whichever Emirs, Obas, Shehus, Sardaunas, Alafins, Alakes and other kinglets who more or less kept order and demonstrated that they retained clout among their own people. Many native rulers had a stake in seeing that indirect rule under the colonial regime was maintained.

Indirect rule left the fabric of traditional Nigerian societies more or less intact. In fact, the colonial administration helped consolidate many indigenous customs and power relations through establishing native courts and codifying native law. Multiple marriage and the complex sets of duties and rights among kinsmen, traditional obligations and rights of inheritance and above all ownership of land were left largely unchanged. In comparison to what many peoples elsewhere experienced during the roughly seventy-year period of British colonial rule in Nigeria, it was a relatively benign regime, if not as beneficent as it was once portrayed.

The great majority of the Nigerian population remained in the countryside as tribal-peasant cultivators tending their subsistence and cash crop plots in the context of variously modified traditional arrangements. A low-level cash economy permeated most regions of Nigeria during the first half of the twentieth century. Although most rural Nigerians could still cover most of their food requirements by their

In an old district of Lagos, capital city of Nigeria, circa 1957.

own labours on their own land and in conjunction with their own kinsmen, the need for small but crucial amounts of cash became near universal. I am using "Nigerian" here in a rather schematic way since the great majority still identified themselves more closely with their particular ethnic and "tribal" origins than with any nation called Nigeria.

In the cities traditional social relationships and cosmological conceptions were melded with new ways of life. Cities like Ibadan and Lagos became the mud-brick Babylons of men and women who were ready to sample new worlds. They became the refuge for others who could find neither a livelihood nor justice in the countryside. In that they became true cities, even if crammed with people living in seemingly traditional ways. Inhabitants of Ibadan and Lagos and other Nigerian cities were as much vocal patriots of their towns as any New Yorker and viewed the charms of village life with patronizing disdain.

The cities became the locus of a heterogeneous spectrum of petty and no so petty traders, labourers, artisans and others who survived by assorted miracles and ingenuities reminiscent of Lazarillo de Tormes. Among them were the beginnings of a Nigerian working class. Even as late as the 1950s it struck many anthropologists as smart to discount the changes wrought in the lives of African city dwellers. Speaking of a "Nigerian working class" sounded quite ludicrous to them.

During the period of colonial rule an amorphous Nigerian merchant class arose. They ranged from successful wholesale traders to multimillionaire building contractors. Nigerian traders were nothing if not entrepreneurial — buying and selling goods, land and labour. Although there had been sporadic anti-colonial demonstrations since the late 1920s Nigerian nationalism began to emerge only at the end of World War II. It is impossible to say how long it would have taken for the independence movement to sink roots had it not been conjoined with Britain's decision to withdraw from its remaining colonial possessions. By 1957 a forced draft policy of Nigerianization was under way. For the emerging Nigerian middle class the forthcoming national independence was being awaited as an invitation to a permanent feast. Others were hopeful but considerably more cautious in their expectations.

Glimpses of the Raj

About a month after I arrived in Ibadan there was a train wreck nearby at Lalapun so I went down to the new teaching hospital on the outskirts of town to donate a pint of blood. The Nigerian nurses on duty didn't quite know what to do with me so they called the British MD running the hematology section. "Yes, it's alright. Take his blood," she said. She and her radiologist husband, both in their thirties, had been working in the still far-flung corners of the shrinking Empire. It sometimes seemed that there were almost as many dedicated people in the British colonial service as there were Colonel Blimps.

One such anomaly was a district officer by the name of George Shepherd. District officers were the all-purpose administrators of county-sized districts throughout the British Empire. He'd just gotten out of Ibadan hospital after a bout of filariasis, a nasty and potentially fatal parasitic disease caused by a microscopic worm, one of the host of diseases which some geographers called the real rulers of tropical Africa.

Shepherd had a rather interesting history. He was from an English middle-class family carrying on in genteel penury who had managed to go to Cambridge in the mid 1930s only through considerable sacrifice. The spread of fascism in Europe and its appeal to broad sections of the ruling classes almost everywhere, the seeming dead end of capitalism as well as imponderables in his own background brought him over to the left. He'd dithered over joining the British volunteers in the International Brigades but was overtaken by events in Spain. In 1939 he joined the British Army in the expectation of a European war, became an officer and by 1942 was posted to a Gurkha battalion in India. After two years of the bloody jungle campaign in Burma he was second in command. One couldn't find a role much more typical of the British Raj than that.

After the end of the war George drifted around Britain trying to find some footing and hoping that something might come of the Attlee Labour government. Betwixt and between, he volunteered for pick-and-shovel work to help rebuild railways in Tito's Yugoslavia. God only knows how he was viewed there in those paranoiac times.

Back in Britain George finally decided that there was nothing for it except to emigrate or enter the British colonial service. He was posted to Nigeria in the late 1940s as an assistant district officer, the lowest grade in the system. When I met him eight years later he was in a back-water district one grade up. George was the DO for Shonga and Lafi-argi Emirates, two Nupe-speaking Native states of some fifty thousand people on the banks of the central Niger river. Although I was predis-posed to be suspicious of anyone involved in colonial administration, Shepherd and I hit it off immediately and he asked me to accompany him on a visit to his post some 250 miles north, a two-day trip by bat-tered Opel.

As the gods would have it, a day before I left on that trip an incident occurred at the college which ultimately led to the place being closed down and to my departure to live in the old wards of Ibadan and Lagos. "The Riot at the University College", as Nigerian tabloids such as the *West African Pilot* called it in breathless purple prose, occurred the night before I was to go up country. What it amounted to was stu-dents tearing down the wire mesh screens which had been installed on the outside corridors of the student residences. The college had been built five miles beyond the edge of Ibadan to cloister the students from the distractions of city life. You could only get in or out of your resi-dence with a special pass or by clambering over a back wall. When the wire mesh was installed the residences looked like a prison. That was the last straw.

At a "meeting of gentlemen" (and two or three women) the discus-sion raged over what the college administration must think of Nige-rian students to pen them in like animals. Assorted Yoruba maxims were trotted out, to no one's elucidation. Olajide Alo, the most char-ismatic of the student leaders, finally asked all those unwilling to be caged up to remain behind and the others to return to their residences before the curfew. About a hundred or so stayed, including myself.

Most of the students were already mature men and some already had wives and families and responsibilities. I didn't have much to lose but it was a daring decision on the part of Nigerian students. They ran the risk of being expelled when a university degree made the difference between obtaining a position with a fairly comfortable income and being reduced to the penury of the frayed white-collar class.

The long and short of it was that we marched from one dormitory to another and within an hour tore down the offending wire screening. That was all there was to it. It wasn't in the least violent although I suppose that a hundred men tramping along at night with crowbars in their hands may have looked scary. I felt completely at ease amongst them. But all the watchmen stayed in the gatehouses and not a single college warden showed his face until the police arrived a few hours later.

The University College was run along the lines of a British public school with hall wardens and masters and a plethora of hierarchical rituals. The teaching staff and administration of the college was almost exclusively British. "They can run their college any way they want but I didn't come all this way and spend my savings just to live in a bloody British public school," I felt. Turmoil or not, I was going to see what the back country was like. So I decamped with Shepherd.

Lagos, 1958. A crowded street scene in the old market area.

Lafiargi and Shonga Emirates had once been part of the Nupe state whose capital was at Bida. They had split off and made a deal with the Fulani overlords when Bida was conquered in one of the *jihads* of the early nineteenth century. It is a region of savanna orchard brush with remnants of gallery forest along the river margins. The scattered farm hamlets were surrounded with a patchwork of complex multi-crop garden plots interspersed through the bush fallow. Given the size of the Nigerian population, then around seventy million, broad stretches of the countryside were surprisingly empty.

The Nupe were well known to readers of British social anthropology and I'd previously waded through S.N. Nadel's *A Black Byzantium*. If one were expecting a medieval city, something between Fez and Timbuktu, Lafiargi would have been a disappointment. There were towns like that in Nigeria but this wasn't one of them. Lafiargi was an over-grown mud hut village of about twelve thousand people. "This is Byz-antium?"

Since Shepherd's departure to hospital the Emir had been lobbying the British authorities of Illorin Province for another District Officer and the Emir's ears in Illorin had told him that a new man was being dispatched. So when we drove into Lafiargi the Emir came out to receive what he expected would be a more pliable DO. The royal entourage issued from the palace gate — drummers drumming and umbrella bearers bearing as they swirl along beside the Emir — until someone realized that the same old district officer had returned. A stoney silence and then a diplomatic and possibly ambiguous inquiry about Shepherd's health.

The most recent set to between the Emir and Shepherd had taken place over the murder of an old woman who had been accused of witchcraft. Witches are usually isolated people with few strong kin connections. Outbreaks of witch hunting hysteria were a recurrent aspect of many Nigerian cultures. It was a tradition which was suppressed by colonial authorities whenever possible, and rightly so too. No government which is unable or unwilling to knock clerico-traditionalist heads together to suppress certain customs which "have come down from time immemorial" has a right to govern.

This woman had been dragged out of her hut, put through various torture ordeals, beaten by a crowd of villagers and finally killed in a particularly gruesome way. One of the witch hunters had rammed an iron rod up her vagina. All this took place over a two-hour period and within shouting distance of the Emir's palace. Neither he nor his Native Constabulary moved to intervene. That too was part of back-land politics.

Shepherd had threatened to have the Emir charged with derelic-tion of his oath of office as the ruler of a Native State. But the British colonial administration in Nigeria was by then unwilling to become embroiled with local rulers they were preparing to hand over author-ity to. They would leave Nigerians to settle their own affairs after they granted independence. Shepherd was feeling rather dispirited about all this. That may have accounted for some of his perversity.

Shortly before we got to Lafiargi the Northern Provinces govern-ment had circulated a letter to all district officers ordering them to list those persons within their districts they knew to be "hostile to estab-lished order" and those who were spreading beliefs "inimical to the respect for and authority of Native Rulers".

"Do they think I'm going to be an informer for their protégé Sardauna? Our governor seems to have stopped playing Lawrence of Arabia and started aping the Yanks." Shepherd sent back the question-naire with a short notation saying, "Unfortunately only one person in Lafiargi and Shonga Emirates fits the characteristics outlined in your memo as subversive." Then he filled in his own name. Luckily one of the British administrators at Illorin read his report and sent it back to George, telling him that while they understood this kind of response some of the deputies of the new Northern Region government might not; that in the interests of his service record and pension he should destroy the original reply and send a memo with the simple statement "No one".

The incident at the college had grown into a major political debate while I was away in the Middle Belt. When I got back to Ibadan two weeks later I was amazed to find that the incident had become the main topic of debate in the Western Regional Assembly. It led to the closing of the single university then in Nigeria.

One of the more fatuous deans told me to make myself ready to face a college Board of Enquiry. "This is a most serious matter," he said. It was a tempest in a teapot but if it hadn't been for the principal of the college, an English historian by the name of Parry, I probably would have been deported. He decided to back me up and said to me pri-vately, "You will appreciate that there have been certain influences of Mr. McCarthy from your part of the world here as well. It would be best if you were a little more judicious in the future." Of course it didn't end there.

The British Central Investigation Directory was then running the immigration services of Nigeria. They sent a British inspector to pick me up. "You're in serious trouble my lad. It's lucky that you turned up when you did because we've been trying to locate you for ten days. Chief Commissioner Horrocks-Mosley has given us instructions to send you down to him as soon as we have you. Thought you'd flown the coop. Har, harump. Well — see to it that you're down in Lagos in the Commissioner's office by tomorrow morning or you'll get the biggest rocket . . ."

Have you ever seen the film *How I Won the War*, a satire of British officers' war memoirs? There is one sequence in which an addled colonel, veteran of the Northwest Frontier campaigns, drills World War II officer-cadets on the stratagems of "the wily Pathan". That was Chief Commissioner Horrocks-Mosley. *Pukka sahib*, with Sundowner-splotched complexion, thin droopy mustachios and gleaming, gimlety eyes which I presume were supposed to peer into your soul but really only made him look a little demented.

"I want to know exactly what part you played in all this and who else was behind it," says the Commissioner. "We know very well that Nigerian students aren't able to organize an action, as this incident was organized, on their own. We have had reports that a Red Chinese agent entered with that student convention circus at about the time you arrived. [He actually said that.] I'm not at all satisfied with the documentation of just what you are doing here and who the people responsible for sending you are. Not at all . . ."

"Are you joking ?" That was the wrong thing to say.

"This Is No Joking Matter. Let me tell you, Laddie Buck, if I'm not completely satisfied about you in this whole matter you'll be on a plane out of here so fast it'll make your head spin. The only reason I'm giving you this opportunity is because the principal of the University College [a slight curl of the lip here] has assured me that you were innocently caught up in all this. But I'm going to get to the bottom of it." More raving and ranting, some of it blatantly racist too.

I just sat and listened to him. Whenever he asked a question I answered with a non sequitur. There's no point in trying to talk sense to irrational people, especially if they have power. Basically, I think what it really amounted to was that his pride was hurt when for almost

Car park and bus station, Ibadan, 1958.

two weeks his CID couldn't find the single white university student in an almost totally African region. Horrocks-Mosley put on his sternest face and said, "You just keep to the straight-and-narrow from here on in. We'll be keeping an eye on you." Don't blame me if it sounds like a soap opera scripted by Mel Brooks.

New Ogas for Old

In some regions of Nigeria urban life long predated European colonization. The Yoruba had established some fair-sized indigenous cities of which Ibadan was one of latest and largest. It had been established early in the nineteenth century by Yoruba soldiery and refugees fleeing from the collapse of Oyo, the once predominant Yoruba state. By the middle of that century Ibadan had become the leading Yoruba military power, jostling and feuding with the neighboring Yoruba states. By the 1890s, at the time of its incorporation into the colony of Nigeria, the city contained some 150,000 inhabitants and was surrounded by a ten- to twelve-mile perimeter of town walls. The majority of its residents, however, continued to farm plots outside the city walls. This was made possible by the intensification of a complex form of slash-and-burn horticulture. Although there was some scholarly debate about how to view such urban conglomerations, Ibadanis had an ingrained pride about being city dwellers and not "bush people", as the pidgin term for villagers had it.

By 1957 Ibadan contained more than 400,000 people but was still basically an indigenous city. The only modern quarter of the city clustered around the Western Region government buildings on an outer edge of town. The rest of the city was comprised mainly of crowded compounds housing extended families and tenants. A great deal of daily living — washing, cooking, taking care of children, working and lounging about — was done in either the backyards of compounds or along the margins of alleys. Only the sketchiest infrastructure of roads, electricity, sewage or public water existed. There was a single British department store carrying European goods but an incredible number of small shops owned by Lebanese or East Indian merchants selling cloth and a range of goods especially manufactured for the West Africa trade.

Nigerian cities were inundated with itinerant peddlers all selling the same two or three dozen items. Petty traders operated with an eighty-shilling stock of tinned corned beef, canned sardines, *gari* and yam flour. Others hawked Japanese plastic sandals or cheap enamel ware, cigarettes and *kola*, soft drinks or ready-to-eat snacks. In the city you would rarely be out of sight of someone trying to sell something. I could never understand the economics of this petty trading, but then neither could most Yoruba men, except that they knew that their wives' petty trading helped support their families.

The word *oga* was a traditional term of respect applied to any prestigious or powerful individual but it had taken on a secondary connotation of "big shot" in Yoruba parlance. After the University College was closed I briefly stayed in the house of an *oga* named Adewale. He had inherited a two-storey compound in the heart of Ibadan. Adewale was seven or eight years older than me, from an old Yoruba family and a part of the then rising government contractor class. Probably he's a Nigerian millionaire now. He was already well on his way then and was the right person in the right place.

Wale had been sent to England by his father for a no-nonsense education as a chartered accountant had been back in Nigeria for some four years when I met him. At first he'd been disappointed that he hadn't been sent to do a proper university degree in law or economics but had since come to appreciate his elder's good sense. "There are so many boys with university degrees now that some will have to soon settle for teaching school children to make a living."

By 1957 Wale had established his own accountancy firm which

thrived on contracts to audit the books of government agencies scattered from Ibadan to Benin. He had also acquired a young wife and had picked up two child servants who worked as skivvies around the house for their meals and a place to lay their mats at night. The family lived on the top floor of the building while the ground floor was rented out as storage space for merchants dabbling in grain speculation. There were a cluster of huts strung along the inside wall of the compound which were rented out to washermen and a few impoverished old women. After all, "ten shillings rent a month is still ten shillings to the good." Wale also owned a number of taxis and had invested in sundry houses and building plots in Ibadan. There was money for endless rounds of gin and beer for hangers-on but just let his wife ask him for another pound a week for household expenses and Yoruba maxims about domestic frugality would pour forth.

Adewale's parents and grandfather lived in another large compound next door. His father was a distinguished-looking but rather retiring man of about sixty who might have passed for an Anglican cleric. I never heard what his story was but the grandfather, by all accounts, had cut a wide swath in his time. The old man was almost ninety and had come of age before, or better said with, the British colonial administration of Ibadan.

Born in Ibadan when it was an independent Yoruba city-state, the grandfather had gone to Abeokuta as a young man. That must have been in the late 1880s. At the time Abeokuta was an advance base of British missionary interests and the Alake of Abeokuta was known throughout missionary England as the "Christian King", which the Abeokutans turned to good advantage in trade, advisors and imported muskets.

When the British incorporated Ibadan into the expanding colony of Nigeria they left the day-to-day political power in the hands of the traditional council of chiefs. It was into this milieu that Wale's grandfather returned to Ibadan with some sort of church position and a knowledge of British colonial customs. Even cursory familiarity with the ways of the new suzerain power was of value during the initial decades of indirect rule. The grandfather had parlayed his position into one of considerable importance.

The grandfather, who had been ailing a long time, died while I was staying in the compound. What a wake! Messengers and telegrams were sent out in all directions to kinsmen and assorted notables. Chartered vans began to arrive loaded with people come to attend the four-day wake. They set up cooking facilities in the yard and were lodged in whatever space was available. A bonfire was kept burning throughout the night beside the main road and those coming to pay their respects sang and danced to traditional drum bands and praise singers. A steady stream of people came, some dressed in hundred-pound *agbadas* and others in threadbare ten-shilling gowns. There was some crying but mainly it was dancing to praise songs for this *oga* who lay in state in his house.

"If it were a man with young children and his life unfinished we would be sad. But he died after a long life, having done much and seeing his family strong and well planted. That is not a life to be sad about," said Wale, rising above his usual pronouncements.

Travels by Bolekaja

Not much in the way of twentieth century technology had spread beyond a few major cities in Nigeria. In the small towns and villages "modern technology" mainly meant treadle-powered sewing machines, and "imported consumer goods" primarily meant Argentine corned beef, enamel cooking pots and Indian or British textiles. An occasional merchant might have a windup gramophone and a stack of endlessly replayed Highlife records but even radios were extremely rare. There were some places where you couldn't even find a bottle of Coca-Cola!

The most widespread emissary of European ingenuity were trucks — transport trucks were everywhere. When I say trucks were everywhere I mean in bush hamlets where you wouldn't suspect it possible to get one of those underpowered British lorries into, let alone what anyone might find there which could pay for the gas and the wear and tear. On a rutted trail leading to some backland village you might be confronted with a lorry lurching and bumping its way along between the trees in a mechanical dance. Or you might find it sitting forlornly in the village marketplace, the driver tinkering with the carburetor and the swamper sleeping in the back as they waited for a load of shea nuts or sacks of yams or god knows what to materialize which they might profitably haul to the next larger town.

One can hardly overemphasize the role which truck traffic played in stitching the backlands and the villages to the towns, the towns and the regions to each other in the years after World War II. It must have been quite a venture for the mainly Nigerian traders who bought and operated the first trucks. There were hardly any roads worth the name and virtually no gas stations or repair facilities initially. The problems of developing paying routes in a country where most people thought twice and thrice before paying sixpence they might save by walking. But by the mid 1950s many traders had invested in one or more working lorries and some had whole fleets of them. They were usually fitted up to carry both passengers and freight and operated in ways analogous to tramp freighters.

In the "car parks" near major city markets on a typical day you could find a couple hundred trucks loading, discharging or waiting around. Travelers would swirl back and forth from truck to truck, ask about fares, look to see how many actual passengers were aboard and finally heave themselves and their cargo on board.

The driver wanted to have as many bodies on board as possible so that it appeared as if he were loaded and near ready to leave. After a number of real passengers had been enticed aboard and had paid their fares you'd often see the shills drop off and go to sit in another truck trying to get a load together. The swamper, hired partly for his ability to cajole, would work passing travelers with his pitch in Yoruba and pidgin English. "Make fast. We go now, Ker Ker. We go now soon," followed by the string of places they were bound for — Abeokuta or Ijebode, Illehsha or Ijesha, Oshogbo, Obomosho, Illorin and the smaller towns and villages in between, which might or might not be mentioned. Maybe two or three more passengers would climb aboard as the driver gunned the engine. If the wait was more than normally excessive a group of passengers, often incited by a market woman, would begin berating the driver about how he was wasting their time and trade.

There were also old British buses which looked as if they had survived the Burma Road, filled as much with stacked headpans of *gari*, stalks of plantains and covies of live chickens as with passengers. Although these buses never seemed to leave for their destinations, sooner or later they must have because you recurrently saw them broken down along the side of the road with their passengers glumly standing around or shouting imprecations and offering unsolicited advice to the driver-mechanic attempting some Lazarus feat of resuscitation through haywire wizardry.

The trucks were mainly two-tonne British lorries, loaded with as much freight and as many passengers as could be crammed aboard. *Bolekaja* was their generic name in Yoruba, which roughly translates as "Come down and fight". That referred both to the temper of the drivers and the combativeness which jouncing around jambed together created among passengers. "Mammy wagon" was the Ghanaian term, memorializing the market women who originally had constituted the primary users of truck transport.

The vehicle was bought as a bare chassis and the owner contracted local carpenters to add the cab and body. This usually consisted of tiers of wooden benches in various space-saving arrangements, and strong wooden running boards along the open sides for easy access and a sturdy flat roof on which freight was piled. The trucks were painted in a vivid collage of green or dusty yellow with red panels and black stripes or white borders. All had a scrollwork of Yoruba sayings painted on them. *Agbon Pal'o Pa. Eni Agbon Pako Ton' Kan*, meaning "Folly kills many but those killed by wisdom are few." Or you might see the chorus of a popular Highlife tune, "Iyawo Ma Pa Me" which translates as "Wife, don't kill me" but more colloquially as "Stop complaining". There might be two or three such sayings on a truck so you could take your pick.

You might be bouncing along, packed in like a sardine. The *bolekaja* stops along the way and a few more passengers scramble aboard and try to wedge in, berating everyone for not making space, amid laughter and banter. Someone might make a sexual pun and someone else might split *kola* nuts and share them around.

My jousts with the Yoruba language were not very successful. It's not an easy language to learn. Yoruba is a tonal language, the relative tone levels determining the meaning of a word as much as the actual phonemes. For instance, *Oba* (two high tones) means "he meets" while *Oba* (one high, one mid tone) is "he hides". There are yet other meanings of *Oba*, including the generic term for "chief". In addition, spoken Yoruba revels in elisions — the syllables in some words are dropped or run together in phrases. That's familiar enough in English but Yoruba is downright fiendish with elisions. I can't remember any good example now other than in a common name. "Wale" is the elision of *Ade Wa Ile*, meaning "The Crown Comes Home". It alludes to the belief in the rebirth of a powerful ancestor's spirit in the child so named.

Seeing as I wasn't getting anywhere with Yoruba grammar texts I decided to try another approach. I memorized the words and tone patterns of popular Yoruba songs and maxims. Although I did learn something that way it was not enough to carry on a meaningful conversation. People talked to me in anything from King's English to Lagos pidgin and lent a tolerant ear to my attempts to unscramble their language, which most assumed was beyond the ability of Europeans anyway. Pidgin English wasn't exactly a *lingua franca* but it was quite general in the cities of Western Nigeria. That and a collection of Yoruba phrases and a certain alertness to what people intended got me by most of the time.

Ordinary Nigerians were quite self-confident. They hadn't been colonized in their own sense of themselves. I might come wandering down a bush garden path, dressed in a melange of western and Nigerian clothing. Some farmers would hail me from their gardens, stop work for a minute and crack an apt saying, try to strike up a conversation and go back to work. Imagine the obverse, a Yoruba farmer dressed in an Agbada gown comes clomping down the back lanes of some Canadian suburb. He'd be greeted by suspicion and fear rather than with interest and passing homilies.

I don't want to idealize the Yoruba. There were more than fifteen million Yoruba with every conceivable kind of attitude and nature. Given the wrong conditions some of them could be pretty violent. Kinship oriented or not, some could be as miserable towards servants and dependents as any character out of Charles Dickens. Yet somehow there was something full of life about the Yoruba people.

Truck drivers had acquired the aura of the traditional itinerant traders. Footloose, combative and knowledgeable about different towns and regions. Sailors of rutted inland routes. Tough, resourceful and urbane, familiar with the magic of machinery — that was the image they liked to convey. Among the pantheon of Yoruba gods, still vital despite the spread of Islam, the one which truck drivers had a special affinity to was Ogun, the god of warriors and ironworkers. It fit; the trucks, the way they drove.

On the two-lane highway from Lagos to Ibadan and north the *bole-kaja* trucks would race along trying to pass each other. The one in the lead got to pick up any passengers waiting alongside the road. That was the reason for all the shouting and pushing to get passengers on and off once the truck was finally rolling. Considering that the main road was in pretty good shape there was a phenomenal number of pileups and wrecks on it.

Adegoke Adelabu died that way, in a car wreck on the road from Lagos to Ibadan. He had been the leader of the Ibadan-based opposition in the Western Region legislature. Some of his supporters claimed that he'd been killed by witchcraft instigated by his political enemies. "Killed in a smash-up, yes. But who caused the car to smash up?" That's always the tack in witchcraft accusations.

Adel... abu... Adel... abu
Adelabu Alhaji Adegoke

So went the chorus of a hauntingly beautiful praise song that was played at his funeral in Ibadan.

Within a couple of days Adelabu's followers began the violent expulsion of the opposing Action Group supporters in the villages surrounding Ibadan. I was living in the heart of old Ibadan then and commuting to the college during the day. At one point some hundreds of men and boys armed with machetes, spears and few old Dane guns started marching on Ibadan down the main road. The tumult had been going on for a few days but I, with what now seems an incredible foolhardiness, wandered around the city day and night. It was not an anti-white or anti-colonial riot, but a mob is a mob, and people had been killed. Finally, mobile squads of Nigerian military police cordoned off districts and cracked down. They had the thing quashed in a two days. However naive I then was I was not so stupid as to fail to appreciate that there are times when use of military force is absolutely necessary. Had there been a similar response by the Nigerian army a decade later against the murderous mobs which killed tens of thousands of Ibos the Biafran civil war would never have occurred. Samuel Ifaginaw, a fellow student at the University College, died in those later pogroms.

Not long after I arrived at Ibadan, an acquaintance, student leader Sam Oloopitun, said, "You may see us laughing and working together but I'm a Yoruba and he's a Calabar man, so you know we really hate each other." They were actually close friends and the comment was supposed to be a tongue-in-cheek dig at western misconceptions of tribalism, then the bugbear of journalistic philosophizing about emerging African states. But it turned out to be a grimmer jest than any of us could have supposed. Let's end with a *bolekaja* story, because Samuel Ifaginaw was one of the people involved.

There had been a conference of Student Union leaders from developing countries at the University College shortly before I arrived and crates of communications gear were still laying around waiting to be shipped back to the respective countries. To ensure that it all arrived at the Apapa docks intact, Olajide Alo and three other student leaders, Sam Oloopitun, Sam Obumps, and Samuel Ifaginaw, decided to hire a truck and driver to deliver the load themselves. I'm put prominently up front with the driver so that any police we encounter will be dissuaded from pulling us over for an impromptu road inspection, waived on payment of "dash".

As we are rolling along I reach up and touch a small bundle swinging back and forth on the inside of the windscreen, of dried skin with some feathers and blood splotched cloth protruding from it. "What's this?" I ask. An angry glare from the driver.

"Ah — don't touch that," says Jide. "You'd better not go touching things like that here. That's, ah ... a "fetish bundle" I suppose you could call it. Probably from Ogun. It's sacred to the owner and he won't like you touching it."

Sam Oloopitun asks, "Do you know if any of our African practices survived in America? Do you ever hear of some of those things back in your home?"

"No, not in Canada. Not that I ever heard of. Maybe in America. But there was a chant which is part of a Haitian dance tune which was popular a few years ago."

"Can you sing it? We would all be interested to hear what that might be."

We're bouncing along the road down to Lagos, coming off the edge of the savanna country and dipping into the tropical rain forest. The Yoruba truck driver and me up front, the four Nigerian students in a seat behind us and crates of electronic communications gear from an international student union conference in the back. The song is in Haitian French but the chorus goes something like,

Shango-mambo, Shango-mambo.
Eiyeh eh, hey yeh ...
Shango mambo' ... N'Tore.

I repeat it a few times and begin to get into the spirit of the thing.

"Hmm. That's very interesting," says Sam Obumps.

Shango of course is the state god of the Yoruba, the mythical founder of the Yoruba kingdoms. As such he is also a god linked to war and power, symbolized by a double-edged stone ax. The embodiment of his presence is lightning. The lorry driver is looking at me out of the corner of his eye. ("Crazy fool," he's probably thinking.) Not three minutes later, less, there is a cloudburst and bolts of lightening come crashing down all around us.

"Ah," says Jide in mock seriousness, being agnostic about all gods in any shape or form, "It doesn't pay to fool with these things."

In the Big Apple: Lagos

After the great wire-cutting caper the University College was closed down while the authorities decided what to do next. It was ludicrous but it was fine with me — I wanted to be on my own anyway. The main trouble was that I had used up my money in getting to Nigeria and had been relying on room and board at the college. I borrowed a couple of hundred dollars from home but for half a year I lived a very catch-as-catch-can existence.

I had trouble with food in Nigeria. That is to say, for some three or four months I never had enough to eat and sometimes didn't know where my next meal was coming from. Of course, if I had gotten desperate I could always have had myself repatriated to Canada so it was not the same hunger which many people have known. But it was the only time in my life when I was chronically hungry and unable to do anything about it.

There was also an initial problem in adjusting to Nigerian cooking. Yoruba cookery is a combination of starchy doughs and the most fiery sauces in the world. Not the hottest Mexican chili dishes or the most potent Indian curries can hold a candle to Yoruba oil stews. For the first month I could hardly taste anything and my stomach was in constant turmoil but gradually my taste buds and stomach lining acclimatized to the peppers and I began to appreciate the combinations of flavour.

Meat of any sort was relatively expensive and was used sparingly in the oil stews — a few cubes of stringy meat in long-simmering pots of peppered palm oil sauce. Palm oil is a rich reddish fluid pressed from the kernels of the oil palm. It has a subtle taste all its own and is the basis of Yoruba stews — oil, cubes of meat or fish, tomatoes and a ground paste of local peppers ranging from fiery to incandescent. This simmers away over a charcoal burner for a couple of hours. The staples are *eba*, a dough-like porridge made from cassava meal or *hamala* from yam flour; *jollof* rice, a holiday dish fancied up with saffron and flavoured with meat and tomatoes; and *dodo*, a staple made of deep-fried plantains and served with a peppery fish sauce. Delicious.

The main meal of the day is taken in the early evening. Everyone gets a small clay bowl of oil stew and a platter or banana leaf heaped with *eba* or *hamala*. You are supposed to take a bite-sized hunk of dough with two fingers, form it into a disc with your thumb and scoop up some of the sauce without dribbling any on your clothes. A refined diner should have no oil on the palms of his or her hands when the meal is over. Adults made allowance for me as a European but children would watch my efforts with giggling fascination until they were shushed by their parents.

Diende Dipeolu was in his mid thirties, and the closure of the university was a crisis time for him. He had been alloted a two-room flat in the Surru Lere housing project on the outskirts of Lagos because his family had been displaced by one of the first redevelopment schemes in the old city. But they refused to live out in the sticks. Diende finally managed to find an apartment for his family only a ten-minute walk from the Yaba Roundabout. So they let me stay in their allotment at Surru Lere.

Diende's brother was the assistant manager of the local Reuters news agency. It supplied copy to the major dailies in the city (one per political party) and filed whatever news items came out of Nigeria. He was conversant with the manners and fashions of the broader world and played the role of a suave man about town — to the extent possible on thirty pounds a month and an old Vespa motor scooter. Nevertheless, all of the family — Diende, his wife and two young kids, his aged mother as well as Diende's brother and girlfriend — lived together quite equitably in a set of rooms around the inner courtyard of a Moorish-style apartment house.

Lagos proper, the old city, was built on a sandy island and had been the main depot of the Royal Niger Company. It was the rail terminus and primary seaport for the entire country. There were possibly a quarter million people living on Lagos Island itself and as many again in Ebutte Meta, Yaba and the newer districts on the mainland. In the

Canoe Harbour, Olowogbowa district, Lagos, 1958.

close-packed old wards, where the houses were still mainly one- and two-storey adobe compounds, the population densities were higher than in many tenement areas of New York.

The worst traffic jams I've ever seen in my life were in Lagos. Manhattan traffic was quite reasonable by comparison. The main roads were packed with creeping, crawling, honking buses, cars, trucks and hand-pulled *Omolanke* wagons during morning and evening rush hours. Buses would be backed up a mile or two into Yaba. Riders sat glumly looking out the windows as pedestrians and cyclists passed the stalled traffic. The conductors would announce cheerily that the line was beginning to move and make jokes to diffuse demands by passengers who wanted fares returned so they could get out and walk. Passengers struck up bantering or indignant conversations with their fellow riders at these times.

It wasn't that there were so many vehicles in Lagos but rather that there were hardly any roads for them. There were a few main roads leading to the commercial core of the city but the rest of Lagos was a tangle of cement and adobe houses where streets narrowed down to sandy lanes and twisting alleys and ended up in interconnecting backyards.

Although there were few roads there were swarms of taxis — Fiats, Opels, Anglias — their size determined not only by fuel consider-ations but also by the width of the lanes they attempted to traverse. You often shared the taxi with whomever the driver managed to pick up and after some roundabout detour you ultimately would be depos-ited in the general vicinity of your destination. Depending on what kind of mood the driver was in and what fare you had bargained for, the taxi might wind up bumping down a narrow lane, picking its way along an alley twisting between house walls, bouncing across back-yards where women pounded cassava or artisans cobbled away at one thing or another.

If I were going to visit Bisi at her aunty's house and could spare two or three shillings I'd get a cab at the central square in Lagos and tell the driver, "Olowogbowo, Ajao's House." If the driver wasn't sure he'd heard right I'd repeat it and add, "Sal'eko". Sal'eko was a *favela* district down by the canoe harbour, between the Old Custom House and the Carter Bridge. Olowogbowo was a roughly defined area at one end of that district while Ajao's House was a large four-storey building, the landmark of the immediate vicinity. That put me within a few hun-dred yards of where I was going.

Christmas Day, 1957

We had decided that all of us, the whole Dipeolu family, some of their friends, I and anyone I wanted to bring along, were going to spend Christmas day on Victoria Beach, just beyond the edge of Lagos.

It was as paradisaical as anything I've ever experienced. The water was warm and the surf rolled in just high enough to make for exciting swimming once you got the hang of it. The beach was a fine white sand which stretched away as far as you could see. It was bordered by salt-re-sistant grasses and scattered palm trees, enough to provide shade but without the tangle of vegetation which one found on the landward side of the lagoon. There were no flies or mosquitoes or other noxious insects because of the light salt spray carried by a gentle breeze. Fol-lowing the Harmattan and before the monsoons the days are clear and sunny and an even ninety degrees Fahrenheit.

Peddlers wander along the beach carrying headpans of paw paw, mango and more exotic holiday fruits, such as apples imported from the Jos Plateau. There is warm beer and Krola, a favourite Nigerian soft drink tasting like a combination of Dr. Pepper and Coca-Cola. Just awful. Fanti fishermen are selling five-shilling boxes of stogies smuggled in from Dahomey, others are hawking spicy Lebanese meat pies and other treats. It was an almost exclusively Nigerian crowd.

Family groups and other entourages were scattered along Victoria beach, children cavorting in the wash of the surf while Yoruba mothers kept a sharp watch that they didn't go in above their waists. Hardly anyone actually swam and no one at all went out beyond the surf. That should have given me pause for thought. I didn't know what the currents were like, but I'd swim out past the breakers a good half mile.

"Very foolish," said Bisi.

"Ah, Bisi — in my home I lived on the water. I'm really part fish."

Nope. People should stay out of deep water, like the then popular Highlife song said. It was a couple of months later that I learned from a Fanti fisherman that those waters were infested with sharks. They caught them there all the time.

I'd bought some Christmas presents for Diende's family, including a Monopoly set. Who could have guessed that it would strike such a responsive chord. They all became Monopoly addicts. Much of Christmas day there was a circle of Monopoly players sitting under the palm trees, near oblivious to the sea or anything else, debating the relative worth of the properties, wheeling and dealing and making close inspection of the rules at contentious points. Strangers would wander along the beach and edge over to see what this lot were up to; some would stick around to add their advice, much to the annoyance of the players. Seems like I'd tapped into a vein of Nigerian dreams.

One of the players was a boyhood friend of Diende's who had come along. Adu had enlisted in a British regiment raised in Nigeria during the Second World War and had been sent into the Burma campaign. He had risen to the rank of sergeant but had wound up as clerk selling clothes in the Kingsway department store where, eight years later, he was still earning a bare subsistence salary. It was sort of sad to see this friendly man in his late thirties and with the body of a wrestler going to seed, who had become resigned to his fate. But there he was, wheeling and dealing for Park Place or Ventnor Avenue.

Bisi had come out to Surru Lere by taxi and brought along a holiday offering of *jollof* rice, the bowl wrapped in a square of silk. By the end of the day I was in love with her, although at the time I didn't quite know what that meant. So maybe that colours my remembrance.

Bisi Archer and the author, Victoria Beach, Lagos, 1958.

Biograph: Bisi Archer and Native Medicine

We had met shortly after everyone was expelled from the University. Diende and I and some others were at a dance hall in Ikeja when a girl came over and asked me to dance. ("Now what's this beautiful young woman approaching me for? Well, who cares.") We danced, she came back to the table with me and did that traditional knee bend of respect to Diende, sat down and talked. Bisi took my address and said she'd visit one day soon and then left.

Bisi Archer was eighteen and nineteen when I knew her. She had an aura about her, a mixture of schoolgirlish innocence and elder sisterly audacity. If one believed in those sorts of things you'd say she was an Abiku, one of those whose souls have returned. She was more sagacious about people than seemed possible for anyone her age. I won't attempt to diarize the events and feelings of that relationship although many novels revolve around just that. It was the first time I had ever been in love and it knocked me for a loop.

We got to be known as a pair wandering around Yaba and through Sal'eko, where she lived with her aged aunt in a tumbledown shanty. We wandered through winding alleys, past palm wine shebeens, were greeted by neighbourhood people and accosted by prides of Boma Boys, as street corner toughs were then called in Lagos. Bisi had a candy-stripped shift she wore while I'd bought an Italian shirt with an open, upturned collar in a similar pattern. Although I didn't know it at the time it was the type of shirt which Ghanaian Boma boys allegedly wore. "Ole . . . Jaguda" ("Thief and robber") was the cheery shout as we rambled by. "Oh deez Englishmens, dey iss too cunning. Com heah steal our wimens," followed by a Yoruba salutation. But we were never ever hassled.

Bisi could relate to all sorts of people, children and *ogas*, toughs and respectable mothers, native doctors and the notoriously sharp-tongued market women. She fended off unwanted admirers with a mixture of wide-eyed surprise and irony which left everyone's pride intact. But she also had a power she could draw on. I'll be damned if I knew how it worked, except that it did.

For instance, once she and her young nephew accompanied me down to the sprawling truck park at Lagos when I was bound back to Ibadan. Out of nowhere one guy starts speechifying about Europeans who steal Nigeria's wealth and the shamelessness of women who go with them. I'm wondering if I'm going to have to fight him, a tough-looking character and a hell of a place to do it.

But Bisi begins talking to me and randomly addressing a few words here, a maxim there, a smile to people standing around the truck. Putting her arm on my shoulder she said something like, "If there be people who want to harm you is because dey have bad hearts. But God knows you and will protect you. He will turn back their evil so it will strike dey themselves". She followed up with a Yoruba proverb, just loudly enough for everyone around us to hear. After a short while the bystanders began to berate this guy and the driver tells him to shut up or else. She could pull off things like that.

I looked very young and had a wide-eyed sort of innocence too. Maybe that communicated itself to people and they responded accordingly. At the time I didn't have the slightest qualm about going into the worst rookeries, the toughest stews of Lagos by day or night. Well, maybe an occasional qualm. Individuals I had never met before would pop up out of nowhere. "You be de boy who come to Nigeria to go for school?"

Maybe his uncle's brother-in-law was related to someone who had met or heard of me. We might have a bottle of Krola or just exchange a salutation. That sort of thing happened constantly. I relied on it.

Bisi spoke Yoruba, Hausa and Lagos pidgin English fluently. Her mother was Igbira so she understood that as well. Her father had been born in the British Caribbean, Jamaica I think, and was already a middle-aged man when he emigrated to Nigeria in the 1920s. There he became a successful trader in the Middle Belt region. A black, severe, wizened figure in a suit with a stiff collar stared back from a photograph of him.

Bisi had grown up as one of the youngest children in a polygynous household, one husband with a number of wives and their children. Each family had their own rooms in a compound, an arrangement which could combine co-operation, affection and sometimes considerable hostility and fear. In the countryside wives worked plots of the family's farmland. In the city, a wife of a polygynous household often started out in some trading venture which was to help support her and her children. Bisi's mother had become a successful market woman.

When it came to disciplining children, the Yoruba could sometimes be downright brutal. Parents who otherwise were warm and generous people could do some incredible things to their children. For instance, the neighbours of mine in Surru Lere were strict traditionalists in child raising. Their nine- or ten-year-old boy had shown disrespect to his father in some way so they tied the kid up and hung him in a small shed in which red peppers were thrown on a bed of embers. The boy was half asphyxiated and temporarily blinded before they hauled him out. It absolutely amazed me. Quite a few people remembered childhood terrors like that. Ethnic traditions are a mixed bag, they are not necessarily wonderful just because they are different.

As a girl Bisi had gone to the Sudan Interior Mission school at Kaduna. When she was fifteen she became entangled in a love affair and was dismissed from the school. Soon after she was sent away to live with her aunt in Sal'eko. Although she never admitted it I suspect that she'd gotten pregnant. That had happened only three years earlier but a lot of life had flowed under the bridge since then. It's all very mundane. None of it helps to explain how it had produced this remarkable person.

Bisi accepted all kinds of contradictory views and beliefs and people — though not petty wiles or meanness of spirit. She had the same attitude towards a plethora of Christian, Islamic and indigenous Yoruba gods, spirits and supernatural forces. For someone living hand-to-mouth without any security she was generous to a fault. She might have her last ten shillings tied in a silk handkerchief tucked in her *lappa* and give two shillings to a beggar. That was one thing she always chided me about, not giving alms more freely.

Bisi's brother was a handsome, likable, though somewhat timid man in his late twenties. He had inherited an artisanal soft drink bottling business from his father which was in the final stages of going broke. Fermie had also inherited a rambling old compound just off the main road in Ebbute Meta where we stayed for a short while.

There was a reputed sorceress living in the best room in the compound, a husky woman in her early fifties. Everyone living there went out of their way to be respectful and it had been a long time since Fermie had collected any rent from her. She could make medicine for a variety of good and ill purposes, it was said, and had been given a little girl to raise. Asika was about five years old with a strangely mature and watchful calm, taking in everything going on around her. Although I'm not usually fond of children I considered what it would be like to have a child like that.

Belief in magic and witchcraft was nearly universal and was central in the culture of most Nigerian societies. There may even have been an increase in worries about and reliance on witchcraft among those who migrated to the cities. Reliance on "native medicine" didn't obviate attempts at other practical solutions. But there was a plethora of individuals trading in their presumed ability to direct supernatural forces. One of the worst concomitants of the reliance on "native doctors" and medicines was that it gobbled up a significant portion of the income of families who had little money to spare, usually without the slightest objective possibility of curing physical ailments.

In addition to diseases stemming from poverty, crowding and lack of public sanitation, Nigeria had a large complement of tropical diseases which were almost impossible to guard against under the given conditions. They killed and crippled a great many children and adults. Many of the beggars one saw around the markets were victims of one of those diseases. In Ibadan and Lagos there were surprising good outpatient clinics at the public hospitals but they could hardly handle all patients and medical needs in cities of that size.

People both consumed anti-malarial drugs and invested in magical amulets and cures when they could afford it. Many of the supernatural concerns had to do with healing and protection against illness. That was what the Seraphim and Cherubim specialized in, a syncretist Yoruba religious sect composed largely of women who dressed in white robes and danced down to the sea to the accompaniment of drum music to wash away sins and illness. But there was no end of others — "Native doctors" dispensing love potions, money-making medicine, fetishes to protect against sundry threats, alleged cures of venereal diseases or prevention of unwanted pregnancies. The practitioners ranged from outright charlatans to others who believed in their magical powers to yet others dealing primarily in herbal remedies for specific ailments who may have had something useful to dispense.

Bisi was an endless source of information about the native doctors, their specialties and talents or lack thereof. Women ranging anywhere from teenaged girls to others much older than Bisi came by to get her advice about one thing or another, what they might do about some difficulty or illness. Who should they go to see, which *oga* or official they might beg for what favour or which European (i.e., western trained) doctor or which native doctor they might approach for a cure. They would sit and talk intently as I left the room and at the end the visitor might fall on one knee before Bisi.

One of the native doctors who Bisi might recommend specialized in a psychiatric practice. Some time earlier a school friend of hers had become alternately rebellious and catatonic. After assorted cures and beatings, all to no avail, the girl's parents despaired and sent her to the government mental asylum at Abeokuta. There she was classified as incurable, which was hardly surprising since the asylum wasn't equipped to cure anyone.

Luckily, a favourite aunt came down from the north and managed to get the girl released into her care. She then delivered her niece to this native doctor, which did not mean a Nigerian with an MD, who had a reputation for treating the mentally ill. He had a rambling compound in a bush hamlet not far from Lagos and apparently had quite a reputation for success. Wonder of wonders, the girl actually began to recover, returned to Kaduna and got married. Well, that's a cure of sorts. Bisi had a mental file of cases and references like that, including certain practitioners who she considered to be quacks.

The native doctor specializing in mental illnesses collected hefty fees

from his patients' families and was no stick-in-the-mud-hut tradition-
alist when it came to the business of medicine. He had invested some
of his profits in a more or less modern maternity hospital in Lagos
which had Western-trained Nigerian nurses on staff and an MD on
call. It is quite possible to have one foot in magic and the other in modern medicine, as is evident from watching the current doings of Bible
Belt America.

The Paradise Club and Moving Pictures

Smack in the center of old Ibadan, on the lip of a low hill and near
the juncture of the two main roads, sat the Paradise Club, its name
spelled out in partially burned-out electric light bulbs. It was the oldest and best-known dancehall in town and looked like a movie set for
a Graham Greene novel. Splotches of plaster crumbled away from its
exterior walls and a knot of taxi drivers and a scattering of Boma Boys
perpetually hung around its entrance. Street peddlers selling kola nuts
and cigarettes and snacks were spotted along the street at night, their
oil lamps sputtering in clay dishes. Over the back terrace you could see
Baptist House, a notorious lair of righteousness.

"Dancehall" or "beerhall" do not really describe places like the Paradise Club. It was a colonnaded compound with a bandstand and an
outdoor dance floor ringed with tables. Things got going after dark
and ran on into the early hours of the morning. Beer and gin flowed
and receded in proportion to the patrons' conviviality and their budgets. Dancers shook seductively yet somehow demurely to the music,
Nigerian Highlife, a combination of brass, guitars, traditional drums
and bells, all the better for having some of the rough edges left on.

The Paradise attracted a cross section of Ibadanis. Only a daring
unmarried woman would accompany you to the Paradise but younger
Nigerian couples were frequently in evidence. It was an exciting but
friendly atmosphere.

Some of the clientele would be decked out in western togs or rigged
up in traditional finery. There was a fashion of women's *bubas* (short
blouses) printed with traditional or updated Yoruba proverbs. Some of
them captured the spirit of the times. *Ekun Gbe Omo* translated literally as "The Leopard Births Its Child" but meant "I bear leopards, so
don't push me." Another traditional saying one saw bouncing along
on *bubas* was *Okun Kosi Egbe Osa*, meaning "Sea is Not Equal to

Lagoon", or roughly "You're not my equal." A more contemporary saying referred to the process of Nigerianization which was in full swing: *Minister Omo Mo Fe Eh* or "I want a child who'll be a government minister." They weren't intended to be taken too seriously.

When they could afford it the Yoruba really were clothes horses. Lagosians were especially fashion conscious, donning both traditional and modern styles with considerable flair. When fully dressed Yoruba women wore an elaborate turban created of yards of material wound so that it swept around the head in great bows and wings. These were always coming apart. The *buba* is a simple pull-over blouse with wide sleeves, which with normal activity rides up the midriff. But the critical items of women's apparel were the *lappas*, two voluminous skirts which were wrapped around the waist and tucked in, one over the other.

Clothes and cloth were a symbol of prosperity. Among the most prized cloth was that dyed by traditional methods. *Adire* cloth is a kind of stiff, dyed batik. It was produced in one of the host of local cottage industries which still continued to hold their own. Some women's *lappas* were made of heavily brocaded material which might cost thirty pounds each — three months' salary for many unskilled workers. The equivalent for men was a Nigerian version of hand-woven *kente* cloth, at up to a hundred pounds for a toga-like *agbada*. At the time, such clothes evoked more admiration than hostility from those wearing ten-shilling gowns.

Courtesans were an institution of long standing in urban Nigeria. A few of the leading courtesans became influential in their own right and a handful acquired a charisma — an aura developed around their names and doings. They entered into urban folktales and were sometimes alluded to in Highlife music. One such song became a smash hit of the Lagos dancehall scene. It was done in the form of a praise song but was in fact a lively put down.

Titishido was a famous courtesan around Lagos during the mid fifties and moved in the circle of rising Nigerian millionaires and senior legislators. One of her lovers was Bobby Benson, the band leader at the Empire Club, a Nigerian dancehall at the Yaba Roundabout. Benson was to Lagos of the 1950s what Tommy Dorsey had been to American swing in the 1940s. He was known as "Pastor Bobby Benson" because of the teenage girls you'd see hanging around the Empire Club on a Sunday afternoon, freshly scrubbed and decked out in white dresses, strayed from church services and with dancing feet itching to be led into this den of perdition.

Titishido had had a brief fling with Benson, had broken it off and had bruited it about that she considered him just a "small boy", someone without influence or money. Bobby Benson replied by writing a Highlife song which he played at the Empire Club. Other bands around town took it up and overnight people and children were dancing to it in the streets. It was held to be the perfect putdown. The chorus went like this.

> Titishido, do not take shame
> Plenty husband is too much.
> Plenty driver, without labour.
> If she make go nobody care.
>
> If she marry taxi driver, I don't care
> If she marry lorry driver, no I don't care
> If she marry railway driver, I don't care
> Let she marry taxi driver . . . we don't care.
> Titishido!

It had a good tune to dance to and was also an example of the new folklore beginning to permeate the cities. It reflects some of the class distinctions which had emerged. As these things work, it was lorry and taxi drivers who were the most enthusiastic singers of this song.

Decadent? Well, what the hell. I was twenty-one years old and just had escaped from the Comstockery of the 1950s in Canada. The dancehall scene bulks large in later Nigerian literature so I'm not the only one it made an impression on.

The one other dancehall in Ibadan I occasionally went to was the Live And Let Live Club, a ramshackle place on the edge of the city beside the main road heading north. It tended to be patronized by Hausa and recent Yoruba immigrants and could get sort of rough. Uli Beier's Yoruba wife operated a market stall nearby and she might be in the club from time to time. Mary was an interesting woman, very shy if you met her at a party given by expatriates, but in her own setting her vibrancy reasserted itself and she might deliver some pithy comments on contemporary Yoruba ways which were a lot more realistic than the spiritual evocations which Beier savored.

Uli was developing a reputation as a cultural historian and all-round Yorubaphile. He was a German Jewish refugee who had landed in

Nigeria a half dozen years earlier and was then attached to the University College as a research associate. Mainly he was involved in getting out a Yoruba cultural journal and in enthusing about Yoruba cosmology. Old palm wine in old bottles. I don't mean that as archly as it may sound since it was comparable to what most anthropologists of the time were doing. He grooved on Oshun festivals in small towns and not on the lives of people who frequented places like the Live And Let Live Club.

One kind of music you rarely heard in the dancehalls was that of the traditional Yoruba drum bands. In the past the more important chiefs included drummers and praise singers among their retinue. While that had much declined there still were traditional drum bands which made a living playing for funerals and traditional festivities, even in the cities.

Yoruba drums come in various sizes and voices; they are the solo instruments and are backed up by cowrie-strung calabash rattles and brass bells. The music involves complex rhythms repeated with slight but significant variations of phrasing and bursts of improvisation. There may be a band of five or six musicians playing in a courtyard, possibly at night, the scene half lit by flickering lanterns. As the soloists drum and posture the accompanists throw the calabash rattles into the air in such a way that the cowries provide a *tchat-a-tchat* counterpoint.

Talking drums are constructed around a wooden hourglass body over which two drumheads are stretched, one on either end. Thongs connect the two heads and the drummer holds the instrument squeezed under one arm, striking the drum with a curved, bell-mouthed stick. By tightening or loosening the pressure of his arm the drummer raises or lowers the tension on the drumhead and thereby the tone. This provides a fluid range of tones as he glides or leaps from one passage to another. Depending upon your imagination you may hear the tramp of feet, the crying of children, the staccato of hoe beats or shouts of joy.

Since Yoruba is a tonal language the drummer can replicate the patterns of speech in drum tones. These are usually proverbs and stylized phrases which Yoruba expect in drum performances. Some drummers and certain listeners are more adept than others in delineating and deciphering the messages — that's part of the art. You may get two solo drummers talking back and forth to each other while the audience dances and calls out its understanding and appreciation of the phrasing.

While everyone enjoyed listening to traditional drumming, to city dwellers it bore the connotation of "bush music". In contradistinction, the modern and one of the most popular forms of entertainment in Lagos and Ibadan was going to the movies. Almost everyone went to the moving pictures at one time or another — families, women in groups and alone, lovers, government contractors and taxi drivers. Only two bob for a seat in the stalls. What a wonder, what a marvel.

The movie houses consisted of large courtyards surrounded by high brick walls, with an open-roofed terrace for the rainy season. The owners were usually Syrian or Lebanese and the films normally were action-packed adventures which allowed the audience to follow the plot with a minimum of dialogue. They were old, cheap films from strange and exotic places such as the Lazy Q Ranch in the Hollywood Hills or the movie lots of New Delhi. A swath of American Z-grade westerns, a melange of British swashbucklers and an assortment of Indian epics replete with eye-rolling, sword waving and their own brand of singing cowguard antics. Although there would be a sprinkling of London School of Economics graduates on hand the majority of the audience was only conversant in basic pidgin English, if that.

Since most in the audience understood little of the film dialogue there was usually a buzz of conversation as the more worldly viewers explained or debated what was going on in the movie. Occasionally I'd catch a fragment of such on-the-spot interpretation in Lagos pidgin. A cardboard villain in one Hollywood western was a spy for the king of the neighbouring country (i.e., cattle ranch). A woman who appeared as an extra and who had no particular role in the movie as far as I could see was "really" the one who gave the "chief's man" the medicine to ward off bullets and other harm. Some of these reinterpretations were more imaginative than the original plots.

Barclay's Bank, the major bank in the country, had a smash hit with its two-minute cartoon extolling the wisdom of depositing one's savings with them by showing all the dangers which could befall money left outside their vaults. The storyline had a sequence of folktale robbers stepping out of the pages of Amos Tutuola and showed the inroads of money-munching termites and of kinsmen descending upon a cash-cropping cocoa farmer like locusts. Accompanying it was a catchy Highlife tune whose coda was,

Bawklays bank, famah go put yor monay for der
Bawklays bank, you gonna save plentay der.

The all time favourite movies playing in Lagos were *The Jungle Book* and *Sanders of the River*. These two epics were playing to packed houses when I first got there and were still going strong when I left. Some people had seen them three, four and more times.

The Jungle Book is a Technicolor reworking of a Rudyard Kipling *Just So* story. Set in British India as portrayed in the backlots of the Rank studios, it has Sabu rattling around plaster-of-Paris temple ruins, communing with talking cobras, cavorting with elephants, finding hidden treasure and undoing the nefarious plots of Indian thieves (though not those of nabobs or colonial governments) through guilelessness and with the aid of magic. There it was in living colour — proof that magic existed, what Europeans were always denying.

Additional evidence that Europeans knew that witchcraft worked was in a book I had brought along, a linen-bound photo volume of the John Ford/John Steinbeck movie *The Forgotten Village*. It contained some extraordinarily fine photography and was a quasi-documentary intended to support the social programs launched by the Cardenas government in Mexico during the late 1930s. The story deals with the cultural barriers involved in introducing public health into an Indian peasant village under the heel of local *caciques*, who use folk superstitions embodied in the person of a *curandera* to defeat a water purification project. The film intended to expose the political underpinnings and the human costs of some traditional folk beliefs.

But to Bisi Archer, a woman knowledgeable about such things, neither I nor the book had it right. It was instead confirmation that people like the *curandera* do have powers and that in the far-distant country of Mexico there were witches too. Sometimes when one of her friends came for a visit Bisi would take the book out and they'd go through it on their own.

The Jungle Book I could understand being popular as a kind of folk tale. But the popularity of *Sanders of the River* was hard to fathom. One would have presumed that it would have been driven out of any African theatre which had dared screen it. It has an interesting background. Sanders of the River is one of a series of flicks made in Britain during the mid- to the late 1930s by Alexander Korda, a Tory Jewish émigré from Hungary. Yet it is suffused with the most patronizing contempt for Africans. Presumably Korda didn't intend it as a racist movie, which makes it all the more remarkable as a comment on the attitudes of the time.

The movie is set in an all-purpose British colony in Africa of the post-World War I era. The Sanders of the title is a British colonial commissioner who cruises up and down a river like the Niger on a sternwheel gunboat replete with loyal African *askaris* manning the machine guns. His tasks revolve about aiding missionaries, appointing and dismissing chiefs, patting Native rulers on the head and mouthing maxims suited to retarded readers of *Boy's Own Annual*.

Possibly the film's appeal to Nigerians was the fact that it revolved mainly around black actors. The main figure is a Young Chief, played by Paul Robeson, attired in loin cloth. ("Why doesn't that man have his *agbada* on mommy?" I could imagine a Yoruba child asking.) He speaks the sorts of lines then thought suitable for native roles and paddles off to rescue his sloe-eyed betrothed from the clutches of a missionary-munching, thoroughly villainous Old Chief.

"Bisi, how can you go and watch that rotten movie again ?" I say, rolling my eyes.

"Is nonsense you say ? You don't see dis young girl is too too beautiful, no? The boy who save her be strong and sing so deep. Like in Sudan Interior Mission. You don't know der be bad chiefs here like in picture show? Oh we got too many. Shah! . . . Tink now-ah! 'Many days are for the t'iefs, but one day is for de owner of de house.'"

The School Off Yaba Roundabout

During my final four months in Nigeria I taught at a secondary school called Lagos City College which had been established in the mid 1940s by Niame Azikwe, the founder of the National Council of Nigeria and the Cameroons, the pioneer independence movement in the country. It was intended to provide a secondary school education for those Lagosians who for whatever reason could not or would not enter one of the mission schools. While grade school education was fairly general in the cities, secondary education was still the exception. Lagos City College was unusual in that it was a non-sectarian and co-educational school. I was the only non-Nigerian teaching there.

The school was just off the Yaba Roundabout, which was a kind of pivot for many of the people and places I knew. It is the setting of

Cyprian Ekwensi's *Jagua Nana* and when I read that novel many years later it was with a shock of recognition.

The building itself had a turn-of-the-century colonial charm, crumbling brick and cracked wood with open verandas linking the classrooms. Lagos City College enrolled some four hundred students ranging from children to young men and women of eighteen. I taught a class in conversational English and reading and gave classes in geography and civics. If my teaching was no worse than what I myself had gotten in secondary school it was no better. There was a lot of rote learning. "Yokohama is the major seaport for the greater Tokyo region, with some one million inhabitants" (in the 1937 text), that sort of thing.

I seized on a technique which my own teachers had used and spent a third of the class time writing notes on the blackboard which the students were to copy into their scribblers. It was a way to fill up time before going on to elaborate some aspects of the topic for the day. Pretty poor, but the salary was pretty pathetic too, something like five or six pounds a week. How I suffered with that teaching, and my students more so I imagine. But they were well-mannered kids.

Civics was an innovation of Lagos City College and something of a problem since there was no syllabus or textbook available. For the civics class I shoveled in whatever I could remember of a political science course on comparative electoral and party systems I had taken the previous year at the University of BC.

During the previous December my trunk arrived from Canada. Amongst other things it contained a portable gramophone and a collection of books and records. There was a record of Haitian cafe music, some early American blues, Appalachian folk music, songs of the International Brigades and a dash of this and that. Mainly I played them at home but a few times I took a collection of records along to school.

My favourite was Ewen McColl and A.L. Lloyd's *Folk Songs of Industrial Britain* but I could see it was downright painful for Nigerian listeners so I kept it to myself. The Haitian songs were a smash hit and everyone wanted to hear them again and again. But Ma Rainey and Blind Lemon Jefferson also had to go to the bottom of the stack. "We don't like European music so much," said one student and was quite skeptical about my explanation of what the music was. Strangely, Joe Glazier's renditions of Joe Hill songs had a modest following. "It be.

church music," opined another guy, unable to follow the words. They were intelligent enough kids and even a few years later were probably much more cosmopolitan. All those records remained behind and I sometimes fantasized that some fragment might have entered into the music of the Lagos back streets, although I know that's not the way things happen in reality.

Although most of the teachers were dedicated enough there were a number of characters among them. A few were like the windbags you find in the novels of later Nigerian writers. Maybe they had the same teachers, who knows? Victorian rhetoric was alive and well in the class rooms of Lagos City College. At least once a week at morning assemblies we would be treated to someone's over-ripe Churchillian declamations. The *West African Pilot* was full of that kind of stuff.

The bane of many students existence was a wizened old demon who taught Yoruba language and "history". That was an option because many of the students were from other ethnic groups. There was hardly a day when this Ijebu de Sade didn't have a few students up on the mat. They were usually charged with lack of respect and would have to prostrate themselves on the floor before they approached him. No disclaimer, no statement of belief or fact ever made any difference, they all got so many strokes of his cane as he gleefully intoned some proverb.

The principal of Lagos City College was Alade Oneipede and for reasons I never understood he went out of his way to offer me a teaching job when I was completely broke and didn't know where to turn. He'd had a pretty checkered career himself. His views were anathema not only to the British colonial establishment but also to the politicians then on the verge of forming the Nigerian government.

Oneipede was the son of a minor civil servant and had been one of the few Nigerians to have reached university entrance in the mid 1940s. He had gotten a scholarship to one of the Black universities in America and later went on to take a PhD in political science at Columbia University under Franz Neumann, the author of the once-influential study of German fascism, *Behemoth*. Alade's left-liberalism had vaguely Marxist leanings. Such views might not be extraordinary in Nigeria today but in the 1950s they were rare indeed.

Since returning Alade had helped found something called the Nigerian Commoners Party. It was a small circle of people which most Lagosians hadn't heard of and was not even influential enough for the government to attempt to buy off. Its program opposed the remnant feudal and chiefly powers in Nigeria and all schemes tending to entrench tribal divisions. It was for iron-clad guarantees of civil rights in a secular state. Those were dangerous principles then, and probably still are.

Alade had been back in Nigeria for about four years and it was only in the previous year that he'd been able to get the job as principal of a secondary school. For a long time he had supported himself and wife through a low-paid job in an Islamic Amadiya grade school. Considering all the handwringing about the dearth of trained Nigerians one might have expected that a Nigerian with a PhD from a leading university would have been offered at least a lectureship at the University College, but the university administration wouldn't touch Oneipede and claimed never to have heard of him.

My own string was just about played out by then. I was losing touch with many of the people I'd gotten to know. The teaching job barely supported me and I was living in a tenement on the outskirts of town. I saw Bisi less and less frequently. It was an impossible situation. I could hardly eke out an existence for myself let along provide for anyone else. Nevertheless, the relationship with Bisi lasted till the day I left Nigeria. Finally I came down with malaria. So it was almost a relief when the CID descended upon me.

Decamping from the college and living in Lagos was a violation of my student visa, to say nothing of teaching without a work permit. So there I was, back in Commissioner Horrocks-Mosley's lair. "You know me Bucky, I made myself a bet about you when we first met." The son of a bitch is smiling. "I bet you would go native before you left ... But we don't intend to let of class of poor whites establish themselves here."

I had to be out of the country within two weeks or face deportation. Bisi stayed with me the last week and brought me out to the airport to see me off. A very emotional scene. But we didn't maintain contact, and I don't even know how her life played out.

A Quarter Century Later

In the 1980s I uncovered notes apparently scribbled shortly after my return from Nigeria. They are entitled *Ekun Gbe Omo* — the cosmology of an African urban proletariat, and bear the stamp of anthropological phraseology of the day. Except that they mention a "proletariat", a term then held to be ludicrous in an African context. The notes were intended for an account of everyday life in the old wards of Lagos and Ibadan and I planned to juxtapose fragments of life history with diary accounts, domestic budgets and Yoruba spirits, songs and snatches of conversation. It would have been much like what you've just read but the Nigerian voices would have been more immediate had I written it then.

While none of what I've described will seem particularly surprising to readers today it appeared as unbelievably urbane to most listeners in the middle of the last century. The predominant image of Africa then was still of isolated tribal villages where custom reigned supreme, where significant changes would only come over generations. To talk about proto-classes, let alone armed struggles, in Africa then seemed as the most hopeless ethnocentrism.

My account is of a Nigeria which was still a colonial backwater of the British Empire, not the most powerful nation in Black Africa. The largest Nigerian city was Lagos, with a population of some three quarters of a million. Today, greater Lagos has some six million inhabitants and other Yoruba towns such as Ibadan, Oshogbo, Obomosho contain well over a million people each. There has been extensive if uneven industrialization and in some regions, as in the mainland abutting Lagos, where once one was hard-pressed to find a garage there now are factories producing automobiles. There is no question now about the existence of a Nigerian proletariat.

By way of epilogue: the Northern People's Congress party went on to win the majority of the seats in the national elections the year after I left Nigeria and were the government in power when the country gained its independence in 1960. The first Prime Minister of independent Nigeria was Tafawa Balewa, an elderly Hausa and long-time civil servant of the northern emirs. In the years following independence the Northern People's Congress government gradually lost the power to rule outside of its own northern bailiwick. Despite that, the power of the tribal chiefs and emirs was displaced by the rising Nigerian bourgeoisie, whether civilian or military. The cash nexus became pervasive and streams of tribal peasant farmers were displaced into the mushrooming cities. Corruption gripped the country.

The first military coup of 1966 was nevertheless unexpected, swift and singleminded. The new military rulers executed Tafawa Balewa, Aminu Bello the Sardauna of Sokoto, and a number of the NPC government ministers. One of my friends at the University College was killed in the second military coup and the intertribal pogroms which followed.

In 1958 the explorations by major oil companies in the Niger delta were treated as something of a joke. But oil was discovered and Nigeria became the major oil exporter of tropical Africa. Oil soon outstripped all other exports combined and triggered the explosive emergence of a Nigerian *haute bourgeoisie* and a vast administrative middle class. Control over the oil fields was an exacerbating factor in the brutal Biafran civil war of the late 1960s.

The potential for violent conflicts should have been evident even in 1958 but it was combined with a considerable tolerance among ordinary Nigerians. However, with the military coups and the civil war, with the anarchic pocket politics and the divisions between rich and poor, a pervasive callousness seems to have crept into Nigerian life. Symptomatic of this was the introduction of mass public executions of robbers. In the mid 1970s xenophobic defenders of Nigerian traditions launched a campaign against "immoral foreign influences" while a later Nigerian government carried out the ruthless expulsion of some 300,000 resident workers from neighbouring West African countries.

I wouldn't have predicted it but I'm not all that surprised. Yet I too expected something better would emerge in the nations shaking off colonial rule. The Nigerian people certainly deserve something better.

NINE

Picaro's Progress

In the Peace River Country

One late August day I was in Lagos and the next I was in British Columbia. The weather was cool and I unenthused to be back home again. Since I was broke I had to make some money quickly. The first thing which came to hand was driving cab in Vancouver during the winter while I took evening classes at university. During the following summer and part of the next winter I worked in the Peace River region.

I had gotten a job as a labourer in a survey camp for the Peace River dam project some ten miles west of Hudson's Hope, the furthest edge of marginal grain and cattle country. As a kid the phrase "Peace River country" evoked an image of the last homestead frontier, of rafting down the Peace in search of land, of horse-drawn wagons and log cabin farms and so on. I must have gotten that from Ebe Koeppen who had been part of that homestead life there during the 1920s and 1930s. There were still remnants of that not-so-distant world around Hudson's Hope and other outlying hamlets when I got there in the spring of 1959 but it was fast disappearing.

The survey camp was located just above the head of the Peace River gorge but the test sites were scattered at locations half a dozen miles away. It was a realm of rolling hills, lakes and rivers and seemingly endless boreal forest. An old freighter continued to run flatboats to deliver supplies into the one general store settlement at Finlay Forks some eighty miles upstream. He also ferried us back and forth across the river. That locale must now be under sixty or more feet of water but the Peace really was an awesome river — wide, deep and fast-running, with huge boils welling up and shallow, shifting whirlpools. Large logs would race, by and downstream you heard the roar of the river entering the gorge. I'd look at the ferryman out of the corner of my eye and will him to get us to the other bank as fast as possible.

My work involved toting around supplies, delivering diesel oil to the test sites and helping the geologists take soil samples. At one point I was set to dismantling an old tent camp located on a rock ledge overlooking the gorge itself, a gash of boiling cauldrons and churning white water twisting between high rock cliffs. The river punched through the low spine of the continental divide there. Even Hell's Gate in the Fraser Canyon was small potatoes compared to the Peace River gorge. Everything was damp and mossy from the mist and spray which drifted up from the river two hundred feet below.

I'd be working alone on this ledge packing lumber, drill rods and assorted junk over to the cat track from where it could be hauled out. Amid the litter of the camp I found copies of *Scientific American*, one with an article by Bruno Bettelheim on "The Mechanical Boy," a much-discussed study in some circles. There was also a copy of Herman Wouk's *Marjorie Morningstar*, with the last twenty-odd pages missing. I read all that there, in the remains of that camp, during self administered rest breaks. There was a touch of the surreal to it.

The survey project was gradually winding down. After six weeks the camp manager laid two of us off but lined up a job for me with a Boyles Brothers diamond drilling crew nearby. The rig was doing deep test bores for one of the footings of the dam. They were a long ways down and still hadn't hit any solid rock.

It was a small tent camp and we worked around the clock, seven days a week. There were three drilling shifts with three men on each crew. The camp push and the head driller of each shift were permanent employees of Boyles Brothers but the rest of us were casual labour which they picked up and trained on the job. I was put on the graveyard shift. It consisted of the driller, the driller's helper and me. At twenty-three I was the oldest of the lot.

In a small crew like that there is a good deal of give and take but each person's tasks were more or less defined by the operation itself. The driller looked like a caricature of some pool hall habitué, eyes hooded, a cigarette permanently dangling from the side of his mouth, draped over the drill controls like a limp flounder. But it's a job with a good deal of responsibility. It entails a lot of finesse — speeding up, bearing down, going slow, reversing. The driller depends on the feel of the drill to decipher what is going on some hundreds of feet below the ground at the head of a string of sectioned pipes.

The helper worked mainly on the drilling platform, attaching pipe sections as we went down, or "breaking pipe", unscrewing the twenty-foot sections of hollow drill pipe when we pulled up the whole string to replace the drill head. Sometimes both of us would have to lean on pipe wrenches to "break" a length. The biggest worry was that a string of pipe would get away from us when we were doing that and sink back down the hole. But "bending the string" (i.e. getting the drill pipe jammed in the bore hole) can also put the rig out of operation for a shift or longer.

One of my tasks was to mix the "mud", a soupy concoction which was pumped down between the drill pipe and the bore walls as a lubricant. I would also hook on to drill pipe from the stack, guide them up through the tower and then down into the head of the drill. I'd be up in the rig twenty feet above the drilling platform doing that.

"Toss me down a smoke, Ralph. I'll even settle for a Tampax" — i.e. an unmanly filter-tipped cigarette. Although no one read a book in that camp there was a certain vivacity in the endless scatological rhymes they composed. They seemed to have few interests outside of their jobs, their girlfriends and how they were going to spend their pay when they got home. But they were a friendly bunch. To work with they were okay.

After a month or so we had gotten the bore down as deep as we could go but still hadn't hit bedrock. So Boyles Brothers decided to bring in a larger rig. In the meantime everyone who wasn't a permanent employee was laid off. We were supposed to go into Fort St. John, the nearest town, and board ourselves until they were ready to start up again.

"Keep in touch. I'll check in the beer parlour when we're ready to start up again. Maybe in three weeks," says the camp push. If you were on the spot when they were hiring you got back on, if not, too bad. In the meantime you'd be eking out an existence, trying to live on whatever you'd saved, sitting in the beer parlour worrying that you were going to miss the job. The Peace River country was notorious for that kind of enterprise.

Fort St. John at the time was packed with men who had come in on the strength of rumours of jobs in construction and in the sputtering oil industry. The construction phase of the dam project was still more than two years off but all sorts of small businessmen and tradesmen and one-and-a-half-ton truck hauling companies had set up in the hope of being in on the ground floor of the boom when it started. They were alternately boosterizing and fending off bankruptcy. They'd take any kind of contract at rock bottom rates just to have some income and if they hired anybody they wanted them to work for next to nothing.

The place was swarming both with penny-ante speculators and people looking for work. A town booming and busting at the same time. Around the few square blocks of what had been a small northern farming town there developed a sprawl of newly graveled roads, gumbo mudholes, straggled-out trailer parks and clumps of plywood and plaster duplexes. Every remodeled garage and shed which could house men was filled, sometimes with four or more guys kipped into a single room. Unemployed men scrounged a few dollars from their buddies to buy groceries, hoping to hold out till they got a job, any kind of job.

Many of the men floating around looking for work in Fort St. John were from the hardscrabble farms of the region. Six dollars cash for a ten-hour work day is what many of them were used to and if they got fifteen dollars for an eight-hour day, well that was just gravy, they figured. Unions and union conditions existed only on major projects or in agencies whose contracts were determined outside the region. The local business impresarios were incensed about "outsiders" coming in to "spoil it". Although they themselves had in most cases only arrived a few years earlier, they were all for "local control". The Peace River region was becoming archetypal Social Credit country.

"Christ, I'm not hanging around here," says I. So I hitchhiked to Edmonton and through Alberta to see what it was like. I saw quite enough before I got back to Vancouver.

After all of that, despite knowing firsthand what the conditions were, I went back to the Peace River five months later in the dead of winter to take a job on an oil rig on the Beaton River. Don't ask me, I wasn't even sure then why I was doing it.

I'd been driving taxi in Vancouver for MacLure's from five in the morning till about one in the afternoon five days a week, and also carried a heavy course load of anthropology classes given in the late afternoon or evening. Never enough sleep, tired most of the time. Never any money or time to do anything, little contact with anyone outside my classes. I began to feel that it was pointless. So I decided to drop out of university. I wanted to make some kind of stake fast.

Oil drilling in northern BC only got rolling after freeze up. In many areas muskeg conditions brought all work to a halt during spring and summer. Nothing could get through that muskeg after it had thawed. Four-wheel-drive trucks, even cats, got bogged down as the winter roads turned into gloppy, quaking gumbo muck. So during the winter, when they could work, the pace was rather hectic.

All things considered, I'd have to say that those small oil exploration outfits were the cheapest, meanest, most miserable operations I ever worked for. The wages were poor and the conditions terrible. Many of the drilling outfits were owned and operated by family entrepreneurs who contracted to do the drilling for larger oil exploration companies, who in turn took contracts from major oil deities in distant heavens. These family outfits cut all the corners they could get away with. The camp boss might be the owner of the rig and one or two of the head drillers were probably partners. The majority of the hands on the rig were not oil workers *per se* but temporary recruits from the farms and small towns around the region. That was the case on the rig I wound up on.

The drilling camp was about a hundred fifty miles northeast of Fort St. John, a five-hour drive over a winter track looping over frozen muskeg, through boreal forest and across ice rivers. The camp was set in an opening bulldozed out of the dwarf taiga — spindly trees growing so thickly that they were like a stockade. There was the rig itself, tool and repair sheds, a trailer for the boss-owner and his wife and two bunkhouse trailers for the dozen-man crew.

January on the Yukon border it gets to thirty and forty degrees below zero. Guys bundled up with as many layers of clothing as they could get on and still work. You try to cover up every inch of skin with only your eyes and nose peeking out. During free moments at work there'd be a dance of readjusting and tucking in clothing. *Siberia Monogatari.*

Part of my job was to keep the "salamanders" filled and burning properly. A salamander is a sheet metal contraption which resembles a headless samurai standing with arms akimbo. Each one holds roughly five gallons of diesel oil in its base and once you get a good fire going in them they throw off a lot of heat. They were spotted around the rig so that the crew could warm up during breaks. When burning properly a salamander emits a contented snore — *Wrum, wrum,wrumple, wrum.* Not enough air and you get more oil smoke than heat, too much draft and flames shoot out of its headless neck and the salamander begins to shake and possibly even hop around. Working outside on a January day it's really a friendly contraption.

Although I had various tasks outside for a couple hours each day my main job was bull cooking. And I was glad of it. Working on the rig under those conditions was not something I wanted to do. Everything on the oil rig was more massive than in diamond drilling and had to be handled with power equipment. There was chain and cable and winches flying around every which way. It was basically a green crew. Most of them were farm kids from northern Alberta, a good bunch with a talent for getting along with others. But they were happy to have any kind of job during the winter and couldn't conceive that they should have a say in working conditions. "Unions kill an industry," they said, parroting their Tulsa Bob boss. If you looked cross eyed at some job and said it wasn't safe you were told you could do it or clear out. The accident rate on those rigs must have been horrendous.

Incredibly, I had packed along an almost completed manuscript I had written dealing with institutionalized crop experimentation and hill rice cultivation among certain Southeast Asian horticulturists. I even had copies of Freeman's *Iban Agriculture* and Conklin's *Hanunoo Agriculture* with me to check some calculations. The resulting paper was published in a Dutch anthropology journal many years later. I still remember sitting huddled in the corner of the trailer which served as the cookshack, recalculating the ripening dates of swidden rice in a tropical horticultural system while trying to keep my toes from freezing. There seems to have been some rather confused emotions in play.

Not long after that I came down with frostbite while doing outside maintenance work. A spot on my lower jaw froze, became infected and within a day the left side of my face was about twice the size of the right. Even the camp boss agreed I'd better get treatment and the steel truck took me down to a tiny hospital run by nuns on the outskirts of

Fort St. John. They shot me full of penicillin and the next day I headed back to Vancouver.

"Never again! I am never going to work in a camp again, no matter what."

"Ah you've said that before. Don't make yourself promises when you don't know if you can keep them," replies the other me.

"No! I just plain refuse. I won't go back."

"We'll see."

I never did work in another camp. Instead I returned to driving cab and attending university after a two month absence. "We haven't seen you around for a while. Did you have the flu or something?" asked one of my classmates.

Pete Vayda, then a young anthropologist teaching at UBC, and a friend, was the only faculty member who knew I'd taken to the hills. He had the decency not to mention it to anyone else. Vayda was completely uninterested in anyone's emotional flights as long as their academic work was done. About oil rigs on the Yukon border he didn't want to hear.

"I'm going to send a copy of your paper to some people I know at Columbia," he told me when I reappeared at UBC. "You should think about applying there. I'll see what I can do." But it was a few years before I got to New York.

Biograph: A Teacher's Tale

Florian was born on a South Saskatchewan farm shortly before the First World War. He was born into a German Catholic family which had emigrated from the Ukraine sometime before the turn of the century. McAllister, Saskatchewan, was part of that checkerboard mosaic of ethnic enclaves on the Canadian prairies and many of their neighbours had come from the same districts in the Ukraine and had carried their village loyalties along with them. Even before finishing grade school Florian was itching to escape the confines of a close-knit and fractious farming community. That was a recurrent theme among so many of his generation.

He and his brother acquired a library of Julius Haldeman's Little Blue Books, which served up everything from potted versions of George Sand novels to Robert Ingersoll wrestling with the Bible-punchers to Darwin's daring views about the mutability of life forms. They were afraid that their parents might investigate what it was they were spending their hard-earned dimes on and confiscate the books. Reading was frowned upon by his father, who considered it as either a waste of time or as likely to make people discontented with their lives.

It was sort of ironic. Florian could hardly wait to get away from the family farm yet his reminiscences of working with horses, of relationships within the family and between neighbours, of enthusiasms and fights at neighbourhood dances, of the expeditionary aspects of hauling wheat to distant grain elevators in winter and much else of that world were wonderfully alive. He wrote many short stories yet he never wrote about his youth.

The first taste of freedom came when Florian was sixteen and hired on as a harvest stiff on a migrant threshing gang: a couple of threshing machines, twenty or so horses and a dozen men. They wove their way back and forth across the Saskatchewan-Dakota border bringing in the wheat crop of 1928. After that Florian knew he had to get away.

By the early 1930s the first of the dusted-out dry-land farmers were trekking past, possessions piled on trucks and wagons, driving their surviving livestock up to the bush country of northern Saskatchewan to start anew. Florian's daughter-in-law knew something of those conditions too. She had grown up in the Milk River country of northern Montana, a big, good-natured woman who had seen a lot of life in the quarter century since she too had fled the land.

> We were hailed out and hoppered out
> Rusted out and dusted out
> And in the end
> We were busted and foreclosed out.

"On clear winter nights you could look west and see the reflected glow of the big city — Regina — just beyond the horizon." Regina or New York were about equally exotic, urbane and alluring to Florian. By 1933 he had arrived in Regina, broke, unemployed, living from hand to mouth but tremendously enthused about the world opening up around him: libraries to go to, midnight oil to burn, friends and acquaintances crowded into single rooms to drink coffee and debate the way the world should and undoubtedly would be reconstituted. In the depths of the Depression, in one of the most devastated regions in Canada, Florian was awash with energy and possibilities. He became an activist in the left wing of the Co-operative Commonwealth Federation, which intended to create a mass socialist party not just a vehicle for loyal opposition parliamentarians.

At the time the New Deal in the US was getting up steam it looked as if social changes in America were going to surge ahead of anything that seemed possible in Canada. Riding the rods down through the land of the free, Florian and a bunch of others were plucked off a freight and plunked into jail on vagrancy charges. "'There's no law against being poor', they say. There sure is!"

Florian fell in with Americans who had retained an older tradition of regarding citizenship as a creation of the ruling class. He and his comrades all had political visions which they felt would change the world. It seemed to Florian that the sharing, the spontaneous friendships and trust (often abused), the dreams and endless migrations of that time had a certain similarity to what re-emerged among the "hippies" of the sixties. However different they were, he felt a sense of allegiance to them for what they were trying to break with.

Florian returned to Regina and was there in the summer of 1935 when the police smashed the On To Ottawa trek. Ann, the girl he was courting, was caught up in the melée. She had grown up near the Regina railyards not far from the Ukrainian Labour Temple where her mother ran a rooming house. Although quite apolitical, her mother was known for feeding streams of unemployed men passing through Regina. That is on the authority of one of those men who remembered her fifty years later.

Ann and Florian were married not long after and he attempted to become a writer. His first and last story was published in a moderately prestigious American literary journal. According to Florian it was Ann who was determined to find some way through the Depression. That was what brought them out to the West Coast near the end of the decade.

Florian landed a job at St. Paul's Hospital. Finding brotherly love a poor substitute for a living wage he quietly tried to organize a union among the orderlies. It was soon broken through firings when the Sisters found out. He then got on at the expanding wartime shipyards. As for many others of his generation, it was the first regular employment in his life. Two children came along and a process of settling down occurred. My guess is that it was Ann who was the business drive behind them getting into operating a rooming house in Vancouver. By the late 1950s it was keeping them comfortably busy and modestly secure. It wasn't a charity operation but god knows how many people down on their luck she put up for free in that rooming house, including me.

Florian gently mocked the obscurantism of academia and yet was enticed by the university world. For some years Florian chaired university extension classes in literature. His front room was littered with copies of *Canadian Literature* and "Blasted Pine" (the *Tamarack Review*) as well as *Scientific American* and *Monthly Review*.

During his later years Florian felt that he hadn't done much with his life. That came through in the letters from him I got while in Cree trapping camps and Colombian plantation villages. There was a sense that his earlier hopes had somehow been lost without any decision ever having been made. He died in his early fifties and left a trunk full of unpublished short stories behind him. In terms of public accomplishments it was a fairly modest life. But with eight years of education in a one room prairie school Florian had made himself into one of those people who do honour to the title "working class intellectual". Of the university classes attended during that time I remember little and miss even less. But I would very much like to be able to hear Florian's commentary and critique of current developments today.

A Throw to the South

I was in the midst of a torrid love affair. Mary had enrolled at the University of California for the 1960 term and we were going to live together there during the summer. That was still rather daring stuff in Canada. In order to get a stake together I drove cab two shifts a day during the final months in Vancouver. I was constantly exhausted. Maybe that was part of the reason why California seemed so idyllic to me.

A month before we arrived in San Francisco the House Un-American Activities Committee had gotten its first comeuppance after more than a dozen years of inquisitional activity. HUAC had fallen upon hard times, as repressive new legislation and numerous other investigative agencies took over many of its former routines. Senatorial inquisitors no longer enjoyed the same opportunities to trod the boards, sniffing out witches, for the delectation of their electors back home. So there was a move to put the HUAC show back on the road. The billing for the return engagement was "to investigate Communist influence among youth and in our nation's universities." Universities were usually a pushover, an easy scapegoat. The first venue was to be the University of California at Berkeley. There were some surprises in store for everyone.

Instead of the usual routine of victims attempting to wrap themselves in the flag or appealing to the Fifth Amendment and other alleged civil rights — appeals which often resulted in firings and blacklisting — instead of claims to "support the goals of security investigations but not the methods used," instead of people caving in and informing on colleagues and past friends under threat of being cited for contempt of Congress, instead of all those sad concomitants of the American inquisition, the HUAC hearings which convened in San Francisco in May of 1960 were faced with an array of civil rights and student groups who rather than plead innocent to the charge of being progressives actually challenged the legitimacy of the Committee. There could be no doubt about it, they did hold HUAC and all it stood for in contempt. It was blasphemy.

From the first day the Committee was confronted in its courthouse lair by a thousand students and others who demanded that HUAC "go home". In reply, the Frisco riot squad was called in and unleashed in a series of bloody assaults against the demonstrators. However insubstantial that protest appears in retrospect it dissipated the aura of omnipotence which HUAC had surrounded itself with. Dumbfounded that the old tactics weren't working, the Committee members decided to cut short the San Francisco tour and head for greener pastures; but only after issuing a batch of contempt citations against local blasphemers.

Considering the powers which HUAC and its supporters still had it is amazing that once it was run out of town the Committee never did get its act on the rails again. The amorphous fear which had enveloped all dissident political activity began to wane. Those who had been silenced by the right-wing hysteria of the past decade now began to answer back. That was the atmosphere around Berkeley when we got there. You could almost feel it, like a long-delayed spring.

Mary and I were enrolled in a graduate course on Primate Evolution given by Sherwood Washburn, possibly the leading primatologist in the United States at the time, an authority on the evidence of blood chemistry, theories of cusp rotation, the anatomy of fossil Miocene and Pliocene monkeys and baboon ethology. Washburn stopped at the point where the first hominids appeared on the scene, which was just as well. He was a splendid teacher of animal ethology but hopelessly reactionary when it came to people.

We had an apartment in an old house two blocks from Telegraph Avenue and four from Sather Gate. At Sather Gate one was greeted by groups soliciting support for various civil rights issues, for anti-nuclear campaigns, for volunteers to help the Farmworkers Union organizing drive. Telegraph Avenue was packed with bookstores, coffeehouses and a genteel student semi-bohemianism. Lots of talk, lots of poseurship. "What a civilized place," I thought. And so it was when compared to most of North America. Actually I don't trust my reminiscences of the place because to me Berkeley was ... "Do you know the land where the lemon trees bloom?"

Occasionally we trundled over to San Francisco and stayed in an old hotel down in the Mission District and a ten-minute walk from Telegraph Hill. The Haight-Ashbury scene hadn't yet put in its appearance but there were the remnants of the Beat crowd around hang-outs like the Bagel Shop. Sure it was escapism. So what! I had my belly full of hard work and gritty determination.

At the end of the summer we decided to hitchhike down to Mexico City. Off we go, me in a tattered Harris tweed jacket, a seabag in one hand and a guitar slung over my shoulder, Mary in a pea jacket and packing a battered suitcase. Hitchhiking through California was a ticklish proposition. I now wouldn't advise anyone to try it but at the time we didn't even consider any dangers.

We crossed the border at Tijuana and got a ride to Tecate, where an ancient beer truck picked us up and took us to the main road down the Pacific coast. After another day of hitching rides we found ourselves stuck in the middle of the northern Mexican desert somewhere north of Hermosillo. By this time we had given up the idea of getting to Mexico City and just wanted to reach Guaymas and soak in the sea.

Finally a battered old moving van came swaying down the road at about twenty miles an hour. Aguilar Transporte was one of a fleet of tramp haulers which circulated around Mexico picking up and delivering cargo from one town to another, never quite knowing where their next load would take them. They had made a circumambulation around northern Mexico and were ultimately headed back to the capital. We stayed with the ride for the five days it took to get to Mexico City.

The driver was a roly-poly, voluble guy who stopped at assorted shrines and points of interest. We dropped off and picked up freight from dusty town squares and the factory districts of northern towns. Through Sonora, through the back streets of Ciudad Obregon, stopping at roadside cantinas and gobbling down tamales and tacos and good Mexican beer. When passing through towns notorious for police squeeze Mary and I would crawl into the back of the van to avoid paying a fine. We passed through Tepic, Guadalajara, Celaya and other nameless night-shrouded towns. Ultimately we rattled into Mexico City where our driver took us to a hotel which had seen better days but was only a few blocks from the Zocalo.

One of the impressive things about the capitol was that in all our rambles around the town (in addition to everything else I wore a scraggly red beard) hardly anyone looked askance at us. After the responses we had come to expect in small-town California the urbane indifference of Mexico City was very refreshing. Mary and I wandered around the inner city districts without plan. The single most moving incident for me was to walk into an old colonial building which had previously housed the Ministerio de Hacienda and to discover, right on the walls and along the passageways, murals painted by Diego Rivera. Not only that, they were the very murals which I had seen in a book and had gripped me as a kid. Yet they didn't mean anything at all to Mary.

I had promised myself to visit Cuautla in the hills of Morelos State. I'd been on my way there when I was fifteen. Shortly after dawn the rural bus leaves Cuernavaca for the hill towns, a two hour-ride around cornfields and peasant hamlets, past derelict sugar haciendas, through former military garrisons and then into Cuautla. The sun is just coming up over the mountain rim, market women are setting up their stalls, everything is cool and fresh.

In April of 1919 Federal troops had finally killed Emiliano Zapata and had dumped his body in the town square of Cuautla. It was the symbolic end of the Indian peasant phase of the Mexican revolution. However, since the Cardenas era Zapata had been resurrected as a safely dead symbol of that revolution. There was the inevitable statue of Zapata on horseback, and bronze plaques honouring him from a host of Mexican government organizations. I had intended to lay a wreath of flowers but decided against it. He wasn't there. His unmarked grave was somewhere in the hills. Yes, it was a romantic gesture.

I returned to Vancouver while Mary went back to Berkeley. The romance was supposed to end there but instead it sputtered on for another two years from one end of the continent to the other. That love affair figured in some idiotic decisions, particularly that of going to Chicago. Someone adept at writing farce might make something of it all but I think I'll let it pass.

During the fall and winter I shuffled back and forth between Vancouver and stays in Berkeley, enrolled in courses at UBC and sitting in on classes in California. Interspersed were jobs that somehow paid for all this, I don't know how. Cyril Belshaw, the *éminence gris* of anthropology at UBC, felt I was a thoroughly undisciplined student and went out of his way to block me from getting into doctoral programs elsewhere. It might have been better all the way around if he had succeeded.

The following year was so hectic, with so many twists and turns, that it is impossible to convey the myriad moves and false starts involved.

Archive: Fortress America and Southside Chicago

The social and political climate in Chicago at the beginning of the 1960s was worse than anything I'd yet seen or imagined. It was hard to imagine that Chicago once had a radical tradition. The Haymarket martyrs, the headquarters of the Industrial Workers of the World, the home of Charles H. Kerr Publishers. It was the city which Jack London saw as America's Petrograd. Studs Terkel talks about the town as if the aura of Carl Sandburg's Chicago still lingers on and as if soapbox oratory still emanates from some dispersed Bughouse Square.

After Berkeley, Chicago was a descent into the most oppressive of American cold war hysteria. McCarthyism had taken root among broad sections of middle America. There were exceptions, certainly, but Chicago was the kind of place where you might be sitting in cafe with a couple of acquaintances discussing how ludicrous the civil defense program was only to have the manageress stalk across the floor and rail about "disloyalty". "We have a bomb that can fly up and blow all the bombs that the Russians shoot at us out of the sky." She wasn't going to have anybody making peace propaganda in her cafe.

During an initial visit to Chicago in the spring of 1961 I participated in a small and cautious peace demonstration, one of the first to be mounted in the city in many years. Some four to five hundred participants, many of them students, descended on the downtown Loop district for a brief Easter march. The theme was nuclear disarmament and it was circumspect to a fault. But some intelligence agency had gotten wind of the march and had mobilized a mob of sailors from the naval depots around Chicago to confront us. There they were waiting for us in their uniforms, at least two sailors for each peace marcher. I still wore my red scraggly beard. "Castro Communist," they growled. The passers-by also yelled imprecations, enraged that "beatniks" should dare to demonstrate for peace in their city. When we tried to hand out leaflets punches got thrown and for a while I thought that we were going to be badly beaten up. It was the closest thing I've ever seen to a lynch mob.

"Get the UN Out of the US and the US Out of the UN" was a commonly seen bumper sticker slogan around Chicago. "Keep American Strong — Fly the Flag" was another, demonstrating that belief in sympathetic magic wasn't dead among the denizens of the Middle West. "This Is a Republic — Not a Democracy. Let's Keep It that Way" was a hobby horse of the John Birch Society. There was the Committee of One Million who were for rooting out the compromisers who had "lost China" (until it was found again a decade later by President Richard Nixon). "Don't Buy Polish Hams" was the slogan of a grassroots campaign against "trading with the enemy" and in support of one hundred percent American hams. The Liberty Lobby urged Americans to "Let Freedom Ring". The Young Americans for Freedom, a claque of aspirant William Buckleys and stock-jobbing Cotton Mathers, called for greater legal restraint of the "dangerous classes". "Support Your Local Police", cracker barrel radio hosts reminded their listeners; "Keep God In Our Schools", presumably feeling that the Almighty had been ejected and required their intercession.

The Holy American Inquisition was still in full voice in the American heartland. The preeminent bible thumper was Billy Graham. He was packing in the yahoos with his Crusades for Christ, damning sin in its sundry, mainly sexual, guises. Graham's evangelical hokum was comparatively innocuous but there also was one Dr. Schwartz, a Southern California evangelist (from Australia) who had parlayed his Anti-Communist Crusade into a nationwide show which Billy Sunday would have envied. Coming up strong out of Oklahoman nativism was the Rev. Billy Hargis with his own Christian Anti-Communist Crusade. The Rev. Hargis was later reduced to appearing in bit roles on the Rev. Pat Robertson's 700 Club medicine shows after the good Oklahoman was charged with abusing some of his young male crusaders. But there were lots of others to take his place. "Boob Belt snake oil showmen," you say ? They had swarms of breathless followers in cities like Chicago.

The Rev. Karl MacIntyre, that sinister theologian of Christian neofascism, hissed "subversion" in his campaign to bludgeon any remaining liberal church leaders into silence. "Peace Is Surrender" was his watchword. A clear reading of the Bible by his gang was the message "I come not with peace but with a sword." He may have been right about that. The unexorcised spirits of Bishop J. Fulton Sheen and Cardinal Spellman weren't to be discounted either.

There were Armed Forces Day parades and Preparedness Weeks. There were Loyalty Day parades in which ethnic organizations jostled to turn out their membership in order to demonstrate their loyalty as True Americans. Daily Pledges of Allegiance to the Flag had been introduced during the Red Scare of the post-World War I era and were universal. Many public school boards now instituted compulsory civics courses entitled "Know Your Enemy". Among the horrors of totalitarianism they catalogued was the sinister process of "brainwashing".

More than a thousand organizations had been unilaterally placed on a list of "subversive organizations" by the United States Attorney General's office in the early 1950s. They ranged anywhere from mildly liberal to what in America counted as "left wing" organizations. They included peace groups, civil rights groups involved in desegregation campaigns, organizations such as the National Lawyers Guild, and remnants of organizations such as the Committee to Aid Spanish Republican Refugees. The list included the IWW and a kaleidoscopic assortment of others. There was no claim that they or their members had broken any law. In fact there was never any specification whatsoever of what "subversive" actually meant. There were never any specific charges or particulars tendered. Indeed, it was categorically forbidden to bring a court case against the Department of Justice to have the evidence of an organization's alleged subversive nature presented. That would endanger National Security.

The American public broadly accepted the *pronunciamentos* of the Attorney General and the serried under-bosses of the National Security regime (who were revealed in Senate investigations two decades later). Americans accepted that J. Edgar Hoover and the other secret police chiefs should be above the law, able to do what they liked, whenever they liked, to whomever they disliked, with impunity. They accepted that creatures like Everett Dirksen and James Eastland and others like them in the US Senate should be able to determine what would and wouldn't be permissible beliefs.

Anyone defending the rights of individuals to belong to progressive organizations or the right to espouse currently unpopular views was himself investigated and harassed. Either agents of the FBI or private right-wing groups would roll out their smear tactics, make "informational visits" to the victim's employer, associates or colleagues, who might themselves be threatened with investigation unless the offending individual was removed. Those who wouldn't cooperate rendered themselves open to the charge of being "dupes of front organizations" or of being "commie symps". A network of publications conveyed slanders and rumours about the targeted victims into print.

Most labour unions in America went along with this self-immolation in a fit of "me too" mania, occasionally counterpointed with a little poormouthing about "excesses". American labour leaders instigated witch hunts in their own unions. With some honourable exceptions, one has got to say that during this period the American union movement was among the most servile and reactionary of any labour ·movement in the capitalist world.

In addition to the plethora of federal agencies involved in thought control, virtually every state government was caught up in the witch-finding craze. Civil servant jobs or jobs which involved public funds came to require loyalty oaths and security clearances. Government employees at whatever level, teachers and college professors, workers in defense (i.e. war) industries, sometimes even employees of contractors building public projects, had to be "cleared" as to their political reliability.

Security Investigation had become a growth industry. There were hundreds of agencies, public and private, investigating the political purity or taint of heresy of other Americans. "I've got nothing to hide, they can investigate me. Nobody has anything to worry about unless they have something to hide," was a common response of the Great Crested *Boobus americanus* — a species widely distributed in Canada as well. Anyone objecting to this wholesale expropriation of what were supposedly fundamental rights was himself under suspicion. The FBI alone, having investigated some ten million Americans, had a million dossiers in its files of "potential security risks". Americans allowed a cabal of right-wing zealots to determine what ideas could be disseminated and who would or wouldn't be accorded their "constitutional rights".

This was the public milieu of much of middle America in 1961, some five years after Senator Joseph McCarthy had kicked the bucket. McCarthyism had become institutionalized.

What I knew of Chicago first hand was a small slice of the Southside.

I attended the University of Chicago and lived in a black ghetto district for some five months in the spring and fall of 1961. That should be enough time to get a feel for a city. I've been sitting here trying to think of something balanced to say about the place but it keeps coming up monochromatically grim. It was steeped in racism, violence and pervasive reaction.

My introduction to Southside Chicago had come on the first night of my arrival. Walking down brightly lit Cathedral Parkway in the twilight of a spring evening I'm mugged. Four young black guys come out of a bar, walk behind me, strike up a conversation and a few minutes later push me into the foyer of an apartment building before I know what's happening. It was the worst fight I was ever in. I tried to keep in a corner where only two at a time could get at me. I don't know how long it went on; it seemed a long time but probably wasn't. I don't know how many times I got knocked down, had the boots put to my head and ribs and yet somehow managed to get up and fight. I was pretty tough in those days.

"Help! Police." I yelled. And then "Fire! Fire!" I would have given them my money but felt that if I did they would beat me up even worse just for the hell of it. Finally, one of my assailants went through the glass in the door and the rest decided they had had enough fun and took off. I'm punch drunk, can barely walk and can hardly see anything. As I stagger out to the street I spot a police car across the road writing up a ticket for a traffic violator. They phone for another patrol car which rolls up after twenty minutes. I'm asked if I can identify the assailants but clearly the police feel it's my own fault. "You've got no business being down here in the first place," they tell me.

Mary and I wound up living in a decaying black tenement district two blocks west of Woodlawn Avenue and a block north of the El on 62nd street. That part of Southside Chicago was like the stereotype inner city slum which the American media began dishing out some years later in its endless police epics. We didn't move into that neighbourhood in order to partake of the ghetto scene. The Hyde Park district around the University of Chicago was undergoing an urban clearance known as "redevelopment" — block upon block of boarded-up apartment houses and bulldozed lots. What remained was becoming a black middle class district where the apartment house managers would no longer rent suites to whites.

While I was up in Rupert House Mary had gotten a couple of rooms in the basement of a crumbling tenement. You went down a flight of outside stairs, through a brick passageway and into the basement door — Whitechapel *circa* 1890. The superintendent and most of the residents of the building were black Puerto Ricans who belonged to a Protestant sect which played drums, swore off drink, and dismissed the world around them as hopelessly sunk in perdition. They were really quite decent to us.

The clubhouse of the Blackstone Rangers was located at Blackstone Avenue and 62nd, two blocks away. It was reputedly the largest youth gang in the Southside. They were a power there although one didn't notice their presence as much as one might think. The few times I encountered a group of the Blackstone Rangers they were less hostile than many others around. A couple of them were actually interested in where I was from. But mainly they wanted to know what I was doing in their neighbourhood. They later evolved into a powerful ward organization of the Democratic Party.

But the district was suffused with a free-floating violence — just below the surface at the best of times. Since there were virtually no whites in the Southside this anger was played out largely among black people. But there was a level of racial hatred I have never encountered anywhere, before or since. Not everyone was like that but the aura of racial antagonism touched everything. The fact that black people had been the main victims of racial oppression did not make anti-white racism any easier to bear.

It had been only three years since I'd gotten back from Nigeria. I didn't expect Southside Chicago to be Nigeria but I figured that one would be able to make contact with some individuals. By the time I had lived in Nigeria for four months I knew scads of people. But I never truly got to know anyone who was part of the Southside. That is one of the consequences of racism.

The University of Chicago had once been and still saw itself as a centre of American intellectual life. But by the early 1960s it was a senescent and beleaguered academy. The campus was bounded by Washington Park on one side, the Hyde Park clearances on two others and a constantly patrolled double carriageway to the south. Few students ever ventured beyond that preserve.

The university was a stone and brick island of pseudo-Oxbridge gothic surrounded by a reef of student residences. The one memorable feature was Ida Noyes Hall. It had been the palace of some pork packer doge and was filled with the faded accoutrements of the beauty which money could buy — art nouveau carving, Tiffany lamps, threadbare but exquisite Indian rugs and a dancing room with a wraparound mural in which a nubile Isadora Duncan and Grecian nymphs wove through woodland scenes. It should have been preserved as a museum but instead it had been donated to the university for student activities. Ida Noyes Hall was usually empty because the students were too busy with serious studies to waste their time attending a harpsichord recital or listening to a talk by somebody who had recently returned from Cuba. It showed too.

Mainly I had gone to Chicago to be with Mary. But the graduate anthropology program there had something of a reputation. Considering who held that department in high repute I should have been able to guess what I would find — the worst of British social anthropology wedded to arrant American conservatism. Fred Eggan began his course on Social Organization with an invocation to his prophet. "When Radcliffe-Brown came to the University of Chicago in 1934, etc., etc." One Professor Yalman did a Sidney Hook routine, slaying any serpents of intellectual heresy which may have slithered into this midwestern anthropological garden. Commenting on Leslie White's mildly materialistic outline of cultural evolution, our émigré Saint Patrick intoned that, "I have a strong suspicion that there is the coloration of totalitarian ideology hidden in the baggage of cultural evolution." Student heads nodded dotingly. Lloyd Fallers informed us that, "Peasantry and Class are European concepts which are ideological façades when applied to African societies." It was still a continent of tribal peoples and organic cultures, according to his lectures. Talk about being overtaken by events.

A few days before Christmas I got a drive-away car to deliver to Seattle and came back to Vancouver. Mary remained in Chicago and that was the end of that. Bill Dunning had saved my bacon by having my Rupert House field work approved for an MA thesis. I scribbled away at the thesis and tried to round up a research contract to get me into the field again come spring. It was a terribly empty time. I hadn't any inkling that better times were just around the corner.

TEN

Trapping Post Sojourn

Rupert House

Between the spring of 1961 and the fall of 1962 I spent some seven months in two Cree trapping communities east of James Bay for the National Museum of Canada. It was my first real anthropological field work and despite my qualms it proved to be more productive than I had any reason to expect.

The arrival of the first float plane after breakup was an event which brought much of the population of isolated northern posts down to the dock to see who was coming off or passing through. My first sight of Rupert House was from the front seat of a Beaver as we taxied down the Rupert River to the dock. A covey of local teenagers lounged behind the Hudson's Bay Company warehouse, many of them decked out in imitation black leather motorcycle jackets, chromium studs and all. ("This is where I'm coming to research changes in hunting and trapping?") But it was just the summer fashion among the local youth set and by the beginning of autumn they had changed back into work season clothes; baggy wool pants, heavy flannel shirts, parkas and moccasins, while younger children were being cajoled into trying on the rabbit yarn jackets their mothers had woven for them. The trade store bikers returned to being actual trappers and hunters or had gone off to residential school. Rupert House was still primarily a trapping post community.

Although the region was the first to be brought into trade with the Hudson's Bay Company some two hundred and fifty years earlier, East James Bay remained a backwater almost to the eve of World War I. Whereas most Native Indian communities in Canada had entered the world of reserves and various forms of direct articulation with Canadian society by the beginning of the twentieth century, the peoples of East James Bay were then still soldiering along in a manner not strikingly different than that of two centuries earlier. There was one hell of a lot which older people at Rupert House had experienced. People still living in 1961 could provide recollections of hunting with muskets and trapping with wooden deadfalls, could give accounts of starvation and of an almost total reliance on traditional food economies. Such exigencies were central in the social arrangements which had existed until recently. There were individuals who could provide details of life under conditions which now seem like the very distant past.

During the summer the population of Rupert House was some five hundred people. The white "community" consisted of the Hudson's Bay Company manager and his wife, a company clerk, a nurse and her husband at the nursing station, and one Maude Watt. During the school year there were also two teachers. Coming into one of these small communities with their ingrown cliques is always a touchy matter. Normally I left them alone and they left me alone. Maude Watt, the "Angel of Hudson Bay", as a pop biography called her, was the only fly in the ointment.

Her husband had been the last of the HBC factors to hold near-unchecked sway over Indian people around trade posts like Rupert House. The way in which managers like Watt ran their trade post fiefs and how he and other external agencies came to institute government-controlled trapping territories in the region is a matter of debate among fur enterprise historians. A process of beatification is now apparently in the works.

Forty years after her first entry into the James Bay region and having nothing better to do than administer the provincial game quotas and regale the occasional visitor to Rupert House with pioneer tales, Maude Watt came to fasten on the Red Russian threat to Our North. It so happened that an obsolescent radar station was located in Moosonee, about eighty miles to the southwest. Maude was determined to do her bit to protect this outpost of Canada's defenses from any alien menace. Although she had seen my letters of appointment from the National Museum of Canada she wrote to the RCMP detachment in Moosonee about potentially subversive aspects of my presence at Rupert House. What is even more ludicrous is that two RCMP inspectors flew out to check over my papers and question me about what I was doing there.

I got into the swing of field work fairly quickly and easily, more so than I appreciated at the time. Some local people were crucial in getting me off on the right foot. Not everyone was enthused about my being at Rupert House but the response in general was encouraging. What I didn't fully appreciate, nor did others, was how rapidly all of this would be overtaken by events.

I didn't experience any attack of culture shock, a much discussed affliction then. That is a malaise more likely to strike those who have expectations of "tuning in to the inner values and cultural spirit" of a society than those who concentrate on documenting external realities. In my estimation it wasn't possible to commune with cultural spirits nor was it my task to do so. In twenty-six years I hadn't ferreted out the "inner cultural imperatives" of Anglo-Canadian society so it would have been vain to believe I could decipher them among the Cree.

My intent was to record the specifics of more mundane activities, the daily subsistence strategies as people lived them and explained them to me. I would concentrate on hunting and trapping activities, then still the core of economic activity in these Cree communities. Any spirits which chose to reveal themselves were welcome, others could await the brush of some more psychic commentator. That is a more brash attitude than either I or any other practicing anthropologist would actually follow in the field. But it is a healthy counter to those who would have you pursue the most ephemeral of topics while glossing over the complexities of daily reality. Even if I limited myself to a crassly materialistic concern for comparatively objective aspects of trapping organization, that topic was more complex than I could document in a couple of field trips anyway.

One of the misconceptions about field work is the belief that there is always opportunity and time enough to document everything which may be of importance. Later readers always complain, "Why didn't he/ she investigate this or that or the other while it was possible?"

It is difficult to convey the amount of time and effort (and some-

Meeting the cargo plane at Rupert House, northern Quebec, 1961.

times even thought) which goes into acquiring what would seem to be straight forward information. The visits and discussions entailed in acquiring the data on a one-page chart can be enormous. Obtaining the information to produce a chart outlining the kinship composition of just thirty-two trapping groups operating out of Rupert House in the winter of 1960-61 involved dozens of visits and interviews. An attempt to survey the seasonal moves and the game taken by each trapping group was even more time-consuming.

Ethnological field work is quite different from ransacking archives and files where the source material exists regardless of whether anyone uses it or not. In field work the potential data is always far richer and more extensive than anyone could ever gather. It resides in the on-going activities and in the memories of the people you are working with. It entails all the problems and pleasures of dealing with living people, not papers.

Understanding whatever it is you are concerned with requires something more than just opening your heart and mind, just recording what you see and are told. Some readers of anthropology seem to have the impression that monographs spring from the intuition of the researcher and are about as good or bad as anyone's guess. That is a convenient view for those who wish to proffer their own off-the-cuff analysis. It fails to recognize the multiform checks which the ethnologist has attempted to make (although one may be wrong despite everything). But monographs rarely are simple replications of what an ethnologist was told by one informant or another.

You have to devise the pertinent questions to ask and then rephrase them as you yourself learn to appreciate some of the complexities involved. You have to find cross-checking accounts and assure yourself of the translations on certain key points at least. None of this is evident in the final version of the study.

In the course of pursuing some questions one is inevitably led into all sorts of "irrelevancies", some of which are just that while others are entries to other facets of the whole picture. Whatever the topic, one is faced with a maze of interconnected facts. For example, the question of which group utilized a particular tract of land in the previous year gets you into the movements and readjustments by various trapping groups, into a welter of kinship or trapping partner relationships. It will trigger accounts of particular hunts and comments on particular techniques used. It may touch on fragments of family history, provide some deadpan humour and may even summon forth some spiritual forces, possibly all in one evening's interview.

Participant observation can often provide a clearer understanding of the actual processes at work than may be obtained either from records or from purely verbal accounts. However, getting a general picture always requires extensive interviewing. When dealing with the past one is necessarily dependent upon mainly verbal evidence. Compared to the material historians work with there are some stringent temporal limitations involved in ethnological data. You can't directly observe past conditions and you can't gather meaningful oral accounts of events which occurred before the lifetimes of the oldest living members of a community.

Most adult men and women at Rupert House then were functionally unilingual in Cree. But apart from a few phrases and possibly a hundred words, I spoke no Cree and made no plans to learn it. That may seem blindly ethnocentric but realistically there was no possibility of my being able to learn the language. I would never have been able to begin field work if it had to wait upon fluency in Cree. My study was geared to having an interpreter and dealing with topics for which approximate translation would suffice to gather useful material.

The interpreter was Willy Wistchee, a man in his early thirties who had spent a decade in a tuberculosis sanatorium down south and had returned to resume some semblance of hunting and trapping despite the fact that he was badly crippled. There was a touch of the suicidal about Wistchee. He had the reputation of being a daredevil canoeman who would cross the dozen miles of open water from Cabbage Willows to Rupert House in a fall blow when others stayed put. But Willy proved to be an astute translator, interested in the work and ready to follow up details. He might point out a salient aspect I had overlooked but was sometimes as nonplussed as I about certain accounts.

You have to give yourself and your informants enough time. Memories can't be pulled from storage on demand even with the best of will. It's only through a series of interviews, with time between, that most people can begin to recapture what is stashed away in their memory. A mixture of patience and inquisitiveness, a sensitivity to nuances and a thick hide are the everyday qualities needed. That and a genuine, visible appreciation of what you are being told.

Most important of all was the willingness of older informants to recount their experiences, in what at times must have seemed like painstaking repetition. The head of the Jolly family, a twenty-member, four-generational group which trapped on Charlton Island, was determined to see that I got down accounts of the past correctly. Mathew Cowboy, then in his late eighties and the oldest person at Rupert House, was amenable to discussing his life, and varied from being lucid on some topics to confusingly cloudy on others. A widow in her seventies became enthused in reliving events of her youth and we repeatedly had to ask her to slow down so Willy could translate. Some half dozen people provided reminiscences of a Cree hunting and trapping society in the early twentieth century. Whatever the quality of the interviews virtually all of them added pieces to a broader picture of what life had been like then.

There was David Salt, then a man in his mid sixties with a wife and young son to support. His father had been a full-time "servant" (wage employee) of the Hudson's Bay Company and Revillion Freres at Rupert House during most of his adult life. The Hudson's Bay Company once maintained an elaborate infrastructure of artisans and wage employees on its major posts and Rupert House was long as much a regional entrepôt as a fur trade post. David himself had been employed as the courier between the East James Bay posts but in the early 1930s the HBC dismissed most of the local employees at their posts as a cost-cutting measure and the bottom fell out for people like David. He had never primarily been a trapper or hunter and had only survived that very difficult transition by being taken into the trapping groups of unrelated families. Twenty-five years later David was still a "coaster", one of the families engaged in subsistence hunting and

*An elderly couple
with whom I stayed at
Nemiscau, 1962. The
conical tent is much larger
than it seems here.*

marginal trapping in the coastal areas. His history struck me as an unusual turnabout but I later came to understand that David's experience was not as unique as it seemed.

Then there was John Blackned. Born in the mid 1890s, the still-active head of a trapping group, he was able to provide systematic accounts of life during the First World War period and earlier. Blackned was an articulate memorialist and an enthusiastic story teller. The only problem was sorting out which was which at times. If you could keep him off allegorical tales (viz., what the first Indians to see white men, some three centuries earlier, had said to each other) and focus his accounts on what he had experienced himself, you really had something. Blackned was a fount of information on such topics as how caribou had been hunted in drives with muskets. We did some interviews together and I was intending to get back to him after I had gathered contemporary accounts from the other trapping groups on the post. But time ran out.

So little of the human relationships involved in field work come through in my own and most other monographs. For instance, during an early evening Wistchee, Blackned and I are sitting talking and drinking tea in the shack I lived in down beside the Rupert River when the first flight of Canada geese are heard in the distance. That wheezing, creaking, honking, joyful sound. Everybody comes streaming out of their tents and cabins. Blackned edges down to the river bank and begins making a goose call through cupped hands. *"Snn Auk*

... Sn Auk ... Auk, Auk." Believe it or not, a string of geese begins to descend, circles and comes in at about thirty feet before it spots humans and then scrambles up again, wings screeking and flapping. People are laughing goodhumouredly and Blackned saunters back, ostentatiously nonchalant.

Somewhat later we were talking about trapping techniques before steel traps were available. After numerous attempts to explain beaver deadfalls John says that tomorrow he is going to build one in the small creek beside my shack so I can see how they worked. Sure enough, next morning he brings over some poles which he chops into various lengths and begins making a wooden deadfall.

I'm trying to ask halfway intelligent questions about gates and triggers and runways (which really are beyond me) through Willy Wistchee while Blackned provides a running commentary on practical deadfall design — what you should avoid, what is altered depending on specific circumstances and so forth. Soon there are twenty or so younger men standing at a distance, engrossed in the demonstration and tossing in the occasional comment. I later found that many of them also had never known exactly how wooden deadfalls worked, though they had all heard about the technique.

While most younger people at Rupert House were interested in listening to accounts of "how it was in the old days" they were usually not that interested. Most had other priorities. If they, in their late middle age, decry the fact that their grandparents' experiences weren't gotten down on the record one may ask why they didn't lend a hand in doing it themselves. Not romances of some never-existent golden age but the much more sagacious and humanly gripping accounts their elders were capable of telling.

The accounts I got from older men and women were moving and compelling, often detailed and at times contradictory. It didn't require any great cross-cultural leap to appreciate the tenacity, the mutual aid and self-reliance involved in subsistence hunting and trapping. But it was also important to realize the human costs of that sort of economy. Many people had not survived the rigors of that life. In addition to staggering infant mortality rates, premature deaths among adults left almost half of the families widowed before the children were adults. Infectious diseases took a heavy toll and in the not-so-distant past there were cases of outright starvation when families became isolated from each other during bad seasons.

It strikes me as ludicrous that such experiences should now be converted into images of a golden age of cultural autonomy. In 1961 older men and women did take a justifiable pride in having survived those challenges and fulfilled their duties to their children. But they hoped that those conditions would never return.

I regret not collecting one or two life histories of individuals who had lived long and active lives and who were willing to recount their experiences. A life history could have accompanied a more systematic study and would have been something which general readers could have appreciated. It was not what the National Museum of Canada had commissioned me to do but I should have done it anyway.

Living on the post was still a seasonal arrangement for many Rupert House families. A dozen years previously everyone had to be taken out into the winter camps if they were to be fed, from seventy-year-old grandmothers to month-old infants. Once families and trapping groups left the post for goose hunting or trapping camps their social relations changed noticeably. People became more spirited, they talked more and made spontaneous jokes. The lackadaisical postures of teenagers on the post disappeared. Individuals took up their various tasks and a quiet but definite authority was established by the "trapping boss" of the outfit. Of course that "boss" was usually a relative and he was attuned to the individual capacities and quirks of members of the group. But he could be rather definite in laying down "suggestions" when out in the bush.

Most trapping families still kept dog teams for winter travel and canoes were essential during the spring and summer. But by 1961 Cree families had already become inveterate air travelers on the bush planes shuttling about the region. Bush planes had become a part of contemporary Cree culture. If you gave a batch of children paper and crayons and suggested they draw whatever interested them a good proportion of the resulting artwork would be of Otters, Beavers or maybe even an old Norseman, possibly with a sled lashed to one of its floats and loaded with a family setting out on the fall hunt.

I made visits to nearby fish camps but the longest trip was a hundred-mile canoe voyage up the coast to Eastmain. It was a community once closely linked to Rupert House by marriage and summer visits and meetings on the winter trap lines. But the development of band endogamy during the previous generation, as well as new patterns of travel, had pretty much broken the links between these two bands. Wistchee took over and made himself the boss of our expedition.

The coastal shelf around James Bay is very shallow and you sometimes have to run a mile off shore just to have depth for the outboard. With the slightest wind a sharp chop comes up immediately. We were using one of those twenty-two-foot freight canoes which were built at Rupert House, a very big canoe indeed which could easily carry a ton of freight plus four passengers. But we were caught in a squall which came up out of nowhere and were marooned on an offshore islet for two days: Willy, me and two other men from Rupert House. It was a tremendous feeling, traveling up the coast of James Bay by canoe to do interviews at Eastmain post. ("My god. I'm actually an anthropologist.") Although we were welcomed at Eastmain as the first boatload of people to come up from Rupert House in many years, I didn't get much accomplished there.

Back in Rupert House I spent my remaining time digging into the parish records of baptisms, births and deaths. The local Cree minister of the Anglican church had suggested that I look at them. They confirmed the picture of mortality my informants had described, as well as some surprising other patterns. Rupert House had a sixty-year history of apparent population increase and outmigration. This was

Anthropologist at work, Nemiscau, 1962.

also attested to by the kinship charts of Rupert House families I gathered, which showed distant relatives scattered throughout many of the bands of the region as well as others who had seemingly disappeared into the Canadian communities of Northern Ontario and Quebec over the previous three generations.

I left for Ottawa in mid September to deposit my field notes in the National Museum. Then I zoomed back down to the Southside of Chicago. That place was more difficult to adjust to and more alien to me than anything I encountered at Rupert House.

Nemiscau

In the spring of 1962 I was back in James Bay bound for the small, isolated Cree trapping community centered around Nemiscau, about a hundred miles upriver from Rupert House. Nemiscau retained many of the trapping and hunting patterns of an earlier era. I intended to extend the research I'd been doing at Rupert House but things didn't work out that way.

Apart from the HBC factor and his clerk, there were no other whites on the post. However there was a guy we can call Jim Flint who had been the previous factor at Nemiscau who was then living with his Cree wife in a tent on an island a few miles down the lake. Jim was in his mid twenties, a well-read person who allegedly had "gone native", as the old colonial phrase had it. As the HBC factor he had not only lived with a local woman but had begun to press appeals for government relief for Nemiscau families. Today it is well nigh impossible to imagine the Dickensian miserliness, the endless weaseling about by Department of Indian Affairs officials to circumvent payment of twenty dollar a month for rations to individuals in dire need.

The HBC had demoted Flint for his unprofessional behaviour and was about transfer him to another post. He refused to leave and was fired. At the same time the RCMP informed him that he was on the equivalent of an Indian reserve without permission and would have to clear off. At first Jim and his wife moved to southern Ontario but that didn't work at all. So they returned to Nemiscau and were attempting to eke out some kind of existence on Crown land. Naturally that proved impossible and they ultimately split up. But at the time they were still trying to stick it out together. Although it didn't have any

direct bearing upon my work their situation somehow seemed to epit-
omize the general impasse which had been reached.

Government presence, in the form of the Department of Northern
and Indian Affairs, was mainly restricted to taking out older children
to residential school and providing hospital facilities at Moose Factory
for those desperate enough to use them. Welfare payments, subsidies
and other transfer payments were negligible. Wage labour was virtually non-existent. Hunting, trapping and fishing comprised the entire
economy and were the centre of everyone's life. Even many of the historic trade posts had not been as exclusively engaged in hunting and
trapping as Nemiscau was.

Apart from one elderly couple the entire hundred and fifty-mem-
ber population of Nemiscau dispersed to trapping and hunting camps
scattered over thousands of square miles for almost ten months of the
year. Members of some groups might come in to the post for supplies
at mid winter but band members were together for only two months in
the summer.

There was little in the way of material goods used in Nemiscau which
one couldn't have found around a northern trade post of circa 1912.
About the only exception was the country music emanating from a
station in Wheeling, West Virginia, which droned out of two or three
portable radios for as long as the batteries lasted. Nemiscau trappers
were not in fact living in the pre-World War I era, but the general
round of life at Nemiscau in 1962 seemed rather like that described by
Rupert House elders in their youth forty and more years before.

Following the misconceived anthropological dictum of living
among the people you are working with, I managed to wangle myself
an invitation to stay with a couple with two young children. They were
the junior members, dependents almost, of one of the largest trapping
groups operating out of Nemiscau. The head of this outfit was a force-
ful character and I had a near run-in with him at one point. Luckily he
turned out to be a generous and high-hearted person.

Some snarl-up had delayed the supply plane getting in and the HBC
stock at Nemiscau was down to little more than flour, lard, baking
powder and matches. This resulted in a greater than usual reliance on
country foods. There was lake fish in abundance but even people used
to fish as a staple had had enough fried fish, bannock and tea. Extra
effort was devoted to snaring rabbits and the remains of preserved

game came out of cartons and oilskin containers. Selling country food to fellow band members was still unthinkable but the remaining stocks of preserved meat were shared within close circles of family members.

So I was on a bannock and fried jackfish diet too. The trapping boss who occasionally hassled me about living with his people nevertheless sent over some winter preserves. Oiled caribou meat looks ghastly but is very tasty. Even better was dried moose — black, stringy and slightly sour. You chew it and it leaves a delicate flavor in your mouth for an hour afterward. Smoked beaver wasn't too bad but muskrat is definitely a one-time thing as far as I was concerned.

A gaggle of teenage, not quite marriageable girls hung around together in search of anything which might relieve their summer boredom. They were waiting to see how I took to the smoked muskrat. It actually tastes muskegy. A couple of them trotted out their quite adequate residential school English to ask, "Did you like the ... rat? Hee, hee. The mushrat? Giggle, giggle." Unless you are used to it the oil has the effect of a strong cascara infusion, a powerful laxative. A half hour later my stomach was roiling and I was making repeated dashes into the bush. Such reminiscences may seem gallingly anecdotal but they are part and parcel of field work.

Matthew Ottereyes, the band chief, was in favour of my work. But that didn't carry any weight outside his own family. The trapping

Three girls making bannock, Nemiscau, 1962.

groups clustering around extended families were the all-important social groups. A few of the older men at Nemiscau, usually those beyond their active trapping years, were amenable to talking about their past experiences but the interviews were all quite fragmentary. I gathered data on fur incomes and game take as well as recording the composition of trapping groups during the previous year.

At Rupert House my work did proceed well despite the limitations of language but at Nemiscau it didn't. Most people in Nemiscau were not particularly interested in discussions about how they lived. They knew how they lived and their children would learn quite naturally, they felt. Nemiscau trappers didn't see why any of this should be written down or that it was really anybody else's concern. My stay was an imposition on their hospitality, I knew that. Some didn't mind talking about their hunting and trapping arrangements providing they didn't have something better to do and as long as the translation wasn't too tedious. I kept saying that other people like themselves had seen their lives change a great deal within less time than it took for a child to become a man and that much can be lost if it's not written down. But nobody really believed that.

There were still men alive and active who in the 1920s had worked in the canoe fur brigades which then delivered supplies and took out furs from inland posts. Luke Mettaweshkum was quite willing to talk about his life. Mettaweshkum was known throughout the East James Bay region and was invariably described as "definitely over a hundred" or "at least a hundred and twenty years old". "Well, let's say he's ninety and still lucid and willing to talk to me," I said to myself. "He would have been an adult and hunting and trapping by 1890 in what were essentially the same conditions as applied in the late eighteenth century. Christ, what I could learn from him."

Mettaweshkum turned out to be a jovial, hearty guy who must have been a giant of a man in his prime. Although now somewhat arthritic he was still going out into the winter camps with his middle-aged great-grandchildren. I never did pin down his exact age but he must have been at least ninety. The trouble was that events were tumbled together in Luke's memory so that descriptions of how to quick-load muskets of sixty and more years before were juxtaposed with events which had occurred in the last decade. He didn't have any hesitation about describing the way he used hunting magic and divination, telling me how he relied on dreaming while drumming to locate game rather than reading burnt scapula. That kind of "supernatural" material was of considerable interest to me because it effected what people actually did on the ground while hunting. But it proved impossible to follow up in any meaningful way.

At the time I berated myself for this impasse but there was something beyond my own limitations involved, I now believe. At Rupert House, people past middle age were clearly aware of how much their lives had changed in the previous generation: a day school and a nursing station had been established and a growing number of families lived on the post for most of the year, seasonal wage labour was not uncommon and "rations" were available in emergencies. The Canadian world loomed just beyond the band trapping boundaries at Moosonee. At Rupert House there was an impetus for older people to record their experience of the past. In Nemiscau on the other hand, always an isolated post, the observable changes in peoples lives to date had been comparatively minor. There was little sense of the changes imminent.

While I was in the field I tore my hair and strove to assure that the information I obtained was reliable. In the end it didn't matter because facts and evidence are selectively used, refashioned and dismissed as the intellectual fashions of each period sees fit. A decade later, during the hearings involved in the James Bay Agreement, any journalist's wisdom on the topic had more influence over the public's conception of native land use than a study like mine did.

Just when I was most frustrated with my research at Nemiscau I received Edward Rogers's unpublished study of hunting groups and family territoriality among the Mistassini, a group just east of Nemiscau. It was a topic and approach close to my own — except that Rogers was the leading authority on the area. At first I was thunderstruck, even a little jealous. But what I mainly came to feel was relief. I had believed that either I collected the information or it would be lost. Rogers's study was a weight off my shoulders.

On evenings when I had had enough of all the anthropological treasures around me I might paddle over to John Flint's camp and listen to his shortwave radio. I vowed that the first thing I would do when I came south was to buy a Zenith Transworld radio. One of the stations which came through strong and clear was Radio Habana Cuba. One night there was a rebroadcast of Fidel addressing a rally at the Plaza Jose Martí.

What the hell was I doing in a place like Nemiscau trying to document a world passing out of existence? Certainly I appreciated the intricacies of the culture and the decency of people in northern trapping communities. Yes, I found the task of ethnography important. But that wasn't what I wanted to do with my life.

If this were a more dramatically written memoir you would now see me depart from a round tent where I am chewing on oiled caribou to descend on the Upper West Side of Manhattan. It was almost like that. But first I put in a stint with the Department of Northern Affairs doing a strictly defined consumption survey of a "model village" established for an Ojibwa band on Wunnimin Lake in northwestern Ontario. I think that's all I want to say about that! It was from Wunnimin Lake that I took the fish plane out to Sioux Lookout, the train to Ottawa and then down to Nueva York. Though I didn't know it at first, New York was the place I'd been looking for.

"Changing Social and Economic Organization Among the Rupert House Cree" was ultimately issued by the National Museum of Canada. It is mainly a descriptive survey of the social organization of trapping among this Cree band during 1960 and 1961 and only touches on the changes experienced within the lifetimes of surviving band members. Half a century later my account of the then-contemporary conditions reads like distant history.

In the late 1990s I received a request from the Cree Regional Council's historical research program asking whether I had any photographs of Nemiscau in the 1960s. The band members had scattered to surrounding groups after that post was closed and part of their territory flooded by the James Bay hydro project. The historical program was collecting oral histories from older people and felt that photos would help in eliciting recall. That says a lot about the changes which have occurred in the intervening years. I wish them well.

ELEVEN

New York In the Sixties

Archive: The Rome of Our Age

If New York was "the Rome of our age", as some boosters claimed, it was Rome in its senescence. The city was crumbling at quite a clip. The physical decay was the result of decades of dwindling investment in the infrastructure of the city, much of which had been laid down in the four decades preceding 1930. The social disintegration was partly attributable to the continual increase in the number of unemployed, underemployed and underpaid people in the city as runaway shops moved to cheap labour locales in the sun belt. Whole strata of industrial jobs, totaling hundreds of thousands, had been removed over the years or had been replaced by service jobs which offered bare subsistence wages.

There were still something like twenty thousand "old law tenements" in the city, tenements which had been prohibited by building codes in the first decade of the century. When it became more costly to provide services and make repairs than profits warranted, when deterioration passed a point of no return some owners simply abandoned these buildings. They let the buildings go unserviced and waited for the opportune time when the site could be sold and the building demolished. There were areas in the South Bronx and in the Bedford-Stuyvesant district of Brooklyn which looked like scenes from Hogarth.

The Lower East Side which I rambled through had been built in the half century before 1900. Buildings of that age when properly maintained can be perfectly serviceable, exciting even. But the rationale of profits hadn't warranted such maintenance for a long time. At McSorley's Old Ale House, that all-male beer joint at the edge of Little Italy, arguments raged as to whether slum conditions created the people in them or whether people created their own slums. Beery *philosophes* from the neighbourhood pontificated, to the enlightenment of no one, about how their mothers or sisters had scrubbed the stoops of their tenements, allegedly demonstrating how some people (i.e. their own) once maintained a respectability in areas which now had become slums. Similarly in the White Horse Tavern, where a crowd of fourth-generation Irish-American Brendan Behans held forth.

New office blocks, burgeoning luxury apartment complexes and the federal "urban renewal" projects scattered throughout the city added to the devastation. The redevelopers condemned a swath of buildings, gradually evicted the tenants and then demolished or boarded up the houses in preparation for rebuilding — which might take place years later. When such projects entered a district the remaining apartment buildings often began to deteriorate through a combination of processes. Neighbourhood and tenant organizations struggled to retain some still-viable section of their communities as the wrecking cranes battered away nearby. It was only the fact that New York was so huge and its natives so schooled in local politicking that much of the previous urban environment still remained. But New York's landlordocracy wasn't going to await the coming of some kitchen cabinet Nero. They would sack the city quite nicely on their own.

The city's public infrastructure was crumbling. The then sixty-year-old subway system was constantly breaking down, hardly one in four public telephones worked. Public services in general were pathetic. Public parks, some showing the faded glory of what they had been, were battered, littered and often unsafe. Garbage sometimes lay in bagged heaps on the streets because the city Sanitation Department and its fleet of aging trucks could not handle it all. Most of the docks around the periphery of Manhattan, once the lifeblood of the city, were derelict and the Port Authority couldn't afford to dismantle them let alone rebuild them. The West Side Highway, an elevated roadway along the western edge of lower Manhattan, was an incredible stretch of sagging and potbellied roadbed resting on crumbling concrete piers. It was only closed, years later, when sections of it threatened to collapse.

There were almost twenty-five thousand regular policemen in the New York Police Department, plus an additional ten thousand in the transit and housing police forces — a medium-sized army. They were a lackadaisical power unto themselves which no one really relied upon. They were faced with an impossible task, to be sure. Crime had become part of the fabric of society, from top to bottom. Laws didn't protect the many elderly people, who lived in fear of muggings and break-ins. This was the seedbed of the neighbourhood vigilante organizations, the first of which appeared in Brooklyn's Crown Heights with Rabbi Meir Kahane at its head.

The public health system was a shameful anachronism from the nineteenth century. In any other advanced country the US medical system would have been considered a criminal scandal. Public health care was suffused with a charity ward mentality without the charity wards. Unless you could pay the clinic fees, unless you were enrolled in a private or social security scheme which paid for medical services, you got no treatment at any public health clinic. I know that from a visit to the Ear and Eye Clinic in the Lower East Side as a patient. It was unchanged from when it had been established as a charity clinic during the first decade of the century. In more modern public clinics the treatment you got was just as degrading. A phrase in an old Blues song says,

> If living were a thing that money could buy,
> The rich would live and the poor would die.

On a statistical basis, the American health system accomplished just that. If you are old or poor or outside the charmed circle, America is not the greatest country on earth. In fact it's a rather third-rate country in terms of medical care and social services for over a quarter of its people. Still, most of them are proud to be Americans.

Despite the above, New York was in fact the Rome of our age, the booming, festering, smug, corrupt, cosmopolitan heart of the greatest imperial power in the world.

Archive: Beyond Bread and Circuses

It's difficult to get a handle on America during the 1960s. Everything seemed to be in motion. There was so much which was interconnected and which affected the understandings and responses of the time. There's no way to summarize it all. Naturally, developments don't just start and stop at the turn of a decade. But there was something phenomenal about the period.

If one wanted to dramatize the changes over the course of a few years one might compare the everyday understandings in vogue in 1960 with those of only five years later; the changes in outlook, the liberation from endless cautions, the deepening anger and then the mass opposition to and confrontations with the American state. It was a lesson on how people can awake from a seemingly fathomless somnolence. Few would have predicted what was in the offing at the beginning of the decade.

The first breach in the ramparts of Cold War America was the black civil rights movement. It began in the mid 1950s but only came to fruition in the early 1960s. The desegregation campaign was symbolized by the Montgomery bus boycott and the long-drawn-out court actions which ultimately required the use of federal troops to get a handful of black school children into Little Rock schools in 1957; the at first sporadic but always heroic confrontations of civil rights demonstrators with local police in the South enforcing what were constitutionally illegal Jim Crow laws even in 1960; the black voters' registration drives, the sit-ins and marches. When police power did not suffice, the hardcore segregationists resorted to bombings, vigilante violence and murder.

The bombings of black churches which supported the civil rights movement in the South, most notoriously one in Montgomery, Alabama, where black children were killed during a Sunday service, was only one of many such outrages. The murder of Schwerner, Chaney and Goodman, three young civil rights workers involved in the Mississippi Summer voter registration campaign. Murdered at night along a country road by a mob of Mississippi townsmen led by their local sheriff, beaten to death while chained to a tree. Few of the perpetrators of these crimes were ever arrested and if arrested usually were not convicted.

An unending stream of civil rights workers were murdered in the South during those campaigns. They included blacks and whites, priests, housewives, students, men, women and children. Mrs. Viola Liuzzo, come down from Michigan to participate in a voter registration march in Selma, was murdered on a main highway by a gang of segregationists. Throughout all of this the FBI not only did nothing to halt the vigilante violence but instead mounted a campaign of intimidation against the civil rights workers.

The most bitter and most sustained confrontation of the civil rights movement arose as late as the spring of 1965. Selma, Alabama police chief "Bull" Connor used dogs, fire hoses and teargas, and unleashed mounted State Police troopers armed with clubs and cattle prods to club down non-violent black marchers demanding nothing more than the right to be registered as voters.

It's impossible to recapture the extraordinary heroism but also the bottomless viciousness of America of the time. Don't read a revised history of the period; read some of the better newspaper reports from that time. I don't know if they will today convey the anger which so many of us felt at a regime which allowed official vigilantism to go on unchecked, year after year, outrage after outrage.

History makes many detours. By the time opposition to the war in Vietnam had emerged the alliance between the white and black supporters in the civil rights movement was being shattered by the urban ghetto riots which began in Los Angeles during the summer of 1964. They were outbursts of blind anger directed more at the panoply of economic disenfranchisement than at any specific civil rights abuses. They demonstrated a frightening degree of pent-up anti-white hostility.

The Kerner Commission, set up by President Lyndon Johnson to provide some sort of "investigation" of the phenomenon, later tabulated almost two hundred "urban disturbances" between 1964 and 1967 which involved mobilizing the National Guard. "Uprising" is not too strong a word to use for a dozen or so of the most serious confrontations. The scale of some of these risings may be difficult to comprehend today. They developed from scattered street clashes with police, escalated to battles with paramilitary police units and led ultimately, over the course of a week, to the introduction of up to twenty thousand National Guard troops in a given city. The forces of law and order used sniper teams, armoured personnel carriers, jeep-mounted machine guns and armed helicopters. At least in one city, Detroit, the National Guard even deployed a battery of artillery.

Hundreds of thousands of rounds of ammunition were fired by the army and police in some of these "urban disturbances". Casualty lists of twenty to thirty "Black rioters" were published during each major confrontation but what the real toll was anyone's guess. Black neighbourhoods involved in the riots were ravaged by fire and shot. A black tenement district in Newark, New Jersey, where I briefly worked a year after the riots, looked like a bombed city. It was almost as if Jack London's *The Iron Heel* were being tried on for size.

A few years later when I was again driving cab in Vancouver, an Alberta government economist hired me to take him out to Chilliwack where he had a private land deal to conclude. It's a long ride and we got to talking. Mainly to annoy him, I said, "Those Solidarność guys are lucky they aren't trying that in America or they would really know what repression means," "What do you mean by that?" he demanded. Although this guy had gone to university at the very time the American ghetto risings were going on he thought I was making it up out of whole cloth. For him, as for many others, these massive confrontations had just not happened. I don't know how one deals with such self-administered amnesia.

Correlative with the ghetto risings was the upsurge of "Black power" and "Black pride" ideology. It became a vehicle of the black ethnic bourgeoisie and while some militants referred to this trend as "porkchop nationalism", it came to dominate the rhetoric of the movement. Those whites who supported the civil rights movement but were unwilling to abase themselves, those who refused to carry the can for "White exploiters", parted company with this new direction. By 1966 there were two disparate streams of protest in America whose membership only partly overlapped — the black revolt and the anti-war movement. Relatively few blacks mustered in the anti-war actions and progressively fewer whites took part, or were even welcome, in the black struggles. That is an oversimplification but it is basically true.

Another event which had shaken America at the end of the 1950s was the triumph of the Cuban revolution. The fact that a small Latin American country could stand up to the USA offended many Americans' faith in their country's omnipotence. We now know that those minding the store during the final years of the Eisenhower administration had launched a campaign to overthrow the Castro government less than a year after it came to power in 1959. We now know of the attempts to assassinate Cuban leaders, of the CIA-supported *contras* in Cuba who murdered "enemies" like the fifteen-year-old literacy *brigadista* Conrado Benitez, of the sabotage campaign involving sending letter bombs into Cuba. We now know all that from the files of the Central Intelligence Agency opened in Senate investigations after the fall of the Nixon administration. However, at the time that this state terrorism was being carried out anyone who charged US agencies with doing what they demonstrably were doing was dismissed as a left-wing paranoiac.

The campaign against socialist Cuba culminated in the Bay of Pigs invasion in the spring of 1961. Overlooked in the stream of events following the defeat of the invasion was the admission by the senior editor of the *New York Times* that he had knowingly run completely fraudulent reports of the course of the invasion written by CIA hirelings before the assault began. It was one of those times when "the interest of our country had to supersede simple truth," said the *Times* editor. That went in spades for the rest of the news media in America.

The Cuban missile crisis of October 1962 may seem like just another Cold War squabble but it brought the world to the brink of nuclear war. It sent a shock wave through the saner elements of the American population. Many Americans began to back away from appeals to nuclear brinkmanship. There were still proponents of "nuke 'em back to the stone age" but the Cuban missile crisis brought home to many Americans the reality that their cities, their families, their lives might be wiped out in a nuclear war. Some began to reconsider just where the previous decade and a half of Cold War had taken them.

The Lamasary on Morningside Heights

I had been saving New York in my inspection of places to live. While I was pleased about my acceptance into the doctoral program at Columbia University I would have gone to any university in the city. It was New York itself which attracted me.

Columbia University is primarily a graduate school drawing its students from throughout America and the world. The campus is located on Morningside Heights in the Upper West Side of Manhattan. It is jammed into two city blocks, three if you count the affiliated schools, between Amsterdam Avenue and Broadway. Clustered around a small plaza are blocks of late nineteenth century classroom buildings and residences. The first impression I had of it, coming up by cab from Grand Central Station on a rainy fall day, was of the Dalai Lama's palace in Lasha. But it turned out alright.

I don't intend to write about graduate students and university life at Columbia in the 1960s. There's enough of that sort of thing around and I don't think I could say anything novel about that scene. The place had its share of sycophants and opportunists and those who despite transparent mediocrity were convinced of their own mental wizardry. But Columbia was a great university with a core of true scholars who pursued the thrust of their investigations to wherever (within limits) it took them, even to taboo conclusions. That is rarer in universities than you may think.

It may seem that my years in New York revolved around exploring the city, friendships, protest demonstrations, and anything but study. But I invested quite enough time in classes and in the stacks of Butler Library. Columbia University was notorious for the way it dragged out its doctoral program with endless exams and ancillary requirements; some two thirds of those who entered the doctoral program failed or dropped out along the way. There were course requirements in all four fields of anthropology — archaeology, linguistics, physical and social anthropology. There were always papers to write and endless exams: comprehensive exams, language exams, orals, defense of doctoral research and dissertation defense. Prying a doctorate out of Columbia was not a matter of clipping coupons.

On top of that was work as a teaching assistant during the winter as well as teaching at suburban colleges during summer. In addition, I wrote and published my first articles and a monograph while a student at Columbia.

The long and short of it was that Columbia proved to be more fulfilling than any other university I've ever been at. The intellectual milieu of the department was one of unparalleled openness in the contribution of ideas. Marvin Harris, Pete Vayda, Morton Fried and a number of other professors, along with a group of senior graduate students, were engaged in a quasi-collegial reformulation of anthropology along materialist lines. Many of us were not typical graduate students in that we already had fairly extensive anthropological training and some practical field experience behind us. We were rather bumptious at times but it was an intellectually exciting undertaking to be part of.

Part of the endeavor revolved around de-romanticizing anthropology and providing materialist analyses in place of the exoticism so prevalent in the field. This did not merely involve philosophizing but entailed a great deal of painstaking research into previously accepted shibboleths. It involved analyses which made the cultural features of tribal and peasant societies less exotic but more generally understandable.

Marvin Harris, then a young and frenetically productive professor, was engaged in a fundamental reconsideration of many misconceptions in anthropology. It was a tremendous apprenticeship to work with him. Marvin tackled topics ranging from the religious cargo systems in Mexican Indian communities to the sacred cattle of India but recast them in materialist form. A detailed consideration of the ecological underpinnings and material consequences of often well known cultural phenomena frequently placed them in a totally different light. It pointed up a host of causal relationships which had been totally overlooked in more traditional accounts. Harris had a gift for getting to the core of a topic and of showing how re-evaluations were not mere nitpicking but challenged the cultural relativist obscurantism which had so badly distorted anthropology and, more importantly, which misinformed Euro-American views of the non-industrial world in general. There were some blind alleys and excessive claims made, certainly. But the studies we were engaged in were long overdue and for the next decade this broadly ecological approach had a considerable impact on anthropology.

As one of the established old-line universities Columbia had weathered the Cold War purges better than some other institutions. It was in public colleges such as Brooklyn College and City College that McCarthyism had taken root. The City University of New York system had become a boot camp for Cold War indoctrination. The president of Brooklyn College was a notorious witch hunter who personally saw to it that even part-time faculty signed the loyalty oath. I was almost fired from a summer job there for refusing to sign. I told him that as a Canadian it would be "treason" for me to sign "a pledge of allegiance to a foreign power" — meaning the US. That nonplussed him and he allowed me to complete the term. But the college never hired me again either.

Columbia University had circumvented the worst of that although there were some sinister elements around Columbia as well. For instance, the gang connected with a brownstone building on a side street which housed the Institute of Communist Affairs, presided over by Pan Zbigniew Brezinski. Often you didn't know who or what was behind a scholarly agenda. But all major American universities have sinister elements. So do most Canadian ones.

Today, with the seemingly all-pervasive swing to the right, Columbia University may have changed. But I was proud to be a part of that audacious intellectual milieu of Columbia in the 1960s.

Notes From the Upper West Side

The Upper West Side of Manhattan, loosely defined, is the area which extends from just south of Columbia University to Columbus Circle and from Riverside Drive to Central Park. It was a collection of disparate neighbourhoods containing everything from the haunts of monied professionals to residence hotels along upper Broadway which had turned into rookeries of crazies who might drop a bottle on you from a tenth floor window just for laughs. Within the confines of the Upper West Side were old Irish working-class enclaves giving way to Puerto Rican *barrios*, islands of luxury co-op apartments, neighbourhoods which still were Jewish silk stocking districts and sections which were plainly *in extremis*. There were tiny bodegas making four-dollar sales of bread, rice and sardines on credit to established customers and stores like Zabar's delicatessen, where a chauffeured Rolls-Royce might be parked outside while a clerk politely assured the customer that their Scottish smoked salmon, at eighteen dollars a pound, was excellent.

Riverside Drive curves along the western spine of Manhattan island and was a "good address", as New Yorkers put it. At least it had been. There were moldering mansions from the 1870s, brownstones and swanky 1920s highrise apartment blocks jostling along its three miles. About a week after my arrival in the city I managed to get a place which New Yorkers were on the constant lookout for, a room with a view. It was in a four-storey stone mansion built some time before electric light had become all the rage. It had been divided into apartments and rooms long since. The building was on the corner of Riverside and 106th Street and my room ran along the front of the building, a twenty-by-twenty-foot self-contained housekeeping room with six windows overlooking the Hudson River. The rent was $85 a month. "That sounds reasonable," I said.

The Hudson is a mile wide at its mouth. The Palisades rise from the New Jersey shore, rock cliffs with a narrow band of waterfront industry below them. I could look up river and down for seven or eight miles and watch tugs, tour boats, and the ever-changing face of the river. Riverside Park slopes down towards the Hudson and is spattered with groves of trees, ornate walkways and monuments to late-nineteenth-century beautification schemes and sentiments — such as a marble plinth dedicated to "the firemen of New York and their brave horses". Immediately below my windows was a wide, park-benched boulevard. On sunny days, children overseen by watchful mothers played in sandboxes while strollers decked out in an array of fashions trundled along.

My fellow tenants were a mixed lot, ranging from embattled defenders of frayed white-collar respectability to others not far removed from the booby hatch. It took me some time to realize that theirs was well within the range of normal behaviour in the city. But most of them had learned to mind their own business and let you mind yours. My next door neighbour was a well-educated Haitian working as a chauffeur for his country's UN delegation and hating it. There was an aspirant painter given to temper tantrums below me, a middle-aged black woman on the ground floor engaged in singing off-key opera and watching for burglars, and a pod of *luftmenschen* pursuing whatever it was they pursued.

After I got my sea legs I managed to live better in Manhattan on three or four thousand dollars a year than I ever had before. The trouble was that my income from part-time teaching jobs and scholarships fluctuated and was never assured. There were times when I didn't know where the next month's rent was coming from and a few times when I had to hock my radio to get eating money. It was actually a genteel sort of poverty but at the time it seemed quite luxurious.

New York was littered with ridiculously overpriced restaurants but one could also find cafes serving great meals for very little. One of my favourite eateries was a tiny Puerto Rican place on Amsterdam Avenue, across from where I later lived. They only had four or five main dishes but they were the kinds of meals one could eat regularly. You'd get a plateful of saffron rice with a choice of one of their bean toppings, along with a large portion of delicately flavoured meat stew and a half loaf of French bread. I might eat it there and listen to neighbourhood banter or pack it home in cartons to make two meals of it. The price — about a buck and a half.

Man doth not live by Red Hots, seltzer and pizza slices alone — though some New Yorkers seemed determined to prove that you could. Possibly it is too mundane to exemplify the near endless variety which existed in New York by the narrow span of the stomach.

Twice a week I'd wander down to the Thalia Theatre. Want to see a rerun of *The Grapes of Wrath*? Interested in a film by Pudovkin or Dovschenko or examples of 1930s Mexican cinema? Just check your Thalia program guide and sooner or later they were bound to turn up. People young and old, film buffs out of a Jules Feiffer cartoon, people of all shapes and sizes and backgrounds mixed together in the audiences.

I hate to sound like a booster but New York has museums great and obscure, libraries and concerts abound. All sorts of people went to them. I once attended a performance of Othello mounted by the Shakespeare in the Park repertory group in a temporarily converted basketball court on Amsterdam Avenue. Sitting around me were mainly residents of this mainly Puerto Rican barrio, some sneaking swigs of wine, others engrossed in James Earl Jones's histrionics. "How can a country which facilitates something like this also demonstrate such appalling barbarity in other areas ?" I asked myself.

Then there was WBAI, a listener-sponsored radio station which operated with a volunteer staff and on a quarter-million-dollar annual budget drawn from its subscribers. It was an eye opener to what radio could be and just how abysmally vapid the commercial mass media in North America, even public broadcasting, is by comparison. Of course WBAI had its quota of drivel and Ginsbergian hipsters too. But this one-horse station put out more informative and exciting programs than all the commercial radio and television networks combined. I mean that quite literally.

Maybe it had something to do with the pool of talent they could draw from. Possibly it was because whole realms of thought never got aired on the major networks. But it was also due to WBAI's audacity and their determination not to talk down to their audience.

The first program which caught my attention as I twiddled the dials of my shiny new Zenith Transworld radio, sitting in a place of honour in my Riverside room, was a serialized reading of a history thesis done at Columbia University. The author had dug into events which had swirled around him as a kid in Manhattan. It centred on the wave of rent strikes and tenant organization which had occurred in tenement districts of New York during the 1920s. "Is this supposed to be a joke, reading an old MA thesis to an American radio audience?"

It was superb. What a great introduction to the city. Streets and districts, squares and buildings, names of places you could still identify and visit cropped up in the reading. The author alloyed scholarship with passion and an ability to write. The account wove together the times and the background of that struggle, it chronicled the events and sometimes resurrected the lives and voices of those engaged, forty years previously, people who had inhabited areas of New York I walked through.

There was a series of readings from Langston Hughes's poetry and a thrice weekly book hour which resurrected works such as Leo Grassic Gibbon's working class trilogy *A Scot's Quair*, read in a lowland Scotch dialect. At one point Eric Bentley had a series presenting the plays, poetry and music of Bertholt Brecht and Kurt Weill. Where no recording of a Brecht piece was available Bentley would haul out a wheezy harmonium and in a gravelly, atonal, voice would croak out Brecht's songs. Just perfect.

There was some exceptionally fine news reporting and analysis on WBAI. One finally got to know what "reporting in depth" could mean. They kept at a topic and followed through its ramifications until you had some idea of what all was involved. Not only did they cover topics usually passed over by the news media but they ferreted out expertise which really did have something intelligent to add.

That was what later got the station into hot water. At the start of the Reagan era they had some close brushes with the Federal Communications Commission which threatened to cancel WBAI's broadcast license for allegedly engaging in "political advocacy". The multi-billion-dollar corporate networks and the right-wing preachers spouting off on television stations across the country were not political advocates of course.

But best of all was New York itself. I'd take a subway somewhere, get off and walk around, sticking my nose into whatever was of interest. That was time well spent. A part of me begrudged those hours spent wandering through the back corners and out-of-the-way places of the city, telling me I should be studying. I'm glad that I resisted that voice of dedication and took myself for walks. Those who entombed themselves in the stacks of Butler Library and swotted over anthropological tomes didn't seem noticeably the wiser for it.

When I first arrived in New York in the fall of 1962 I'd worked for a dozen years, had been around the world some, had done anthropological field work and had never suffered an attack of the Dreaded Lurgi — culture schlock. But the city threw me for a loop. I was taken aback by the surliness and aggressiveness of New Yorkers. I still don't know why that had such an effect on me because I later came to thrive on the pace. What depressed me, I now think, had little to do with New York itself but was rather the feeling that I once again had to establish friends and connections from scratch. Strangely enough, it turned out that New York was the easiest place to make friends I ever lived in.

Biograph: Siskind and the Sullivanians

Janet was a native Manhattanite and a fellow student at Columbia. She was administering the registration procedure in the anthropology department when I arrived and knots of students were standing around in corridors waiting for faculty advisors to give approval for their course selections. I figured that I could make a better choice of the courses than any faculty member who didn't know me or my work. After listening to the discussions for a while I signed my registration cards with my own illegible signature. "You can't do that. You have to have a faculty member check it and sign," said Janet.

"Don't worry. Who is going to check signatures in a Registrar's Office anyway?" And of course no one ever did.

You would think that there would have been a leaven of Bohemianism among anthropology students in New York during the 1960s, but they were a terribly career-oriented bunch. Siskind stood out immediately in a crowd of graduate students for her easygoing quizzical humour. It was only university regulations she took too seriously. There was an unspoken attraction between the two of us almost immediately but for the first two years we were merely fellow students.

Janet was in her late thirties when I knew her, with a twelve-year-old daughter and a younger son. She didn't look it. Martinis, cigarettes and the occasional game of tennis were the secret. She had a piggy bank to safeguard the funds allocated to the weekly supply of gin and vermouth, because next to therapy two double martinis in the evening were the sine qua non of a bearable existence. Janet had been married just long enough to realize that life as an exurban middle-class housewife was not what she wanted.

Janet lived in a state of genteel impecuniousness. It was a marginal kind of rentiership which was fairly common in New York, the last remnants of a family trust fund supplementing child support payments and wages from part-time jobs. For instance, she hadn't bought any new clothes in years, lived in a shabby rent-controlled apartment near 98th and Broadway, and was normally broke before the end of each month. But she made sure that her kids were sent to summer camp every year. A less attractive aspect of that lifestyle was that Janet hired a woman to do housework and cook (albeit hamburger and macaroni dinners) while she worked and took classes.

Any extended stay in Manhattan inevitably leads to some passing acquaintance with psychoanalysis and its communicants. It was an endemic ideology and a major local industry, one riven by assorted sects and followings. An incredible number of people I knew had been involved in psychotherapy at one time or another.

Janet had been undergoing therapy with the chieftain of the Harry Stack Sullivan Training Institute for some seven years. Sullivan was an American MD who attempted to put psychotherapy on some sort of realistic, non-Freudian basis. Like everyone else involved in psychoanalysis Janet claimed that only it had allowed her to "find herself" and break free from her earlier life. I had heard variations on that theme so often that I had learned to shut up. You might argue with individuals themselves but you could never criticize their therapists or therapy since that was their hope for salvation. Whatever the reason, Janet was more free-spirited than most of the twenty-three-year-old cuties around campus, and also a lot easier to be with.

Our backgrounds weren't in the least similar but we got along well. God knows what the mutual attraction was based on. If it hadn't been for her kids we might have lived together, although that sort of attachment was against the main principles of her psychiatric set. Most of the communicants of the Sullivanian school had either broken up with their former spouses or had determined never to be married. Apart from their children they were dead set against family or other exclusive personal ties.

The core of this group was composed of some thirty or forty therapists, clinical trainees and veteran patients. Others from outside this circle gradually joined it or floated in and out of a relationships with members of the group. Exclusive love affairs were frowned upon as regressive and rather anti-social. A main principle was that one should never put all one's emotional attachments in one basket. They shared each other's friends and lovers in a way which normally I would say was impossible. But these arrangements did provide an emotional support for members of the group which was missing from the lives of many New Yorkers. It was a defence against isolation in an alienated society and it seemed to work quite well for those involved in the whole *schmeer*.

They all went to the same therapists, they were constantly at each other's parties and they sometimes looked after each others kids. They summered together in Amagansett near the eastern tip of Long Island, sharing outrageously overpriced summer cabins and trekking out on weekends to be with their crowd. The sect's central doctrine was that each person's career should take priority in whatever decisions she or he made. The Sullivanians held that careers must not be sacrificed or undercut by any personal commitments, that one's job and income were the most stable and important basis of self worth. It was a rather novel view among therapists at the time. But whatever else they did or didn't do they never lent each other money and they always paid their therapist's bills. Those were basic principles too.

The guiding light of this group was a Doctor Saul, whose surname I've forgotten. He was then in his mid fifties, originally from Toronto, a man who had emigrated to the United States in the 1930s and who had fought in the Lincoln Battalion in Spain. Not only did he not apologize for that during the McCarthy era, he'd even defended his actions. Saul had made the shift from left politics to "radical" therapy while studying under Harry Stack Sullivan. When Sullivan retired Saul headed up the clinical training institute which dispensed the pure stuff. All the therapists of this group had come out of that institute. Recruitment, training, patients, friends and lovers — all in one pond. It seemed to work as well as any other procedure.

What put me off most members of this circle was their know-nothingism. Politically and historically they were ignoramuses weaned on the pap of American imperial liberalism. Even Saul spoke of the Second World War as the "second war for democracy". The war in Vietnam and everything else since Roosevelt was somehow an "aberration" of what America really stood for.

Although they were intelligent enough people they were strangely provincial and seemed to think that anything much different from their own lives in New York wasn't quite real. At one of their summer parties out in Amaganssett an elderly woman psychoanalyst overheard me say that I had grown up in the camps in British Columbia. "Camps" meant one of only two things to her — concentration camps or children's summer camps. I'm explaining a little about what logging and mining camps were like to someone else when I notice that this lady analyst is taking it in as if it were a fantasy.

"Come now. You should hear yourself. 'That there were no children where you grew up.' It seemed that way to you as a child. But you are a man now and know that is not possible. There are no places, not the smallest village, where men and women live where there are no children. You must examine that illusion you still carry with you," she said. I just looked at her with incredulous amazement but I suppose that life in the work camps was difficult for New Yorkers to visualize.

Another time I got into an interesting debate with Saul over current misconceptions about fascism, only to have a gaggle of his adherents converge to change the subject. Hear no evil, speak no evil. "Just how realistic can all this therapy be if they understand so little of the world they are living in?" I groused. To be fair, a number of them did participate in some of the more respectable civil rights and anti-war marches. But it seemed a sad retrogression for a man who at one time must have had broader views. That's America. It's able to ingest and co-opt almost everyone and everything over time.

Janet and I gradually drifted apart and she later became what she had been striving to become for so long, a professional anthropologist. By all accounts she was good teacher too. Her fieldwork among a hunting group in the Peruvian Montana turned out to be an unusually human account which emerged in book form as *To Hunt in the Morning*.

On Spring and Greenwich

Have you ever seen the movie *On the Waterfront*? It's set around the New Jersey docks but it looked a lot like where I later lived in the Lower West Side of Manhattan. It had once been a pre-tenement working-class district but most of the buildings had long since been converted to ramshackle warehouses. The enclave was basically a dockyard zone and not a residential area. It was totally different from the Upper West Side. In retrospect I'm not sure why I moved down there.

My place was about a hundred and fifty yards from the Hudson River and its docks and a block from the western end of Canal Street.

It was on the edge of Little Italy, below Greenwich Village and on the edge of what later became the chic Soho district, then a melange of old loft buildings, some of which housed artists and sculptors support- ing themselves by driving hack and other odd jobs. At the time it was a rundown backwater of the city, one known to few New Yorkers let alone tourists. You're right — with an introduction like that I've got to have liked it.

I lived on the corner of Spring Street and Greenwich Avenue in a crumbling brick structure containing three apartments. Throughout the day and night longshoremen, warehousemen, truck drivers and others circulated along the street, moseyed in and out of the bar-bean- eries and coalesced under my windows to hash over events. The apartment had a half dozen narrow windows stretching from floor to ceiling: they let in a lot of light but at times it almost seemed that the streetcorner debates going on below had moved into my front room. The area operated full-tilt twenty-four hours a day.

Within a one and a half block radius of my place were some nine bars and three cafes. At night they were oases of light amid poorly lit streets. All the bars served food and most of them were open around the clock. They were always filled with guys coming on or going off shift. If one took care not to get into arguments the area was prob- ably one of the safest in New York. I had no hesitation in wandering around those streets day or night. It was no place for a mugger — there were always tougher types around.

There were loan sharks, crimps and the foot soldiers of criminal organizations. There were corporals of the International Longshore Association and the Teamsters, the agents of the gangster-run com- pany "unions", floating around among these working stiffs. The bar patrons railed about their pet peeves, usually in some reactionary vein or other. They were all two hundred percent Americans even when it was apparent that their parents still spoke the language of some "old country". Draft resisters and demonstrators "should be jailed or shot". "The niggers on welfare were dragging the city down." Repression was their proffered solution to most problems, real and imagined. Jeez!

It wasn't the kind of working class I'd ever known. Of course, this was a very skewed selection of working people in the city. The New York waterfront had been a recurrent battleground between real unions and gangster-run labour organizations. The thugs had won out and over the years those with a more progressive outlook had probably learned to keep their ideas to themselves. Who knows what some longshoremen down there knew or were thinking. I even met a guy there who remembered working on Terminal Dock, part of my playground as a child in Vancouver.

On Sundays the area shut down and became deserted. During weekdays I didn't visit the waterfront much because I was attending classes. But on a summer weekend the abandoned docks were a pleasant place to take the sun. There were two crumbling docks within three blocks of my place. Compared to the beach at Coney Island or the Far Rockaways they were a haven of tranquility on a hot summer day.

People would wander over from the nearby tenement districts. They might bring along a folding chair, the *New York Times* or the *Daily Newsless*, a few bottles of beer and possibly a fishing rod — though I doubt that anyone would have been rash enough to eat any fish taken from the Hudson. You could look across the river to Weehauken and Hoboken on the Joisey shore or watch old harbour tugs come burbling along. The inevitable sellers of red hots would come by on their three-wheeled bicycles, as well as peddlers of Eskimo (not Inuit) pies and maybe a street vendor of Italian ices with his block of ice, shaver and bottles of flavors on a hand cart. And people would actually talk to each other.

I was an enthusiastic walker at the time. A fifty-block hike around the city was nothing. What I mean to say was that it usually was quite something. In Manhattan the character of districts can change drastically within a few blocks. There were still some archetypal ethnic neighbourhoods such as Little Italy, but the seeming homogeneity of such areas was often more apparent than real. There were people who lived in what might be called "urban villages" but that was more a state of mind than a matter of physical locales. God knows there were enough Archie Bunkers about, but there was also an impersonal, tolerant indifference which allowed some Americans to breathe free for the first time in their lives.

I would wander up to Sheridan Square to get a *Times*. The Greenwich Village of 1920s literary fame lies all around there but had become either a tawdry tourist trap or a kip for professionals with a taste for a modulated bohemianism. Maybe I'd mosey over to Washington Square and detour back by way of McSorley's on the other side of Houston. On a longer ramble I might walk east to the Cooper Union auditorium and on to Second Avenue, where something of the earlier Lower East Side immigrant life still held sway. Down Delancy and possibly over to the East River by the Williamsburgh bridge. It's probably all gone now — gentrified or converted into office towers.

It was during that time that I joined a karate group which trained at the Hudson Settlement House. Some people had approached a friend of mine to train them in self defense. Frank was a sculptor who lived just off Canal, sustaining himself with a variety of jobs, who had a black belt in karate. There were about twenty to twenty-five of us, men and women, all somehow involved in "de left". Our concern was not so much personal self defense as the desire to be able to help protect demonstrations from attack.

It might have been a good idea if it weren't for the fact that most of our bunch were quite unsuited for getting into fights, regardless of how motivated they were. They didn't have the build for it and most of them probably had never been in a real knock-down fight in their lives. There was a disproportionate number of young women. True enough, the one real natural at karate who emerged in our group was a young woman. But having a combative spirit and a big mouth doesn't count for a hell of a lot when the fat is in the fire.

We met twice a week for two-hour sessions and worked out at home for at least a half hour each day. That's what it actually amounted to mainly: purposeful exercises. They put you in top shape. Kicks, double punches, push-ups on your knuckles, endless knee bends. The trouble was that it tended to make you overconfident. I wondered if that ever got anyone into trouble which he or she might otherwise have avoided.

After every class a number of individuals would announce the assorted vigils, petitions, sit-ins and similar impending events in the city. It must have been one of the only karate classes where you ended with a calendar of the coming week's protest demonstrations. Our group was composed of a wide variety of New Leftists, ex-Party lefties and undefinable others, none of them crazies. Usually this was a mixture which one couldn't have in a room for ten minutes without fulminations and political quarrels of earth shaking significance breaking out. But not here, strangely enough. Everyone knew not to debate any issue if we wanted to keep meeting together.

Some of us poked fun at individuals who had five separate locks on their apartment doors and were constantly concerned about security. In the more than five years I lived in Manhattan and wandered around almost everywhere, day or night, I was never mugged, robbed or even threatened. Christ knows there were enough loonies, junkies and petty thugs about. But things apparently got a lot worse over the years. I later heard that even Frank acquired a pistol which he kept loaded in his apartment for the protection of his family should anyone try to break in.

Biograph: *Vivian and Her Family*

Vivian had been a red diaper baby. One of her childhood memories was of being dragooned by her parents to hand out flyers for the Henry Wallace Progressive Party campaign on Brooklyn street corners. She'd grown up as part of the Jewish Communist left in New York during the McCarthy era. Where to begin?

New Yorkers have a thing about sending their kids to summer camp. Vivian had gone to one called Wòchika (Workers Children's Camp) and despite some contradictory feelings about it, it was her Eton. In a disorganized way she still kept up friendships initially made at Wochika a decade and more earlier. It sounded like any other children's summer camp according to Vivian's reminiscences: artless crafts and talentless talent shows, nature walks, spurious Indian lore, home sickness and the much-touted "fresh air and sun". But there was a theme of left-wing philosophy running through these doings at Wochika. Vivian, as I resurrect her account from the dusty storeroom of my memory, tells it this way:

"We learned things which were held to be progressive at the time. Like, on our nature walks the counselor would tell us how the Pilgrim Fathers only survived in America because of the help of the Indians, who showed these settlers how to plant corn by burying cod fish as fertilizer with the seed. We were so impressed by that that nobody thought to ask how it was they'd got so much fish to spare that they could go around using it for fertilizer.

"Or in crafts we might hear about the Negro — and it was definitely 'Negro' then because racists used the word 'Black' — how this Negro mechanic working for Henry Ford was the one really responsible for devising the assembly line system. I suppose you could say that those sorts of stories were allegories. They were at least as true as the stories you were told in school.

"We'd learn about the great working class struggles, like the early

Vivian Moser and the author, New York, 1964.

labour movement in America or an aspect of the Russian revolution and maybe the part that some Jewish heroine or hero had played in it. But it was made clear that these were class struggles and not specifically Jewish, because whatever the failings of the party, ethnic chauvinism was not one of them. We got enough Jewish background from our own families but we were, yes we knew, by the time we were ten and eleven and twelve years old, that we were internationalists. After all, if you don't feel that by that age when will you know it?

"Singing is something we did a lot of. There was one round, where everyone joins in at different points, that was really beautiful. Even when we sang it. It went like this,

> Sing me not of other towns
> Of towns that twinkle and shine.
> Excuse me, but there's no village like mine.
> Dressed up in her browns and pinks
> She's milk, she's honey, she's wine.
> Excuse me, but there's no village like mine.

"Another song was almost our anthem at Wochika and begins with,

> I'll sing you one oh, high fly the banners oh.
> What is you one oh?

One for workers' unity which evermore shall reign oh.

Vivian would be wistful at this point.

"We'd also do folk dances, traditional ones that the counselors knew or had thought up the week before. Then there was the general hell-raising like in any summer camp, which was the most fun of all. Raiding the neighbouring dormitory or doing whatever it was we were told not to do.

"There were a few other progressive summer camps around then. Camp Kinderland is still in existence but that was where middle class progressives sent their kids. They had horses to ride and paid big fees and were quite luxurious. We had just what we could devise amongst ourselves. We knew that we were better than them, because we were all from working class families.

"Wochika was very select. Children of labour organizers, children of party people who were threatened with jail, kids whose parents had suffered some outrage in the South — they were the kind who'd be at Wochika with us. We were pretty smug about it. But then, it was something to be proud of.

"All that I'm sorry for is the way we treated some kids from totally different backgrounds who somehow got in amongst us. We made fun of them and bossed them around and were pretty rotten to them so that usually they'd want to go home by the end of the first week. And I was one of the worst doing that. All I can say, why I was so mean, is that we were getting this treatment ourselves in school. So were our parents. And this was the only chance we had to gang up on somebody else. But I'm sorry we acted that way."

Vivian is going to hand the reminiscence back to me now, so it won't be the way she would tell it. Wochika was closed down sometime in the early fifties not long after a mob of Peekskill patriots attacked an outdoor concert at which Paul Robeson sang. It was right-wing vigilantism pure and simple. The police who were on the scene just stood by while the attack by club-wielding goons took place. It was only with the greatest luck that none of the audience were killed. The mainstream press held that the Communists had "brought it upon themselves by appearing in public." That too was part of the political repression generically known as McCarthyism, which reached far beyond Senate Investigating Committee hearings. It terrorized many ordinary Americans to the extent that most became too frightened to even sign a petition let alone to sing "One for workers' unity".

Vivian's mother had been born in Brooklyn and had lived there all of her life. Sunday morning brunch with the table decked out with bagels and lax, liver sausage and other delicatessen was when she was in her element. Does that sound like a stereotype? Probably. But somehow I never got a fix on her except as the family peacemaker and a not very hopeful optimist.

Dorothy's mother, Vivian's grandmother, was different. Her I remember clearly though we only met a few times, a tiny, quiet woman in her mid seventies who still spoke mainly Yiddish after being in America some fifty years. Born in the late 1880s in a city of Russian Poland she had not been part of and had never lived in a *shtetl*. That she wanted clearly understood! She and her girlhood friends were modern city people before she ever came to America — that she wanted understood too! Although from a religious family she had grown up during the epoch of the Jewish secular enlightenment which blossomed at about the time she first began work in Poland, shortly before 1905. It amazed her that girls of her granddaughter's age, here in America, were now enthused over romances of Polish *shtetl* life. To her that life had been little more than poverty, disease and superstition.

Vivian's father must have been close to sixty but he looked much younger. He had been born in a village of the western Ukraine. His mother had died when he was an infant and his father had been killed either in a pogrom or in the general butchery which swirled through the Ukraine during the Russian Civil War, I'm not sure which. Sol and his sister were saved by a Ukrainian peasant family who raised them until some distant kin could be found. I know it sounds clichéd, but that is the way reality is at times.

Sol got to Odessa and after staying with not overly receptive relatives, somehow managed to get to America just before it closed off mass immigration in the early 1920s. He landed in the Lower East Side when the district was still largely a Yiddish-speaking community of a quarter million people, and worked in produce warehouses for the next two decades. But it seemed that the 1930s were the most vital years of Sol's life. Most of his reading, understandings, phrases and outlook were consolidated in that decade. While he was a Communist of that era he was not one of those who maligned and dismissed the earlier working-class socialist traditions.

Sol contained enough contradictions. You quickly learned that he didn't hold with the Jewish chauvinism which was then emerging in New York. But he was constantly on the alert for perceived evidence of antisemitism everywhere. You had to think thrice before criticizing anyone or anything Jewish, although he did so himself all the time.

"We had'em. We went through all that like every immigrant group did. Hoodlums? We had to fight them every step of the way when we were reorganizing the garment workers that had fallen away into open shops during the thirties. You want to know exploitation? You should have seen how some of those Jewish shop owners pressed out Jewish men and women who worked for them, using Jewish gangsters when we came in to organize. We'd remember that, you'd think. These same shop owners going to Temple and being praised by the rabbi for donations they made. We had them all. Maybe you don't understand that."

That's about as close an approximation as I can get to one of his extemporaneous lectures. But it doesn't capture the stance and tone of the man speaking, as much to past comrades as to me. If I'd been older, say my present age, and had known him better, I would have said. "Come on. Give it a rest Sol." But of course I didn't.

During the 1950s Sol had been hounded by the McCarthyites. The "revelations" about Stalin's crimes were pretty shattering to him and he left the party some time after 1956. But he hadn't changed his basic ideas and wouldn't co-operate with the witch hunters. Even a decade later he felt stranded as the movement which had been a major part of his life withered away. Blacklisted and without a job, Sol and Dorothy had come to operate a small liquor store. It provided a living but was a bitterly absurd end of their earlier hopes.

During her childhood Vivian had gone to an afternoon *shul* which taught Yiddish and Jewish history from a secular humanist perspective. One ironic consequence of having gone to *shul* was that Vivian wound up teaching in an ultra-Orthodox separate school when she was desperate for a job.

Beth i Jacob was an outfit which considered the other Orthodox institutions too worldly, their kosher foods not kosher enough and the separation of the sexes not strict enough. How they ever came to hire Vivian is beyond me. Well, she had a lot of spunk and was good with young children and there weren't many people her age who could speak Yiddish fluently and teach it. The Beth i Jacob school taught in Yiddish because Hebrew was profaned by using it in everyday life. When we met Vivian would regale me with the latest inanities of and her set-tos with the Mullahs and Malamuds of the school. It came to a head and she was fired because a fellow teacher complained to the school director when he overheard Vivian teaching her charges the old Yiddish labour song "Tsreis Di Keytn des Sklaven Zwank." Or maybe it was "Shnel Loyfn di Rede."

In the five years I knew her Vivian was constantly starting and quitting night school classes while working at various jobs. During those years she was in and out of psychoanalysis, careening between "fresh starts" and fighting with her family and friends and despair. None of it was very reasonable. Yet when it came to political matters she could put aside her craziness and make some astute judgments. Although I didn't always agree with her I came to take her estimations seriously. I valued her as a close friend but she wanted something more and we gradually drifted apart.

The last time I heard from Vivian was a dozen years later as she was in the process of splitting up with her latest husband. She had had a couple of children, was ensconced on a stump ranch in northern Maine and was scratching by on supply teaching. She had just adopted two wild donkeys from Grand Canyon National Park to save them from Department of the Interior hunters. It sounded like the same old Vivian to me, although she wouldn't have wanted to hear that.

A Time to Remember

Some two months after my arriving in New York and moving into the Upper West Side, two Puerto Rican youths were arrested not far from where I lived. They had been handcuffed, frisked and placed in the wire-enclosed rear compartment of a police cruiser. Then, at the 98th street underpass, they were shot and killed by their police escorts while "trying to escape". It was not the first nor the last such killing, but given the outrages in the South a wave of anger ran through the Puerto Rican community. The funeral for the two victims was held in Spanish Harlem a couple of days later, a sunny but cold December morning in a decaying tenement district. Because of my experiences in the Southside of Chicago I had some qualms about going, but I went.

There were more than a thousand of us waiting on the street in front of the funeral parlour. After an hour the two coffins are brought out and carried down to the hearses. People are shouting, red and black flags are raised, the mother of one of the victims is sobbing, in the crush one of the coffins is almost dropped. We set off to march past the local police station. *"Asesinos Policiacos ... Fuera Asesinos"* was the call which went up. It built into a roar of real hatred which I hadn't heard in any of those Ban the Bomb marches. There were Puerto Rican socialists with their own history and traditions among that funeral crowd.

In 1962 and 1963 it was still Cuba and Latin America which held the centre stage of American foreign concerns and the Black civil rights movement which generated the most bitter confrontations at home. With some two hundred US military bases abroad, the war in Vietnam was little discussed despite the fact that there already were more than twenty thousand American "military advisors" there. It was only after the assassination of President Kennedy that massive troop commitments were made to Vietnam by President Johnson. That was when the shit hit the fan. But even in the spring of 1964 the initial anti war rallies were quite small.

The newly formed Progressive Labor Movement became active. It was amazing what these few hundred people could do. Their audacity initially gained the PLM the support of many people who felt something had to be done, even if they bridled at the dogmatism of this bunch. PLM launched into street corner orations around the fringes of the Upper West Side, in Spanish Harlem, down in the Lower East Side. A couple of speakers, a dozen supporters, maybe a few dozen people in the audience and some hecklers. They mounted the first anti-war march in the city, down Broadway to Times Square, despite being refused a police permit for a march. There were some three thousand people on that march and although miniscule compared to marches only two years later, it provided the spark of open opposition to the war.

Over the next few years underground streams which had never quite dried up began converging. People for whom some hypocrisy or atrocity had been the final straw began to speak out. Others, from whose eyes the scales had just fallen, were outraged to perceive how they had been lied to. Individuals who were virtually unknown outside their immediate circles began to emerge on the broader canvas, people like Dave Dellinger and A.J. Muste of the War Resisters League. Muste was a militant pacifist for more than forty years. Or Dorothy Day of the Catholic Worker movement, a small group of progressive Catholics standing opposed to the reactionary American church heirarchy. Or people who left no names behind them. At one anti-war march mobilizing in Central Park I stood beside a couple of elderly women and overheard them reminisce about how as girls they had rallied in almost the same locale to oppose Woodrow Wilson's drive to take America into World War I. Amazing. But then I remembered that my own mother had been part of the general strikes and mass demonstrations in Berlin during the same period to take Germany out of that war.

The reception those anti-war marches got from New Yorkers was generally supportive, despite the sputtering anger of a few. The only exception was when a demonstration edged into the financial district of the city. During some of the later marches however we encountered organized groups of uniformed Marine Corps Reserve veterans massed at points along the route and shouting threats. Talk about faces filled with hate and bloodlust. At those moments you were glad that there was a police presence.

Generally it didn't take much courage to be engaged in anti-war protests in New York. The people I really take my hat off to are those who came out, first a handful and then in larger numbers, in the small towns and suburban backlands of America. Coming out for peace and against American imperialism in such places took real courage, whether it was to give a talk at a local church or to staff a table at a shopping plaza or to stand in a silent vigil. It took more courage than our sometime physical confrontations with war patriots.

The Fifth Avenue Parade Committee was a loose confederation of the dozens of anti-war groups which emerged in the space of two years. It organized some huge marches down New York's Fifth Avenue but also became a coordinating centre for other rallies, educationals, petition drives, sit-ins, draft resistance and lobbying efforts. An organization of Cold War liberals called SANE, the National Committee for a Sane Nuclear Policy, attempted to strong-arm the parade committee to oust groups and individuals whom the Sanitizers held to be "communist influenced". That had always been a surefire ploy in the previous decade. But instead SANE was rejected out of hand. It issued dire threats, stalked out of the Committee and soon lost whatever influence it had had. That was how rapidly things were changing.

The anti-war march of the 1965 Easter-Passover season drew some twenty thousand people, and the next fall some fifty thousand turned out. The New York establishment's editorialists pontificated about the peace movement having "shot its bolt" and "passed its peak". Next spring somewhere near one hundred thousand marchers were out demanding the end of the war in Vietnam: grandmothers and fathers, young mothers pushing strollers, people of all ages, sizes, colours and backgrounds. University students did play the central role in the anti war movement, in its mobilization and organization, in facing arrests and in keeping the pressure on. That was why it seemed, despite all previous experience, that university students were becoming a progressive force.

Chants of "Stop the war. Bring the Troops Home" rose from a forest of moving placards and banners. Hired sages, with the sinking feeling that they were no longer in control of shaping public opinion, snarled "What do crowds of naive marchers hope to accomplish with demonstrations? No government will give in to the undemocratic pressure tactics of protests in the street." But the movement grew and grew and a deepening anger against American imperialism began to show itself, and not just among the fringe of lefties. Chants which had originally scandalized the majority now began to reflect the tenor of broadly held sentiments.

Hey, hey, LBJ
How many kids did you kill today?

Thousands of people chanting that with a real rasp of hatred. Well, why not? The evening news was replete with the body count of "Viet Cong" (and therefore not men, women and children) killed that day or week or month by the US armed forces and its allies. According to Great Intellects like Irving Howe all this anti-war protest indicated a "terrible disease of self hatred" among American youth. But we didn't hate ourselves, we hated them — the technicians and apologists of mass murder.

It wasn't just one or a dozen anti-war marches on set days of the year. There was a constant swirl of activity which began to take on the quality of a culture of resistance with hundreds and thousands of foci as people harnessed their talents and passions to anti-war activities. *Fire* was the title of a wordless mime play staged by the Bread and Puppets Theater, a street theatre group which broke loaves of dark rye bread with their audience and operated out of a stripped-down apartment in an old tenement in the Lower East Side. They could only seat forty or so people at a time yet thousands saw their performance in the course of two years.

Cloaked in larger-than-life-sized *papier-maché* puppets, they wordlessly recreated the history of a single Vietnamese peasant family from old grandfather to new born infant, their daily life and hopes and travails, until caught up in and burned to death in a napalm raid. The figures wove tongues of fire created by dyed cloth streamers and moaning cries around themselves as we sat in that dark, crumbling tenement. Jeez!

Maybe those sorts of things can't be extracted from their times. But even the professional critics who normally derided performances like *Fire* kept their traps shut.

Fire was only one local item of a cultural revolt which surged forth over the course of a few years. I wish I'd kept a record of some of it. The Free University blossomed forth in a loft building on 14th Street and mounted some twenty or thirty courses ranging from "Fundamentals of Marxism" to "The History of American Labor in Art" each semester. It was always on the verge of bankruptcy but attracted a surfeit of aspirant cadres ready to tangle verbally with anyone at the drop of an incorrect phrase.

Literally hundreds of oppositional journals and weekly newspapers arose over the course of the decade. Anything from the *Berkeley Barb* to *Viet Nam Report* and *Desafio Challenge*, containing work which ranged from silly to sagacious. They covered the ferment which extended beyond opposition to the Vietnam war *per se*. Individuals and circles emerged to contend with what had long been passed off as history, to provide exposés of the workings of the secret government at home and abroad, to tender proposals for more fulfilling and liberated relations between human beings. If some of this was juvenile it was rarely as vicious as the prevailing orthodoxies.

The official keepers of the Marxist flame in America were just as nonplussed by all this as anyone else and sniffed their suspicions about "petit-bourgeois affectations". While there was something naive about the whole counterculture movement it also had a vivacity like nothing in the preceding generation. For a Canadian it was wonderful to see.

If much of this was evanescent and if its participants often didn't quite believe what they themselves were saying, they were not short on audacity. Maybe it was an audacity which sprang from not having had to learn the lessons of past defeats. The underlying flaw in all of this was the bemused belief that, despite everything, America was still "the greatest country on earth", that beneath all the militarism, chauvinism and racism and violence there was another, a "real" America, the shining City on a Hill.

The anti-war movement overlapped with many other strands of opposition to Cold War Americanism and its ventures at home and abroad. You might cheer support groups of liberation struggles in Latin America or hail the group with signs reading "Free Fannie Lou Hamer — No Extradition to Klanolina" or applaud a phalanx of men and women bearing the banners of District 62, one of the few remaining progressive labor unions in the city.

To me it was, and still is, America at its best.

The largest anti-war demonstration I was ever in took place in the early summer of 1967. The press estimated some three hundred thousand marchers. What a sea of humanity. The lower end of Central Park was filled with people and every bus and street was packed with more people streaming in. For two hours a solid mass of marchers proceeded down the route to the UN Plaza, and by the end there were more people waiting to march than when the parade started. The White House released a statement saying the President wasn't impressed with numbers, but a lot of other Americans were, including Senators.

Some ten thousand of us split off and marched straight through the heart of Manhattan. Everything went fairly well until we passed a highrise construction site north of Times Square and some dregs working there threw rivets and chunks of wood down on us. But it was a couple of blocks east of the New York Public Library that we ran into organized trouble. Busloads of the much-feared NYPD Tactical Police had been rushed in and were waiting to break up our march a few blocks from the UN Plaza.

The police were going to show us who was boss. Using police buses, they had thrown up constrictions at two street corners. They would allow a few dozen marchers to surge forward and then trap them. Then the police line reformed and we could see some of our people being beaten up. One guy was down on the pavement with half a dozen cops pounding on him with their fists and batons. His girl friend was hanging on to his leg and screaming to us for help. A beefy cop with snow-white hair, a sergeant or something, was sitting on his horse immediately in front of me laughing his head off.

You would think that with the thousands of us there we'd have broken through and rushed them. That's what should have happened. But the few who tried it were clubbed down themselves and dragged away to paddy wagons. The damn thing was that despite our numbers and our determination we were so disorganized. Everybody acted on their own in the final analysis. It was humiliating: not the physical confrontation, but the fear of tackling the police.

I got it at the next corner, hit by a club and slugged in the jaw by another cop. I was so angry that I hardly felt it and was about to tackle him. But then I came to my senses and split back into the crowd. The one thing which always worried me about participating in these demonstrations was that I would be arrested, reported to the US Immigration Service and deported. That would have wiped out all those years of work I'd put in for a degree at Columbia. But in the end it didn't matter any more.

By the time Chicago Mayor Daley's police and the National Guard launched their bloody assault on anti-war protesters at the Democratic National Convention in Chicago in 1968, I was back in Canada. I was dismayed but not overly surprised to hear my colleagues at the University of Manitoba cluck about "American excesses" and "disrespect for the law". They didn't mean the American war crimes abroad or the attempts to suppress opposition at home, but the actions of those Americans who fought back against that.

TWELVE

Colombian Earth

Archive: Land of a Thirty Year's War

Between 1964 and 1966, during two separate field trips, I spent some nine months in a sugarcane workers' hamlet in the Cauca Valley of southern Colombia. How I came to go to Colombia was somewhat accidental. I had specialized in Latin American anthropology, had done a considerable amount of reading on plantation agriculture, and was intending to do research in Cuba for my doctoral dissertation. I planned to study the labour process in the sugarcane industry within a socialist economy.

Despite the US government's ban of travel to Cuba, I won one of the few scholarships privately funded by Columbia University to do that research. The university's support under those conditions greatly impressed me. But in the end I couldn't get permission from Cuban authorities to do field work there. During those years I always seemed to be in situations where one decision was dependent on others, none of which were predictable beforehand. I now realize that I should have gone to Cuba regardless, and made whatever arrangements for research I could while there. Something useful would have emerged from that. But the necessity of getting into the field quickly led me to do research for my doctoral dissertation in Colombia, which I knew from earlier work.

The Cauca Valley lies between the western and central cordillera of the Andes. It is a semitropical highland valley with a year-round summer or late spring climate. Sugarcane is grown and harvested throughout the year. The Cauca region was the center of slave- and peon-worked *haciendas* and plantations since the seventeenth century. It remained a bastion of plantocracy long after the civil wars of the 1850s brought legal emancipation from slavery. Some of the powerful families in the region during the 1960s were a continuation of the plantation owners of the previous century. However, one should not be misled by this into the common stereotype about Latin America which sees a stable, quasi-feudal landlord class stretching from colonial times to the present. The ruling classes of Colombia were anything but stable.

During the second half of the nineteenth century the Cauca Valley was already an arena of conflict between Conservatives and Liberals, groupings as difficult to sort out on class lines a century ago as today. There was endemic conflict between combinations of regional *caudillos* who were not simply classifiable into categories such as "large landholders", "commercial capitalists", "emergent middle class" and so forth. Lands, wealth and power constantly changed hands among contending sections of the ruling class through court actions, financial losses and gains, and in civil wars. While the great majority of the population remained peasants and landless farmworkers, they did not escape being dragged into this turmoil.

Between independence in 1830 and the end of the Thousand Days War in 1903, Colombia was rocked by recurrent outbreaks of fighting. Disregarding local "political" feuds which sputtered on continuously there were some nine national civil wars, fourteen regional civil wars and two wars with Ecuador — as tallied by Diego Montaña Cuellar, a Colombian Marxist historian. He suggests that alliances of large landholders and commercial capitalists failed to fuse into a single ruling class because of the limited profits available in the restricted national markets. Whatever the reason, armed struggles to defend or seize political power are not an invention of revolutionary socialist movements during the second half of the twentieth century in Colombia.

None of these earlier conflicts were the comic opera coups which seem so humorous to Woody Allen and similar wits. But none of these struggles were as bloody as the inchoate conflict which began in 1948. The modest advances made by some sections of the urban and rural working class over the previous decade were being challenged by an increasingly reactionary Conservative government. When it seemed likely that Jorge Eliécer Gaitán, the populist leader of the Liberal party, would win the election he was assassinated.

Gaitán's assassination resulted in the *Bogotazo*, a spontaneous uprising in Bogota which, when it was crushed, ushered in a *de facto* Conservative dictatorship. That was the beginning of an amorphous civil war euphemistically referred to as *La Violencia*. It was fought with a pathological ferocity between groupings which called themselves Liberals or Conservatives; it was fought mainly by disparate sections of the peasantry and by members of the rural *petit-bourgeoisie* who by family inheritance or social accident were linked to one faction or another of the regional landlordocracies. Over the course of a dozen years *La Violencia* resulted in the deaths of some two hundred and fifty thousand men, women and children. No one knows the exact figure. Only a relatively small proportion died at the hands of the military. If one adds the maimed, those who lost family members and the dispossessed the conflict touched a large proportion of the rural population of Colombia.

In 1953 General Gustavo Rojas Pinilla seized power, and his regime soon became the vehicle of the most reactionary landlord elements. The army was launched into a campaign of bloody repression in the peasant areas. Most unions were banned, all vaguely progressive organizations were declared illegal, major national newspapers were closed. Even the traditional Colombian ruling class was threatened by the grab-bag looting of those sheltering under the military dictatorship.

Rojas Pinilla was overthrown in 1957 by a National Front composed of the leaders of the two traditional parties. The worst of *La Violencia* gradually began to wind down after 1958 when the leaders of the two contending parties came to an agreement to share power nationally on an alternating basis. Along with a desire to reestablish their own power, the leaders of the Liberal and Conservative parties were frightened by the emergence of revolutionary guerrilla forces. One strategy of the National Front government was to use former guerrillas and gunmen, as well as the police, to suppress those designated as "antisocial elements". Violence and bloodletting had become institutionalized by 1965.

Some of the most protracted fighting centered on the Tierra Dentro and Tolima del Sur regions, within a day's ride of where I lived. These areas had been engaged in sporadic armed struggle almost continuously since the late 1940s, a veritable Thirty Years War. Listening to some people's accounts I had the eerie feeling of hearing contemporary versions of "Hörch Kind Hörch."

You don't hear much about it now but during the mid 1960s Colombia was the client country most entangled in the Alliance for Progress. That involved aid from the US in the form of intergovernmental loans, scads of Peace Corps volunteers, a swath of paper reforms cogitated in Washington and Bogota, a plenitude of interest-bearing loans from US banks, and a stream of American experts in development. And lots of military aid.

The Alliance for Progress was a major policy initiative of the Kennedy administration. It was a response to the shock which the Cuban revolution had sent through both the American and Latin American ruling classes. The openly expressed fear was that a similar revolutionary trajectory could develop in other countries in Latin America. For reasons that are still unclear to me, American strategists in the early 1960s believed that Colombia was one of the countries where the next revolutionary upsurge would break out. The Alliance for Progress was going to help contain it by effecting a "Revolution within Democracy". The strategy, as I interpreted it, involved strengthening sectors of the lower middle class, especially in the countryside, and linking their interests with that of the National Front government.

A conjoined development of the early and mid 1960s was the massive importation of American food surpluses. You got the ludicrous situation where a region like the Cauca Valley, which had long been a region producing food for other parts of Colombia, began importing trainloads of US corn, rice and flour as regional farms shifted to growing cotton or sugarcane for export.

Practitioners of the Dismal Science always have some incantation of "competitive advantage" handy which irrefutably demonstrates that such changes are to the ultimate benefit of all. But a few dissident economists outlined how the package of US aid and bank loans would cost Colombia and other Latin American nations heavily. Part of the aid funds were tapped off into service fees and purchase stipulations which flowed back to US firms. The bulk of the "aid" was actually a series of loans which had to be repaid with interest, and Colombia became deeply indebted to American lending houses. By the end

Weekly market scene in a small town in the cane belt north of Cali.

of the decade the benefits of the Alliance for Progress proved more ephemeral than even its severest critics had predicted. American concerns became focused elsewhere in the *Mare Nostrum* and Colombia continued in its trajectory of exploitative chaos.

In conjunction with the Alliance for Progress, Colombia received a consignment of American consultants, advisors and assorted "experts in development". Some actually were beneficial — the medical doctors in particular — while many were merely costly inconsequentials. But others were clearly advisers on sustaining the Raj.

One of the latter was a guy we can call Oliver, an affable and wholesome-looking American who had recently gotten a PhD in anthropology and had become the director of social research for an American-funded institute in Cali. His initial research involved charting changing land use in the Cauca Valley over the previous century through perusal of remnant stands of biota and photographic mapping. "Photographic mapping?" you ask

It turned out that Oliver had started his career in the US Air Force assigned to photo reconnaissance and target evaluation during the final days of the Korean War. The Air Force had sent him to school to pursue his specialty in "anthropology". As of 1965 he was broadening the scope of his studies to the mountains southeast of the Cauca Valley, which by coincidence just happened to be an area of guerrilla activity. In conversation he left no doubt where he stood on the use of American military support for the Colombian government and army. The last time I heard of him Oliver was attached to a major American university and was giving a paper at a scholarly convention. Sometimes you don't know what lies behind academic scholarship unless you see the campaign ribbons.

Still, when all is said and done, it was not American experts, nor was it loans nor even military advisors which kept the fat out of the fire in Colombia. What did was the traditional use of plodding repression and policies which retained the support of crucial strata of the lower middle class. That and the disbursement of penny-ante perks which more or less assured the loyalty of the army and police to the National Front government.

The Federal Police force was a fair-sized army in it own right, organized along the lines of the Guardia Civil of Spain. Its ranks were filled largely by ex-Indian peasants and volunteers recruited from the southern highland regions after a tour in the regular army. They were the everyday face of state power in the cities and in the countryside. In a photograph, the Federal Police might have struck an observer as quaintly anachronistic with their battered model 1898 Mausers and their dated "Bolivian"-style uniforms. But in the flesh, met on some empty side road, they definitely weren't to be trifled with. How safe you were depended on how influential you appeared and on whatever may have happened in that locale in the recent past. As a scruffily dressed foreigner wandering around hillside *favelas* you would soon have a couple of these Federal Police trailing around behind you until they decided to examine your papers.

An ironic turnabout, you may think, members of the exploited Indian peasantry serving as the first line of defense of the exploiters.

It's nothing new to a Colombian or Peruvian or Salvadoran, etc., etc. The Federal Police treated Indian, black, white and *mestizo* peasants and workers with equal callousness.

If a couple of these policemen stopped me I halted in my tracks, turned slowly and looked directly at them without saying anything. Dead eyes — these guys all had dead eyes. Don't reach into your pocket unless you are ordered to, never argue, never show fear or emotion of any sort.

Coming back from Popayan one night the bus I was on was stopped by an army patrol. We are all taken off and lined up with our hands on the side of the bus, under the muzzles of submachine-gun-toting soldiers. ("Oh, oh. What was it I was going to do in a situation like this?") In fact, there is nothing you can do. While the regular army wasn't quite as trigger-happy as the police they could be just as ruthless.

A particularly blatant case of the murder of "subversives" by the army occurred in December of 1965 near the town of Buga, in the center of the Cauca sugarcane region. Four teenagers had been captured in what was alleged to be a hideout of the Workers, Students, Peasants Movement. *Voz Proletaria* had a special edition on the streets the next morning calling for public vigilance to assure that the prisoners would get to their trial alive. No weapons had been found and no resistance had been offered. The charges of supporting a guerrilla movement might not stand up in court and were not likely to lead to long term sentences if they did. To its credit *El Tiempo*, the leading newspaper in Bogota, also got on the story and made it national news.

The prisoners had told army interrogators that they were relatives of certain leading families in the region and apparently this was why they had survived for two days. Even army commanders weren't eager to mix it up with powerful families, who had their own means of settling accounts long after matters were officially forgotten. But when it became clear that the youths were not after all related to these notables, all four were taken out in the middle of the night to where they had been captured under the pretext of showing where the non-existent weapons were hidden. And naturally all four "attempted to escape" and were shot and killed.

It was intended to be that blatant. It was done to show everyone that in matters of left-wing "subversion" the army itself was the law and was not bound by any legal rights or courts. Comparable crimes by the forces of public order occurred all over the Cauca region, to say nothing of the mountain districts, although usually without witnesses or reporters heard from.

In a Cane Workers' Hamlet

The Cauca Valley was the locus of some of the earliest labour unions in the Colombian countryside. First formed in the mid 1930s, unions of sugar mill and cane workers had been through a roller-coaster ride of legality and repression. Since the collapse of the previous dictatorship they had reorganized and on the larger sugar plantations a left-wing union federation, Fedetav, had again become a significant force. But by the mid 1960s it was under assault by employer-backed company unions, which invariably dubbed themselves "Free" or "Democratic".

In ways both simple and complex, the gains won by the sugar worker unions were a major factor in critical changes in agricultural prac-

Back of the mill at Trapiche Amarilla, 1966, collecting the bagasse *used for firing the kettles.*

A cane cutter for Ingenio Maria Luisa, north of Cali, 1964.

tices, investments and labour utilization by the owners of the sugar plantations. The larger sugar cane mills increasingly came to rely on a burgeoning class of cane growers for their cane supply, since they paid much lower wages and could produce cane at lower prices. That was a central theme explored in my dissertation so I suppose it is incorrect to say that it was solely a study of cane agriculture.

During most of my stay in Colombia I lived in a couple of rooms near the centre of a cane workers' hamlet in the heart of the sugar plantation zone of the Cauca Valley. Chicharro was a settlement of about sixteen hundred people strung along a secondary road. Within a radius of a few miles were one huge sugar central, two old *ingenios* (older, smaller sugar mills), a half dozen primitive sugar *trapiches* (small mills producing *panella*, sugar cake) and the farms of numerous cane growers. Clusters of smallholder plots were scattered between the cane fields. They were usually planted in tree crops — assemblages of tall shade trees with an understorey of banana, plantain and coffee shrubs. From a distance, in an early morning mist, these hamlets looked like islands rising out of a sea of sugarcane.

Chicharro was my home base to go traipsing around the country-side talking to itinerant cane workers, sugar mill staff, union activists, "peasant" farmers and the variety of individuals who squeezed a living from the interstices of that society. The overwhelming majority of the men and families living in Chicharro were engaged in one sector or another of the sugar industry, most of them as landless cane workers. The small-holder plots were farmed by families whose members frequently hired out as agricultural labourers and who were often as poor as the cane workers.

I didn't cut or load cane and didn't hang over a hoe in the Cauca Valley cane fields. You only learn something that way if you've never done such work before. I had had enough jobs like that during my youth. It is true that if you actually lived as a cane worker, with the same income, the same worries and fetters, the same illnesses and indignities for a few years you would learn things no observer could. But anthropologists, as distinct from millions of immigrant workers in the past, never carry participant observation that far. In point of fact it would be very difficult to both do research and be a cane worker at the same time.

What you find out depends, in measure, on what you ask and whom you ask. But it also depends in part on how you respond. What you learn depends on what people feel they can tell you. With some individuals you develop a mutual trust, with others you don't. There is nothing wrong in that. I would suspect anyone who claimed he/she was on equally good terms with everybody.

Anthropologists sometimes claim a Buddha-like neutrality which is both impossible and unnecessary. It is sometimes not even desirable. Trying to be all things to all people is both patronizing and may make you appear like a sneak or toady. I was going to work with my own understandings and outlook intact. Naturally, I was ready to listen to everyone and prepared to change my perceptions as part of the research. But if I found some people standing on their heads I was not prepared to join them in their view of the world just because that was where they were at. That may sound sensible enough but it was tantamount to heresy in certain anthropological circles.

What you learn depends on what you observe personally, on what people tell you and what emerges from sifting bits and pieces of information. You only gradually learn what to ask and how to ask it, when to follow up certain hints which are dropped in a conversation and when to shut up. Much of what you learn never gets written down. Spontaneous discussions, humorous and bitter accounts, unpredictable reminiscences. Such discussions are sandwiched between repetitive daily events. You hover between periods when you seem to learn nothing new to meetings where extraordinary things are revealed in an hour or two.

There are also times when you wish you could expeditiously remove yourself from a situation, however informative it is. For instance, an encounter with a bunch led by an ex-army sergeant who had become an employee of the local politico for a nearby sugar central.. They invited themselves and their bottles and their .455 Webleys — which one of them ostentatiously loaded and unloaded — into my rooms. They were going to sound me out and generally let me know how thing ran here, to inform me "who my real friends were". But usually you didn't even know where real danger lay.

I relied mainly upon taking notes but had an old Wollensak tape recorder for doing more formal interviews. The recorder was of only occasional use, firstly because there was usually no electricity available but more importantly because people were understandably leery about having their comments recorded. Nevertheless, it was surprising what people who barely knew me would tell me.

There was a wide range of experience among those living in this small village. Many had made peregrinations from job to job, region to region, before arriving in Chicharro. Men who had been underfed and overworked children on peasant plots in the mountains beyond Pasto. Some who had begun their adult lives as twelve-year-old miners in eighteenth century gold mines. Others who had been voyagers to the eastern Llanos or dwellers in Bogota slums or had sojourned on Magdalena banana plantations were now cane workers at the seasoned age of twenty-five. Women who had left jungle hamlets of the Pacific coast to follow a husband or their luck through the luckless regions of the Cauca Valley. Others who had fled *La Violencia* in Caldas or Tolima and had seemingly worked in almost every crop grown in Colombia at one time or another. People who had lived through near constant hardships in ways which made every week a lesson in courage and tenacity. All now in Chicharro — a typical cane workers' hamlet.

Black descendants of slaves, Indian ex-peasants from impossible mountain cots, men and women who were as European as any land-less Andalusian landworker: they were all in Chicharro, living and working together — or against each other. They toiled at the same kinds of jobs under the same conditions. They spoke regional dia-lects of the same language and drew on variants of the same Colom-bian rural culture. It was allegedly naive to say so but they were all members of a heterogeneous rural proletariat, a proletariat, moreover, which merged with other sectors of the broader Colombian working class at certain points.

Some in Chicharro had determined to do the best they could for themselves and their families within the confines of "their lot" as they saw it. Others lived for the weekend and would trace a brief private comet across a narrow sky. Yet others were sober, capable of calculated guile, and would, as one old union veteran put it, "sell out his work-mate for the boss' favour."

But there were also others who, despite having been taught their les-son time and again, somehow refused to learn it, refused to be beaten. People who described themselves as "poor illiterates" but who pains-takingly read contraband magazines kept hidden under their mat-tresses and mulled over dangerous ideas with friends around evening cooking fires. People who were, lo and behold, blood of our blood, flesh of our flesh. Or so it seemed to me.

Biograph: Some Colombian Voices

I still am unable to write about life in a Colombian plantation village. No brief overview seems meaningful or true. There is so much that has to be said that I find it impossible to say anything general. Why that mental block applies to my stay in Colombia I don't know. Instead of an overview, let's look at some extracts drawn from work histories and informal discussions with Valle Caucano caneworkers. Even alone, they convey something of the Colombian countryside at the time.

They include an outburst of apocalyptic rage, some cautionary accounts, a capsulated work history, and a sagacious account by one cane worker of how the previous dozen years were to be understood. They convey emotions and include phantasms which were part of the social reality. But mainly they describe conditions which were objec-tively true.

"A Strikebreaker's Story" suggests how individuals with similar histories and even similar understandings of their own exploitation may come to very different conclusions about what options they have. It brought home to me that the ranks of the opposing sides are often filled with people who are only slightly different from each other. On the other hand, "Why we live like this" emanates from a man who, despite considerable danger and desperate poverty, was engaged in secretly collecting funds for medicines and supplies to send to the embattled peasantry of Marquetalia.

Today I have forgotten most of the specifics of cane agriculture which filled my dissertation. But I can still often remember the locales of these conversations, who the speakers were and what their histories were. Given the vital statistics for cane workers in the Cauca, the speakers are probably no longer alive. However, all of the names presented here are pseudonyms and details have been disguised in a few places.

Backroom Cautions

Zembrano: "So Don Tulio told you how he strictly avoids politics? Well I know him from a way back — he's an old *pajaro*. A good friend of mine knew of him when he was in Pradera, seven or eight years ago. He was a gunman for the bosses there. Who knows how many people he's knocked off in his days.

"He's quite friendly — and I'm always friendly to him. But I keep away from him. He's still got close connections with *pajaros* on the go and with the police."

Guillermo: "He likes to drink and chase women. Last January, one Saturday night, I was in Florida with some of the boys, drinking in a bar. Don Tulio came in drunk. After awhile I had to go to the urinal and he came over to piss too. When he opened up his jacket I could see a revolver stuck in his belt. I looked straight ahead, finished and went over to the table and said to the boys, "Let's get out of here."

Zembrano: "Sure. Whenever he goes to Florida or Pradera or Cali he has a pistol. That store, the truck, his land and all those cattle — and he has money. He didn't get all that on a truck driver's wages. He has a real arsenal in his house. Not only does he have a revolver and a rifle, he also has an automatic carbine, the kind the army has. One can say a machine-gun, that's more or less what it is. Luis, he was working on Don Tulio's truck and saw it in the garage.

"But listen. About a year ago there was a *cuadrilla* [an armed band] here led by Ricardo Paja. What, you don't know of him? Well they were waiting here for three days and nights to get Don Tulio. Right near Chicharro.

"He was in that bitch's house, drunk, and they thought to get him when he left. But he must have known that somebody was out there. He didn't leave that place for five days, not even to piss. After three days the *cuadrilla* had to leave but one of these days somebody is going to kill him."

Guillermo (to me): "See. It's like I told you. You have to know who you are talking to. Otherwise it's 'Good afternoon. How's it going?' and nothing more. This isn't like your country. There are all sorts of types like this around."

Zembrano (to me): "Look, these are the types that have the say so around here. And it's the same everywhere in the Valle. He is a Conservative, the police inspectors are Conservatives, they are friends of the local Conservative chiefs and they in turn are connected with the agents of the oligarchy. They all support each other.

"Let's say that you are doing something that one political chief or an employer doesn't like. Maybe you get into a fight with him or you find out things about him that he doesn't want anybody to know. Or maybe you are an important worker in the opposition to the Frente Nacional. Well, some day when he is having a drink he meets one of these types, a *pajaro*. Maybe they are old friends. They have a drink or two and the political boss tells this guy, 'Fulano is doing such and such. What do you think of that? Do me a great favour and see what you can do about it?' Maybe he mentions some profitable business deal that he can get for this *pajaro* or maybe he mentions a loan — a loan that is never repaid.

"So maybe this *pajaro*, or one of his companions, comes to beat you. If you defend yourself he shoots you. Maybe he'll shoot you anyway. If somebody sees him doing it he tells the police, 'This Fulano attacked me with a machete and I had to kill him to protect myself.' If you don't have any important connections the police come and look, go back to the police station and write up a report saying that 'Fulano was killed while trying to rob.'

"But let's say that someone else saw everything and tells the police, 'No, that's not the way it was. It was this way.' They may arrest him as an accomplice. Since all the judges take the word of the police, no matter what political party they say they are from, he'll likely get sent to prison unless he has a lawyer or someone powerful to support him. That's the way it goes here in Colombia."

Guillermo: "You know how that Muncho was shot. He was making things too difficult. That guy didn't have any fear. He told everybody just what was what. Remember those two police who were here until about six months ago? The Indian one said that Muncho attacked him. But that's a lie. He would never have done that, alone on the street, at night and with two police."

Zembrano: "No, no! He said that the police were waiting for him and that he couldn't get away. [To me:] They shot him in the leg — he lost his leg below the knee. I went to give him some money, to help him out a bit.

"He's in Cali now, I saw him there just a few weeks ago. He's selling newspapers and periodicals and has a nice room downtown. He has a lot of friends in Cali and seems to be getting along quite well now."

Guillermo: "But those two police, the ones that did it, they were killed outside Florida just a little while ago."

Zembrano: "No. Those weren't the same ones. I don't think so."

Guillermo (to me): "See, I told you that it was highly dangerous in the mountains around here. That was just in Pedregal and you wanted to go to Herrera. That is even further. No sir."

Zembrano: "I have some friends like that too. You remember that big guy who was visiting me on Sunday about two months ago? A real innocent with the face of a boy. He was carrying around a briefcase all the time? Well, he's an old Liberal *pistolero*. That day he was coming from Miranda trying to sell a revolver. He had a really beautiful little revolver, short barrel and everything. A Smith and Wesson .38-calibre. All he wanted for it was two hundred and fifty pesos and fool that I am I didn't take it. I had the money too but I didn't want to take the risk.

"That guy is pretty dangerous. He stabbed a police in Puerto Tejada who was about to arrest him. He said that at that moment he didn't care if they killed him or not. No sir! There are some people like that — one can say they are friends but if they come and ask me for twenty pesos I give it to them without any questions about when I'm going to get it back. Because if you don't give to them, friend or not, they may just attack you and take the money."

Guillermo: "There are too many like that in Colombia. Whether they call themselves Liberals or Conservatives they are damaged, rotten.

They started in that life to revenge a father or a brother killed or for political reasons or in self defense. But after a while they just become animals, whatever they call themselves."

Zembrano (to me): "Listen ! Do you know what the *corte de franela* is? How they cut your throat here? Or the *corte de corbata*? ... Ugh. Poor Colombia."

Eviction

Luis: "Don Gustavo only bought the *parcela* [small farm plot] a few weeks, a month, ago and already he has somebody knocking it down to plant cane. This one guy has been working all yesterday and all today chopping down the plantain and the coffee and the banana. Someone must be poor indeed to work from morning to night, on Sunday, hardly stopping to eat, to do that. What sort of person is it anyway who takes work cutting down poor people's *fincas*?"

Agapito: "I know. But if your family is hungry, if you can't get work ... what can you do? Indeed, what can you say to somebody like that?"

Luis: "Look at Alfredo here. He's got his house and his one and a half plazas of land [two acres]. Not much, but it's his only support for his daughter and the children. At least here, with some work for his neighbours, they can live. But one person after another sells off, cane spreads on one side and then on the other. He'll be surrounded. Access will be difficult. So he will have to sell too and move into a town, maybe Florida. What is he going to do there? If he buys a hut it will take all the money he will get for his land. And then how will he live? He's too old to get work in the town. If he rents a room in one or two years all the money will be eaten up — and then what?

"As for you, Don Adelberto, you can sell your land and buy a house in Chicharro. You could probably afford one of those small houses they are building there for the price of your land. You could make a living working in the fields for Central Castilla. But the way prices are going up you'd never be able to get any land back again, not here or in any other place in the Valle. Not even for twice the price. We can say that your land would be plain lost.

"It takes twenty years of work to get a *plaza* or two of land — if you work and live like an animal. And even then you don't get it. The people here won't even sell it to you or me. Just because the cane lords can give them the money immediately they sell it to them. They'd rather see the land go under cane and have their money quickly than take payments and have the land remain as a poor man's *finca*. They don't even get any more for it.

(A silence.)

"A week from now everything around my shack will be knocked down. I've got a month and when they bring in the bulldozer to level the land my shack will be knocked down too.

"They and their *mayordomos* treat us like dogs at work. We live in semi-slavery as it is. Now they want to make the slavery complete, like in the times when they brought people chained together, bought and sold them like cattle, chained our hands together at night, like this, so we couldn't run away. Now they want to drive us off the land into the villages, into their barracks. Then if you say anything against them, if you don't bow in front of them when you ask for your wage, if you don't accept what they throw you or maybe if they just don't like your face, they can tell you to get out and you'll have to go.

"This is all going to be a sea of cane, the whole Valle. They're going to knock down all the small farm plots, cut down all the coffee and plantains, plough under all the maize and beans. We'll have to learn to eat cane, like the cattle do. There will only be the rich, their hirelings and their slaves who work in the fields. We'll be living again as in past times — in complete slavery . . .

"There is only one thing I hope for, only one thing that I pray to God for, every night. And that is a final world war, a world war of the poor against the rich, a war in which we will clean them out once and for all. Yes, in truth. I'm ready now, right here, right now. By God I am. I may not have anything but I've got a big heart. I've still got spirit. I'm not a dog that they can kick and it comes back to lick their boots. I don't have even a shotgun and I'm alone. But if it should start . . .

"That's the only thing that can save us — a revolution. I don't care if they kill me. By God I don't. I'm old, I'm not afraid. I don't have a wife. Maria can find someone else like me to live with. I don't have any children to worry about. I have nothing — only my dignity. And before they take that they'll have to kill me. I'll be better off then anyway."

Agapito: "But look . . . Colombia has had years of that. And what did it serve? . . . One poor guy killing another — for what? There were enough peasants in the mountains who tried to defend themselves. They were killed by the ton. I never heard of any of the rich being killed during that time. And today the oligarchy is more powerful than it was before."

(A long silence.)

Luis: "Well then ... What do you say then, Don Adelberto? What about going off into the jungles and making ourselves *fincas*? I've had about enough of this Valle. Just wait a bit, pretty soon now and I'm going to leave this place. I'll go back home to Guapi. In my village we were poor but there were no bosses to order us around. Everybody has his *finca* even if it is small. And things grow there ... Oohee. Maize, yucca, bananas. And pigs, they really are pigs, not fattened dogs. If you can't do anything else you can go into the jungle and clear a *finca* for yourself. Maybe sickness will get you. But while you live you can at least be free. There aren't any bosses there — no sir! "

A strikebreaker's story

"I left the house of my father when I was twelve years of age. I left my father's *finca* high in the mountains of Nariño and went to work in a gold mine. He used to punish me a great deal. One night I was still away from the house at eight in the evening. I decided that if he beat me I'd leave, good enough. If he didn't punish me, good enough too. Well, I went back and he punished me. I didn't say anything. I went to bed and waited. When everyone was deep asleep I got up and left. I didn't have money or food or any clothes except those I was wearing.

"I walked all that night and the next day before I came down to the road. The only way of traveling there was by foot or on horseback. That night I slept a few hours in a field and then continued marching because it was too cold to sleep outside without a jacket or blanket. I walked all the next day and at about six in the evening came to the *campamento* of the Porvenir mine. I went up to the woman in charge of the kitchen and said, 'I'm hungry. I haven't eaten in two days.' Since I couldn't pay she gave me a cup of coffee as a gift.

"In the morning, early, I asked the foreman for work. They weren't hiring any men at the time but the foreman took pity on me. 'All right, you work with these men. They are putting in timber.' We went into the mine a long way and I worked with some of the others. Although I was strong for my age the work was very difficult for me since I was so small.

"Besides the difficulty of the work I had no work clothes. No rubber boots or stockings or a jacket. There was a lot of water in some parts of the mine, very cold water because it seeped through the walls from mountain streams. We started work at six in the morning and lunch was at eleven. By lunch time I had nearly collapsed. The only thing I'd had taken in over two and a half days was that cup of coffee. I was numb and wet from the water. When we came to the surface I wrung out my clothes but since I didn't have any others, I had to put them on again. Well, so it went. I continued working at that mine for a year and lived in the *campamento*.

"After a year I returned to my father's house and worked on his *finca*. But after two months of staying there, with all the quarrels we had, I had enough and left to work in another mine, the Albanero mine.

"The conditions there were about the same as at Porvenir but I had a different job, working on tunnel drainage. There were about a hundred to a hundred and forty men working in each of these mines but the individual people were always changing. Some would work for a few weeks, others for a month or two, others for just a few days. All the mines there in Nariño are about the same. Even today the basic wage in the mines is about four pesos a day. They don't recognize any social security laws. We worked from six in the morning till six in the evening with two hours off in the middle of the day. Most of what we got paid went to buy food. After some eight months I returned to my father's *finca* again."

(The cycle of return home, quarrels and departure to work in yet another mine continued over a number of years.)

"I returned to Porvenir mine and was given a job working above ground shoveling the ore dumped from the carts into other carts. After a few months I was shifted into the mill itself and worked around the crusher and on the sorting belt. After about eight months, one day, I was working near the belt and got caught. The belt caught my arm and tore off the skin all the way up my arm and off part of my right shoulder. It was only by the will of God that I didn't lose my arm or my life.

"But some friends at the mine took me into their house until I got well. It was more than a month before I could work again.

"In Nariño the companies don't recognize any responsibility to the workers. They don't recognize sick pay or loss of limbs in accidents — much less any other kind of social security payments. What you can read in government laws are unheard of there. They don't even pay for hospitalization if you are injured at work. There, the 'law' is 'If you are sick, cure yourself. And if you can't cure yourself and haven't got the money for doctors and medicine, then die.' The administrator of Porvenir mine not only didn't pay me for that accident, he even robbed me of part of the pay I had coming. I had to accept it. I needed the money. There is nothing one can do anyway.

"National laws hardly enter Nariño. Here in the Valle there are what they call 'company unions' and 'workers' unions'. But in Nariño there are neither. People working in the mines usually just stay for a short while — they usually have their own *fincas* but need extra money sometimes. I never heard of a strike or a union in any of those mines. The foreman says what he wants done and the workers do it. Anyone who doesn't like it can leave. There are always more who are looking for work. A man relies on the help of his friends or on nothing.

"After that I drifted around doing different jobs and working on *fincas* by the day for a while until I finally came to work in a diamond mine. There I worked with water, handling the sluices and the flumes for the hydraulic operations. Later on I was engaged in transporting timber by mules, in drainage and all kinds of other work for the company.

"One day I and some others were transporting timber when we met some friends. We went to this one house and started drinking. After a while along came some others who had an old quarrel with these friends of mine and, out of vengeance, attacked us. Before I could defend myself one stabbed me in the wrist. A second blow struck me in the thigh and the third was to my stomach. With that I almost died.

"But my present wife took me into her father's house and tended me and cured me. It was then that I decided to marry her. For more than two months I couldn't get out of bed but when I was better and could work again I asked her to marry me. She said, 'Well, you better talk to my father.' So I did and he said alright.

"We got married and I started to work privately, transporting firewood with horses. I used to get up when it was still dark in the morning to care for the horses. Then I would leave for high up in the mountains to load the firewood. Often I would get back home only after it was dark. I was doing that and we were expecting him [points to his three year old son] when one day one of the horses got sick. Within a month, of the five horses we had, only one remained.

"So I started working on the *fincas* again, taking whatever job I could get. I did that for about half a year and then said to myself, 'This isn't resulting in anything.' I had heard from people who had been up in the Valle that there were jobs here and that they paid something. We already had the boy then and I said to my wife, 'I'll go to the Valle and try to find a job. If I do find one I'll send for you; if I don't I'll return.' I think she was worried I would run off.

"Well, I came to the Valle and after not too long got a job on Central Providencia. While the wage was good in comparison to Nariño I didn't like being a cane cutter. You can injure yourself badly. It worried me a lot in fact. After some time I heard that jobs were available here at Central Castilla. The social security payments are better here, they have bonuses for each child and hospitalization payments if you are injured. Maybe all these things are required by law, but still, different companies pay them very differently. I got hired at Castilla the day after handing in my work papers. It's not that jobs are easy to get, it is the personal luck of each one."

(In fact, he had been hired during the bitter Castilla strike and was known to be a strikebreaker.)

"After that my wife came to stay with me here. One suffers alone. When one has friends and family with him all things are easier. Things don't effect you so much.

"Anyway, now I am thinking that one of these days I'm going to leave Castilla. When I have a little money saved, one day I'm going to go to Cali and try to find some job, it doesn't matter what, where I can learn something. I don't want to spend the rest of my days working in the cane fields hanging over a hoe.

"I would like to learn to be a mechanic but here in the cane fields it is almost impossible to improve one's lot. The only way an ordinary person can improve his position here in Colombia is with the help of someone of importance. Otherwise I would say that it is impossible for a worker to make a better life for himself.

"One lives day to day. I have no expectations or illusions. The only thing that I will plan for is to save enough money in the Valle to return to my home in Nariño, where my family and friends are, and buy a plaza or two of land. Nothing more. To do that one works and saves here all the time and returns home for a visit every few years. Others who hope for more end up with nothing."

'Why we live like this'

The speaker here was an older, very sagacious, rank-and-file union supporter who had recently been fired from a *trapiche* when the supervisor learned of his past involvement in the Central Castilla strike.

"It's very simple. I'll tell you why we live like this, crushed in poverty and misery. Because we are divided, one worker against the other. If you try to do something or say the wrong thing some of your own work mates will betray you.

"If you talk with four or five of the people you work with and say, 'Look, things aren't right here. We need better wages, we aren't getting the legal benefits we are entitled to. What we need is a real union and not a bosses' union.' Well, the next day the foreman comes up to you and says, 'I hear that you were talking against the company and that you don't like it here. Alright, you can leave as of now.' You have to leave and you will be lucky if you get your full pay.

"If some workers get together quietly in someone's house, at night, to discuss what should be done, there'll always be someone there who will disagree with you. Maybe he will agree with you to your face but that same night he'll go to the foreman and tell him, 'These persons were in that house discussing such and such.' Even if not all of those who were there are fired they and others are too scared to do anything more after the foreman comes around and tells them he knows what they have been discussing. Let me tell you what happened here at Central Castilla.

"A little over two years ago I and a lot of us you see around Chicharro were working there. There was a union there which was no more than a marriage of the bosses and the priests. Well, some of us decided that what was needed was a union that was for the workers. So we talked to our friends and our workmates, making sure that no one said anything to the known stooges. Before the company knew it we had the majority of the workers on the Central signed up in our union. We held the first assembly, all the paperwork and legal steps had been completed and we received official recognition from Bogota as representing the workers at Castilla. Right after that we affiliated with Fedetav [Federacion de Trabajadores del Valle, a militant labor federation of the region]. At the same time this was going on other people were organizing at Ingenio Maria Luisa and a union was established there which also affiliated with Fedetav.

"Not long after that there was a new contract to sign with the company and we asked for a two peso a day increase in the basic pay and a forty centavo increase in the rate for a ton of cane cut. Castilla simply refused to negotiate. So, after all the due processes we went on strike.

"At that point we had more than twelve hundred of the seventeen hundred people working at Central Castilla in our union and all except forty or fifty were for the strike. The same thing happened at Ingenio Maria Luisa. It was smaller, there were about six hundred men there then, but an even higher proportion of the workers were in the union. They never had a union there before, not even a company union.

"We set up strike camps on the main entrance ways to Castilla and Maria Luisa, with tents and banners and with enough people at every entrance so they could stop the companies from bringing in strike-breakers. One month passed, two months passed with the companies refusing negotiations, and we knew that they would try to conquer us with hunger. The men on strike couldn't get any work even when they weren't in the strike camps. A few got maybe a day or two work here and there. The families of each man, and friends who were working elsewhere, helped as they could. Other unions of Fedetav helped. Public collections, like you see going on now along the roads to support the strike at Hacienda San Jose, they brought in some money to buy food. The situation was very tough but still the majority of the workers at Castilla were determined to carry on the strike. It was a question of survival for our union.

"In about the third month the company started telling everybody that they could work if they came to Castilla and signed up with another union that the bosses had brought in, one they had created. The one they have now. Castilla even offered a higher rate than they paid before — but they wouldn't negotiate with us. One by one workers started going back to work at Castilla, living in the barracks there. Central Castilla is so large and has so many entrance roads that we couldn't be everywhere. The police would escort these strikebreakers in over some back road at night.

"After that the company started bringing in new workers by the truckload. The police would arrive in force to open up our blockade and let the strikebreakers in. It was like a garrison in there — armed guards continually patrolling the fences. But still the strike went on.

Graffiti painted on the side of a house on the edge of Cali, 1965: "A nation that does not rebel against its political associations merits being called 'slave'."

We still had the majority of the original workers at Castilla with us and they were firmly behind the leaders of the union.

"In the fifth month of the strike, that was when some of our leaders sold us out. They were paid off by Castilla and carried the membership lists to the bosses. They sent off a letter to Labour Ministry in Bogota saying that the majority of the workers had left our union and that it no longer represented the workers at Castilla. An official arrived from Bogota, declared the strike illegal and registered the new company union as representing the workers at Castilla. Everyone knows that Festralva [Federation of Free Workers of the Valle] is purely a bosses' union.

"When those leaders sold out everything collapsed. With that the strike at Maria Luisa collapsed too. Those boys over there had it even tougher — there was continual persecution and not a little shooting too. They were counting on us at Castilla to win. Maria Luisa never did start milling again. They now sell all their cane to Castilla.

"After they had broken our strike Castilla made blacklists of all the active members of our union and sent these to all the companies and *haciendas* and *ingenios* in the Valle. Those people either had to pack up and leave the Valle or take work in places where they don't pay anything. Those people lost everything. Even now, after all this time, they still persecute us.

"I know some guys from the strike who managed to get jobs with regular pay. But they have to keep their past a secret and if the company finds out who they are they will find some reason to fire them. The same thing will happen to them as happened to me.

"Since the strike Castilla and the cane farms and *trapiches* around here have begun using labour contractors more and more. These contractors are the most degraded people on the face of the earth. They are dragged up from the human refuse — people who live from the misery of others.

"They go around to the various landowners, or maybe they work for just one, and say, 'I'll do such and such work on these cane fields for eight hundred pesos.' That is probably cheap, so the owner says alright. Well, the contractor gets together let's say ten men, and pays them maybe half of that price. So much by the piece for the work done. He doesn't care who does it, he doesn't take any chances — you get the money when the work's done. The contractors always say, 'That's all I got for this job. I'm not making anything on it.'

"But people have to take the work even if they only make ten pesos for nine and ten hours work. Even if they don't get any *prestaciones* [social security] and don't get paid if they are injured. They have to take the contractor's offer because if they don't take it someone else will. They don't have any money, the wife is hungry, the children are crying because they are hungry and they can't find another job. There are always enough to take the contractor's price.

"But the most basic reason for all of this is that there is no solidarity between the workers of Colombia. We live divided one against the other. You can trust a few friends and no more. One worker will sell out his workmate for the boss's favour. It's not just that there are company unions but that the attitude of the workers allows them to continue.

"Some talk about organizing all the workers in one region, from all the cane farms and *trapiches* and centrals, all under one workers' union. But I would like to know who is going to do this. We tried to organize just two sugar centrals and we failed. The *trapiche* where I worked has two hundred and forty men, more or less. Plenty for a union. But not the least activity. The union at Manuelita has a long history and is strong but most of the other sugar mill unions affiliated with Fedetav are having enough difficulty just maintaining their positions ...

"Here in Colombia the oligarchy commands. They control the government, the police, everything. Those who they don't control they buy off, those who they can't buy off they persecute, imprison or assassinate. If it looks like the popular forces might win an election — we thought that the people would finally have some say with Gaitán — they don't hesitate to kill them. Gaitán's assassination, that cost Colombia who knows how many hundreds of thousands of lives. People died by the wagon load, by the ton. Thousands and thousands. For more than seven years it went on, fierce and bloody slaughter. Men, women and infants. We will never know how many. Nor do I want to know. Dumped into rivers, how many Colombians? Food for the fish, fertilizer for the fields. Colombians were food for the birds of prey, food for the dogs. And it's not over yet.

"During *La Violencia* people were continually being shot down on the streets in Pradera, in Florida, in Corinto, in Palmira — in the open daylight. The killers were never arrested. In Caldas and Tolima where most of the people are poor peasants, where people banded together and fought back against the assassinations, the army went and massacred them. Some fled to the cities and some to the Valle here.

"Many, many people had to flee their homes and land and took refuge up in the mountains. The old Liberal [i.e., pre-National Front] guerrilla bands maintained peace in many of these mountain areas when murder and bloodshed was going on all around. Many people fled to those zones. Often these areas have never been a real part of the nation. They were unoccupied, unworked areas, part of great haciendas that were ruled like the landowner's little kingdom. His word was law and the national law and legal rights were unknown.

"When the Liberal guerrillas and the refugees arrived these *hacienda* owners fled. Self defense committees were established. Well, naturally, because either the old landowners or new political bosses were always trying to attack and rob the people of their land and animals. This is the main reason that we now have so many *pajaros* ['birds', i.e., thugs and killers] here in Colombia. Many started in the hire of large landowners and the local political bosses who wanted to take the peasants' land, to drive them off or scare them into working for the landowners.

"Now they are calling these peasants 'bandits'. You know what is going on in Marquetalia. The press, the army and the oligarchy have mounted an offensive of lies and bullets against these zones and are trying to convince people that the peasants are bandits. There are enough real bandits in Colombia, true. But it isn't these peasants.

"All that the bosses want is to steal the land that these peasant families have made valuable with their work. But besides that, they are afraid of the people having any power. That is what they are really afraid of. You will see, in a few years all of those lands will be back in the hands of the large landowners and the people there will be working like peons for them.

"I don't see any solution. Organizing for workers' unions is becoming more and more difficult around here as the sugar companies get smarter. In politics, when it looked like Lopez Michelson would lead the people against the Frente Nacional they bought him off. We had years of fierce fighting and it only served to set one poor man against the other. Still, if one is a man and not a slave he has to go on struggling. But you see what it has gotten me and many people like me.

"Last Friday the *mayordomo* of the *trapiche* where I was working came up to me and said, 'Listen, the boss got a letter about you from Castilla. It says that you are a Communist and a dangerous subversive. For my part, you've done good hard work here and I'll put that in your work book. But I have to let you go. And it's no use going to Don Jaime's farm because they wrote him the same letter.'

"Look at me. I can't work in that shit *trapiche* for a miserable twelve pesos a day. By God, if they push me any further . . . I'm still a man, I've got balls. If they don't let me earn a living then I'll take what I need. I'll steal. Before I let them starve me to death I'll fight . . . And all that just because we tried to organize a union that would stand for the workers. I'm not a Communist. I've never had any schooling, I don't even know what communism is. A Liberal I am, even an MRL [Movimiento Revolutionario Liberal] Liberal — that yes!"

Hang Fire

Some Colombians may find all this to be a too uniformly grim a portrait. They may feel that it is a derogatory image to convey of Colombia in the middle of the last century, one which reinforces the stereotype which North Americans have of Latin America. Some may feel that the concentration on exploitation and violence does an injustice even to those portrayed. While the foregoing is not a comprehensive cross-section of Colombian reality these accounts do stem from the impoverished and exploited sectors of that country. The fact is that all of those whose accounts which appear here retained a fundamental human decency. They were not the ones who were brutal or mindlessly violent, even if the conditions they describe were.

I scribbled down notes of talks which emerged at night in the backrooms of cane workers' barracks or by the cookfires of peasant huts. I gathered work histories and on-the-spot surveys of labour conditions and wages in the various sectors of the sugar industry. I recorded the experiences of people who had migrated throughout the region in search of a living. There were off-the-cuff accounts by activists in agricultural labour unions as well as surprisingly open accounts by cane growers on how they set about smashing labour organization and bypassing national labour legislation. I acquired masses of material on the exigencies of everyday life of cane workers and their families as well as reminiscences of the maelstrom through which many of them had passed. Very little of this got into my dissertation.

"What was the purpose of my work?" I asked myself. A study of plantation agriculture and labour in Colombia began to seem meaningless. Even if a fine-grained study of sugar cane agriculture were to emerge, who really needed it? Towards the end of my field work I fell into a deep depression.

My work ultimately appeared in a monograph entitled "Sugar Plantations and Labour Patterns in the Cauca Valley". It may be of interest if you are a student of plantation agriculture but is well nigh unreadable if you're not. Few readers are able to infer the broader social conditions alluded to or the people hidden between the lines of the text.

The most fundamental lesson I learned in Colombia was unrelated to my dissertation or to anthropology in general. The lesson was that a brutal and anachronistic society can go plodding on generation after generation. That regimes which rule over poverty and endemic violence and glaring injustice can survive repeated revolutionary attempts to replace them. They can continue despite the heroic sacrifices of so many of their best people. It is not something which is learned from toting up facts. It's not the kind of lesson you are supposed to learn.

I came back from Colombia with a deep distrust of those North American radicals whose militancy revolved around taking "principled positions" and being "tough-minded". I distrusted those who pontificated about "protracted people's war" as if it were some extended protest demonstration. There were many like that around then. I had some bitter exchanges with individuals who presumed to analyse the "errors" of people, in places like Colombia, who just by retaining some spirit of resistance showed more courage and tenacity than most North Americans are ever called upon to muster.

What has happened in Colombia in the intervening decades? The National Front was dismantled and a series of Liberal and Conservative governments were installed through simple majority elections. Electoral support plummeted to the point where little more than a quarter of the population now votes in national elections. No discernible differences are detectable between the Liberal and Conservative party regimes. The proposed land reforms, development and assorted "roads toward progress" bruited about during the Alliance for Progress era are not even jokes anymore.

The one thing which Colombia did acquire was a massive foreign debt. Its governments also acquired the damning reputation of being responsible administrators of the austerity programs and interest repayment schedules laid down by international banking agencies. Despite the deepening social disintegration Colombia acquired the reputation, among bankers, of being "one of the most economically stable democratic regimes in Latin America". This only means that the Colombian government has become the rent collector for external investment agencies while its domestic programs have fallen into a state of near paralysis.

Exports of traditional agricultural goods help pay the interest on past loans. The dollar-a-day labour on cane farms and the twelve-hour shifts in sugar *trapiches*, so reminiscent of the depths of nineteenth century capitalism, persist unchanged. So too the Colombian coal mines with their child labour. Today a portion of that coal is exported, some of it to Great Britain, where it replaces coal once mined in unionized British pits. That is known as free trade.

A new export by the 1980s was the stream of middle class Colombians seeking an opportunity to make a living in North America and Europe. But the vast majority of Colombians do not have the option of emigration; their roads lead only as far as far as the nearest cities.

Sixty years ago no one worried much about the Colombian drug trade and no one imagined it might become a sort of Malinche's Revenge. In the intervening years the export of illegal drugs has generated gangs of murderous and extremely wealthy Colombian criminals who back their financial power with private armies. The pervasive talk about the Colombian drug mafia obscures an understanding of the real forces in contention.

Paralleling the drug *pajaros* are the right-wing death squads. By one estimate there were more than a hundred such organizations operating in Colombia by 1987. They have adopted the genocidal practices of Third World fascism evolved since the Indonesian holocaust. During 1986–1987, these death squads were responsible for some sixteen hundred to two thousand assassinations in Colombia. The victims ranged from ordinary workers and peasants to union organizers to liberal members of the professional middle class. Conditions have deteriorated into what they were during the worst of *La Violencia*.

Against all odds, the armed resistance movement survived and even grew in the years since 1965. It was divided into a number different organizations but the major region of guerrilla strength continued to be in the southern mountains and surrounding areas, including the Cauca Valley. By the mid 1980s the Fuerzas Armadas Revolucionaria Colombiano was sufficiently strong for Belisario Betancur, the then President of the Conservative government, to initiate peace talks with them.

The resulting ceasefire provided a general amnesty and FARC members emerged to form a new party, the Patriotic Union. It proceeded to contest local, departmental and federal elections and to organize regionally around a host of social issues. In 1986 the Patriotic Union elected some fourteen congressmen to the Federal senate.

Following that the right wing deaths squads, with the more or less open support of the Colombian army and police, intensified their reign of terror against supporters of the Patriotic Union. Amnesty International tabulated some three hundred and fifty assassinations of left-wing political figures, union organizers, peace activists, reporters, civil servants, and intellectuals in the vicinity of the city of Cali alone. Those murdered included the leader of the Patriotic Union and three of its Federal and Departmental senators.

One is tempted to conclude that it really is a choice between chains or rifles. However, only those whose lives are on the line have a right to decide what the lesson is and to choose what to do about it. In fact, only they do decide.

Peer Gynt's Return

A Year in Prairie City

I had come to the conclusion that I had to leave New York. Despite everything, it was still part of America. A teaching job at the University of Manitoba came up just as I was mulling over where to jump next and that was how I returned to Canada.

I let everything slide during my last month in New York. It was the one place I had felt at home since I was a kid. I gave my furniture away, packed a couple of bags, said goodbye to a few close friends, didn't answer the telephone and just walked around the city until it was time to leave. Adieu, adieu.

The Winnipeg expatriates I knew were a loyal lot. They said things such as, "Winnipeg isn't just another prairie city you know. It's cosmopolitan. It's really more like . . . Chicago, say, than a town like Edmonton." Or they said, "I envy you. I'd like to be going back to Winnipeg myself. There are such rich cultural traditions: the North End, the Winnipeg Art Gallery, etc., etc." It only struck me later that all the people telling me about the wonders of Winnipeg no longer lived there.

Winnipeg. I had a hard time believing that a city of over half a million people could be that small-townish. Maybe it was the winter, maybe there were all sorts of vibrant social circles around, as Winnipegers always claimed. I can't say because I never discovered any.

The one vital locale I found was the People's Co-op Bookstore. It was run by Floyd Wilson, a quizzical Cape Breton loyalist beached on the shores of the Red River. "What do you mean calling Toronto 'Eastern Canada' — it's Central Canada. You Westerners don't know anything about the traditions of the Maritimes," he might rail.

"Ah Floyd, where I'm from anything east of the Rockies is considered Eastern."

"From BC, eh? Well then its hopeless to try to enlighten you about any other region in Canada."

The bookstore was a tiny hole in the wall joint up near the farmers' market on North Main. It was stacked to the rafters with shelves of books. Amazing what was stashed away in this place. As distinct from the displaced greengrocers who predominate in the book trade Wilson was committed to the importance of books and not just profits. It was one of those undertakings in which a single person can make all the difference.

"Say Floyd, a few years ago there was a film about a Sicilian bandit ... Juliao or something. About the role of the Mafia in Italian politics. Does that ring any bell?"

Wilson would mull it over while talking to another customer about something else. He'd climb on a stool and rummage through the fifth shelf, second layer from the front. "That sounds like Gavin Maxwell's book about Salvatore Guiliano, *God Preserve Me From My Friends*. Is that it?" He'd dredge out some snippets of the theme and more than likely pull out a slightly dog-eared copy of the book you were looking for. If not he could suggest something comparable.

At night I'd listen to my short wave radio. You could pick up Radio Habana and their rebroadcast of the Voice of Vietnam quite clearly. Reports crackling through the midnight winter, interspersed with strains of "Guantanamera" and the reading of names of those who had fallen in Bolivia and elsewhere in a world struggling to be born.

Winnipeg had not yet left the 1950s. The local press, the professoriat and even most university students were more supportive of the tattered hokum about the American way of life than many Americans themselves were. After participating in the rising crescendo of opposition, after witnessing the widespread rethinking which had emerged in America during the 1960s, coming to Winnipeg was like stepping back twenty years. It wasn't just a matter of political attitudes. Zenith City proprieties shaped local attitudes towards sex, authority, social relations, ethnic boundaries and virtually everything which goes to make up a culture.

With a few exceptions my students were determined to hear about "strange peoples and exotic customs". That is what they wanted from anthropology. They also felt, despite the requisite bow to "cultural pluralism", that their little world was the measure of social arrangements and the goal of all human endeavors. Actually the naively conservative students were fundamentally more decent and more open to learning than the squalid group of self-serving "student radicals" hovering around New College. These latter were sons and daughters of the lesser Winnipeg bourgeoisie and "student power" was their shtick, meaning they wanted a say in decisions of who to hire and fire and what was to be taught. I would not be surprised to learn that many of them are corporate lawyers and vehement reactionaries today.

There was only one other Canadian besides myself in the department of anthropology at the University of Manitoba. The rest were imports from the American midwest or Texas. But it could have been worse. In purely collegial matters the faculty were decent enough. It certainly wasn't they who had fastened blinkers on the students. Although I probably didn't enlighten many of my students, the head of the department offered to extend my contract. But I couldn't stand the prospect of another year there.

Do you want to hear about Winnipeg in winter where your tires are square in the morning and you have to plug your engine block heater in wherever you park? Should I try to describe the corner of Main and Portage in early March, or the feeling one gets when the first string of loudly honking geese comes winging in over the slush-sodden fields in spring?

A good deal of my time was spent completing my PhD dissertation, which bore the title "Why Don't You Work Like Other Men Do?" (It's the first line of "Hallelujah I'm A Bum" and alludes to the migratory workers in North America as well as those in the sugarcane fields of Colombia. The song's once generally known response is "How the hell can I work when there's no work to do?")

I defended the dissertation at Columbia University in the spring of 1968. Quite a few people I knew became deeply depressed after they had completed their dissertation and gotten their doctorate. It was almost as if their purpose in life was over. Others acted as if it were something quite mundane. Not me. On getting my doctorate I walked around elated — not because any great vistas had opened up but because I felt that I had finally shown all those sages, from junior high school teachers to Cyril Belshaw, who had told us that we "weren't university material". In my imagination I waved my doctorate from Columbia University under their collective noses.

After returning to Manitoba and completing my teaching stint I quit without having any other job to go to. Carol and I drove through the backlands of BC visiting the scenes of my youth and then I departed to investigate jobs in Toronto. Somehow I'd gotten the impression that Toronto was Canada's New York and thought that it might be the place to live. But I couldn't get work there of any kind, not even an eighty-dollar-a-week truck driver's job. The employers wanted someone younger. I was then thirty-two.

Carol Prefers to Remain Anonymous

Oh you can give marriage a whirl
If you've got some cash in your purse.
But don't marry no one but a Prairie girl
'Cuz no matter what happens she's seen worse.

The one thing which made the year in Winnipeg worthwhile was that I met Carol. My wife comes from a large family and grew up on a hard-scrabble northern Manitoba farm. She could tell you of a world little changed from the 1930s, of one-room schools and traveling down winter roads by sled and caboose, of working with horses and of seasoned thirteen-year-old girl tractor drivers. She did all that and more — and she's a lot younger than me. She might also tell about critical financial decisions involving how to get winter clothes for all the kids in the family. There's a tug of affection in her reminiscences of girlhood on the farm but usually she doesn't want to talk about it. Of seven brothers and sisters not one remained in farming or even stayed in the region. Their parents, who pioneered in that particular district, didn't want them to go through what they had either.

Carol says that her life and that of her family is nobody's business but their own. She says she doesn't want to be pickled on paper and read about by who knows whom. I am enjoined against writing about her. "It wasn't anything extraordinary anyway," she says.

Alright. It would be difficult to do anyway because Carol has been the most important person in my life since we met. That is always the most difficult to capture. The trouble is that a crucial element is left out of the following account. It shouldn't be surprising but it is, surprising what a difference one person can make in your life. It was that I now had someone I could rely on, someone who I knew would be there even if we were apart at times. It's all been said a million times before but it is important. There should be room for the words "love" and "trust" here somewhere. That's what that anonymous song is about.

In the Hall of the Mountain King

I was living in the basement of a retired railwayman's house in East Toronto when, through a series of well nigh miraculous redirections, a telegram arrived asking me to telephone the Political Science, Sociology and Anthropology department at Simon Fraser University. When I heard Jerry Sperling's Runyonesque version of a job offer I jumped at it. In a battered old VW van loaded with all my belongings I clunked and bumped across the prairies, which now looked more beautiful than they ever had while I was stationed there. My van wheezed and sputtered through the mountains, through the Kootenays, and three days later carried me into Vancouver and to the self-styled Storm Centre of the Western World located on the top of Burnaby Mountain.

It beats me why the events surrounding Simon Fraser University during the late 1960s and early 1970s have not appeared in a book. If ventures such as David Bercuson's *The Great Brain Robbery* are any indication we may yet be treated to a fearless adulation of the powers that be and a vociferous denunciation of those who challenged them.

All the interested parties naturally have different, often diametrically opposed, versions of what happened. Few accounts would not be vehemently contested by somebody. Many of the individuals involved remained members of the Simon Fraser faculty until their retirement, while others had to emigrate to find work. I won't even attempt to present a balanced account here.

Simon Fraser University began as a western Canadian version of an American state college. It was launched in the early 1960s as a prestige project by the Social Credit government during its balmier development days. The construction and organization were overseen by Socred braintruster Gordon Shrum. It was an instant institution of higher learning, launched with the flair of any number of other megaprojects around the province being launched at the time. Nothing wrong in that.

Simon Fraser came on stream during a period of university growth in Canada and relied on a captaincy system of recruiting. Heads of the new departments were recruited by a newly appointed college president and the heads in turn recruited more or less whomever they liked as faculty. It was fast. Since the great majority of department heads were American or British expatriates it was not surprising that the majority of faculty recruited also were Americans or Brits. The percentage was open to acrimonious debate but in certain departments up to two-thirds of the faculty were non-Canadians.

The Socred government ultimately got the sort of college it wanted, but in the mid and late 1960s that wasn't as easy to achieve as it would be today. Simon Fraser University was supposed to be something other than a glorified business college. Since it included no professional faculties, since its science departments were weak, there seemed to be a need to sell Simon Fraser University as having some special attraction. A dollop of "experimental and innovative programs" in the social sciences would be a useful ornament.

The head picked to start up the Political Science, Sociology and Anthropology department was a British sociologist by the name of Tom Bottomore. He hired some young Canadian and American teachers with iconoclastic and relatively progressive views, although hardly to the exclusion of others.

Improbable as it may seem today when Simon Fraser University is dominated by business and computer science programs, PSA was then the largest department on campus. A remarkable body of students had congregated around the social sciences. Whatever their fevers many of them actually had a desire and capacity to learn. The graduate students who had been attracted played a major role in changing a barely built suburban college into an at times vibrant place to teach. All that had transpired in the three or four years before I arrived in the fall of 1968.

The social science faculty comprised a heterogeneous array of political viewpoints both within and without that indescribable melange then know as "radical". There were hardly two faculty members in the PSA department who agreed with each other. In fact, it was no more ideological or monochromatic than most other university departments in North America. Only the political spectrum of views was different.

The student movements in America and Europe had a considerable influence on views held on Burnaby Mountain. They were different times. The job situation wasn't so desperate. Students were open to some thought about where they were bound, what was abroad in the world and what they might do about it, if anything. Student radicalism wasn't something conjured up out of a sophomoric mass by a cabal of left-wing faculty at Simon Fraser University.

The predominant outlook took its main direction from the US civil rights and anti-war movements. The dominant element in the radicalism of the 1960s was really a species of left ethnic nationalism, though it was rarely recognized as such. It was alloyed to a rather blind faith in "participatory democracy". Despite nominal bows to Marxism it was race and racism, not class interests and struggles, which made the world go round according to this outlook. In retrospect, it is evident that a great deal of what passed for radicalism could be and was accommodated within the neo-conservatism which came to dominate the ideology of the 1980s.

A general feature of student radicalism at virtually all universities was its distance from earlier left-wing and working-class traditions. I don't mean that they were unfamiliar with once broadly shared understandings. I mean that they usually knew virtually nothing of that past. It was as if everything had to be rediscovered from scratch. You would have thought that any meaningful understanding the world had begun with Our Generation.

"Youth is a class," allegedly. American blacks were a class. Entire Third World peoples were supposedly a class. Only the working class wasn't a class, it seemed. According to the reigning ideology of North American university radicalism, "the working class in the developed countries had become part of and defenders of the system", they had been "bribed by the profits extracted from superexploited Third World peoples".

There were unfailing references to "superexploited" sectors and peoples. Sometimes it seemed like a competition to discover the Most Extraordinarily Superexploited Group in the world. Having done so the discoverers could then dismiss the claims of the vast majority of others as "relatively privileged". Apart from being glib it could be infuriating.

Racism was invoked to explain just about every conflict or system of inequality in the world. This view was sometimes wedded to various "Marxist" analyses as solemnized by contemporary interpreters in shotgun marriages. The war in Vietnam was "racist", as were all colonial wars. "Third World peoples", i.e. non-whites, everywhere were in the position they were because of ethnocentrism and racism. Indeed, some held that "imperialism is a form of racism". Oh me!

"So, you think that the Portuguese regime is a dictatorship because it represents the Portuguese people? And you think that it is fighting a colonial war for its possessions in Southern Africa because it has racist attitudes toward Africans?" I might ask. "Don't you think you have the causes and consequences backwards?" But *reductio ad absurdum* rarely cut much ice.

Those who fearlessly located the primary cause of oppression in the world on racism then figured they had risen above anyone who would not accept this "analysis". Oh the breast beating and flights of hairshirted moral superiority. Racism naturally meant "white racism". It was considered bad form to even mention the serried forms of racial, tribal and caste ideology among non-European peoples and societies. That was explained away with the glibbest sort of apologia. Similarly, bloody tyrants and homegrown exploiters in African, Asian and Latin American countries were typically construed as "compradores", the agents of always external agencies. It was a total misconstruction of the class forces in play in emerging nations. It was as if Europe and America had the patent rights on injustice and exploitation and as if imperialism held the sole export license.

Interlaced with this concern about racism was a heavy dose of ethnic chauvinism — as there always is in any form of ethnic nationalism. It largely went unchallenged. While ethnic solidarity was always a prime virtue, "assimilationism" was allegedly a cardinal sin. It was a variant of what North Americans have been taught for generations. Although most would have vehemently denied it, the underlying world view was that there were certain good, non-exploitive, victimized, etc. nationalities, and certain bad, authoritarian, militarist, etc. nationalities. You'd almost think that it ran in the cultural bloodstream. Elements of this allegedly "radical" outlook drew from much of the same substratum of Great Patriotic War ideology as the right did.

The terms you used were purported to have deep symbolic significance in how you understood a situation and who you "allied with".

For instance, using the phrase "Native peoples" rather than "Indians", or "Azania" rather than "South Africa", supposedly spoke volumes about one's perspective, regardless of what one knew or didn't know about the topic. You still hear that kind of hokum today, the dissection of phrases to reveal supposedly hidden predilections. It's rarely more than a hackneyed ploy.

As a teacher one had to resist demands to focus on issues of burning immediacy. Most faculty managed to keep that within bounds. Although there was some grandstanding involved, the demands for "relevance" (i.e. dealing with issues which did exist, were important and were of present concern) by serious students did stem from laudatory concerns. It was a far better environment for teaching and learning than the jaded indifference I later met elsewhere.

My students became inured to my constant carping that they had to read the assigned material. "It's amazing what you can learn from books if you'll go to the library and read them," I'd rant. Those who remained in my classes usually did so and those who were put off by such authoritarian demands usually switched courses during the first two weeks. That seemed sensible and beneficial for all concerned.

Eldridge Cleaver's *Soul On Ice*, Franz Fanon's *The Wretched of the Earth*, André Gunder Frank's *Development and Underdevelopment in Latin America*, Antonio Gramsci's *Prison Notebooks*, and a few other tomes were dragged into almost every discussion, whether of relevance or not. Someone's estimation of *Soul On Ice* was a good gauge of their gullibility, I found. If they had no qualms about Cleaver's bunkum they were usually high on the cant scale. That sort of bandwagoneering is endemic to university students everywhere. But it could be infuriating.

"It seems that the more grotesque aspects of student radicalism of the time have taken over in your reminiscences," says Mordecai Briemberg. "There was also a commitment to investigate topics which long had been taboo. Surely you don't want to suggest that all of your colleagues and students were bemused by the sorts of excesses you mention." He's right. There was a great deal to be learned from many of my fellow teachers and from certain graduate students. I intended this to be an appreciation of them. Maybe I was expecting more of them than I would of students elsewhere.

Maybe I had forgotten how callow most of us were during our own early college years. The thing was that students in the PSA department were getting, right off the bat, understandings which had taken me and others years to come to. They were by-passing many (though hardly all) of the fallacies and misdirections which we as students had waded through and had to shake free from. Many of our students were doing work at a level in advance of undergraduates at other universities. A few of them could have held their own in graduate classes elsewhere. In one course on the Rural Sector in Latin America almost a half of the forty student papers which came in at end of term were serious and thoughtful pieces of work. In case you don't know, that is an amazing ratio in an undergraduate college class.

That wasn't primarily due to my own teaching, but was an indication of what the department had accomplished in the few years of its existence among a collection of what elsewhere would have been typical college students. Although I felt driven, I enjoyed working with most of my students. Many were the first in their families ever to have gone to college and a number already had been in the labour force. One would have to be steeped in the doxology of the yellow press to write such students off as the children of affluence pursuing a delayed adolescence.

A feature of university life during the late 1960s and early 1970s was the incorporation of student representatives in the decision-making processes of the university, with student representation on the Board of Governors, curriculum and hiring committees, and so forth. Many universities had instituted such reforms. The PSA department had gone further in attempting to put a system of "participatory democracy" into effect than any other at Simon Fraser University. Oh, the bogeyman stories which began to make the rounds of what allegedly was entailed. One occasionally still hears those tales dredged up today, dragons for closet Don Quixotes and their Sancho Panzas. Send for Maurice Sendak!

What most bothered many members of the university faculty, I now think, was not primarily the views but the manners of the more vociferous student radicals. It was the poses struck, the disrespect and loudmouthedness. It was the open lack of respect which raised professorial hackles. It's true that there was a lot of self-satisfied smugness on the part of students. But hubris and posturing is something inherent to universities — and not merely among students either. When one compares the caliber of student work done in the PSA department at the time to that which prevailed elsewhere, it is evident that concern for academic standards was not the real issue.

More than any other aspect of the PSA department, the system of student participation set other faculty against us. Naturally there was no question of course content and teaching being decided by majority vote, although that was one of the more hysterical charges being made. Student representatives could and did initiate requests for certain courses, could raise grievances and make representations on hiring, but they could not determine what was taught or how it was taught. Indeed, anyone conversant with university faculty also knows that any such scheme of ideological control would be quite unworkable.

In any case, participatory democracy turned out to be one of those supposedly good things of which there can be too much. It got to be enervating. The real drawback was the phenomenal amount of time taken up in preparing briefs and reports, attending committee meetings and so forth. Proposals from committees which themselves had gone through endless discussions would be put forward at a departmental meeting. These would be debated and revised, storms in teacups, and irrelevancies would arise and a final (barring later revision) decision would be arrived at. Usually this was a variant of the last coherent proposal made. Ultimately, everyone proceeded in their own way anyway.

Even before the PSA department was placed under administrative trusteeship, both faculty and student representatives were rethinking what was and wasn't possible within the context of a university. The excesses and mannerisms were already on the wane, the posturing was giving way to something more solid. What was responsible for that change is difficult to specify. Given time, a couple of years, the sillier aspects of university radicalism undoubtedly would have been discarded.

It was a situation of considerable promise. Exceptional graduate students from senior universities as well as leading scholars were applying to join the PSA department. That was phenomenal for a reputationless suburban college. One can only guess at what might have developed had the department been allowed to continue. My guess is that a heterogeneous core of faculty and students would have shaken down to become a centre of radical scholarship. They would have demonstrated that those two words are not a contradiction of terms, as most academics since have chosen to believe. But time had run out.

One Good Purge Goes a Long Way

Simon Fraser University was an extreme case of the domination of Canadian universities by foreign faculty. That was somewhat less true in the Political Science, Sociology and Anthropology department than in others. Despite what one might expect, a core of the "radical" faculty in the PSA department were Canadians. But we were not Canadian nationalists and we didn't denounce those wanting to purge the social sciences as American and British expatriates, which is what they were mainly.

However, any suggestion that nationality should be one consideration in hiring was met by howls of outrage by the expatriate faculty and administration. It was depicted as an insidious ploy to water down the precious vital fluids of academic excellence. Oh, the breathtaking twaddle about "academic standards" which some of these holders of degrees from Southern Nebraska U or Dumpling State College came out with. There was a great deal of running off at the mouth about the "smell of burning books" (not meaning bankbooks) and other bits of iconography which one finds on late night flicks.

In the purge which followed, all the Canadian faculty members in the social sciences, with two exceptions, were fired. Consider that. In a Canadian university funded by Canadian tax dollars, a predominantly expatriate administration and faculty fires virtually all of the Canadian professors in the social sciences because of the political slant of their teaching. That would be a *cause célèbre* in most countries. But not in Canada.

The radical phase of the PSA department only lasted three years, if you include the simmering discontent leading up to the original restructuring of the university and the sputtering aftermath of the purge. Moves which had been underway throughout the year came to a head with the administrative trusteeship slapped on the PSA department by the Dean of Arts, who had been shot into the dean's chair by the very "democratization" process which he now decried. The president of Simon Fraser University at the time was an American labour economist by the name of Kenneth Strand. He too had leapfrogged into his position by posturing as a defender of faculty rights during the previous shakeup.

I don't want to imply that the purge was merely the work of a nest of newly minted administrators operating under the aegis of a Board of Governors appointed by the Social Credit party in government. No. The purge did have the backing of the clear majority of Simon Fraser faculty. It's something I always remember when I hear Canadian academics go through their routines about academic freedom.

After the PSA department was placed under trusteeship, the administration set in motion "qualification" procedures which ultimately resulted in the dismissal or departure of the overwhelming majority of the original faculty in the department. The exact figures were always a topic of debate as to who had quit, who had been dismissed, who had just not been rehired and what the individual circumstances were. But however you cut it, at least two thirds of the faculty teaching in the combined social science department at Simon Fraser University in the fall of 1968 were no longer on staff by the spring of 1970.

Among those dismissed were Jerry Sperling and Louis Feldhammer. Reason? Their MA's weren't sufficient academic paper for the new Simon Fraser University. Both of them became senior members and sometime chairmen of the university departments they joined elsewhere.

Also dismissed was Mordecai Briemberg, a former Rhodes scholar and the chairman of the PSA department. Briemberg was one of the most sagacious and stimulating thinkers I had encountered at any university anywhere. He was replaced as departmental chairman by a sociologist with a BA from Leeds, until a more senior retread could be acquired from abroad. Teaching was important to Mordecai and he was a fine teacher. But unfortunately he refused to leave the province. He never taught in a university in British Columbia again.

Tom Brose was an sociologist in the Catholic Worker tradition. Possibly he was not a great scholar but he was the sort of enthusiastic, personal, teacher which any university department should be pleased to have. He too was fired, allegedly for lack of doctoral paper. Brose became a professor and then a dean at Fairhaven College, University of Western Washington. Later he was a co-director of the Navaho Labor Department and helped make that reservation one of the most unionized corners of Arizona. Those were certainly not the sorts of talents which Simon Fraser University wanted.

John Legatt was not dismissed, he just wasn't rehired. But he did have his PhD. In fact, he was then publishing his sixth or seventh scholarly books on American working class life which were widely

The author at an anti-Vietnam war demonstration, Vancouver, Spring 1969.

cited in US academic circles. Few of the Simon Fraser faculty touting scholarly excellence were as noted in their respective fields as Legatt was. I can't remember what reason was given for ousting him — possibly "dereliction of duty" in failing to cross the picket line set up by the dismissed faculty. Legatt returned to Rutgers and went on writing his books, occasionally tossing barbs at the easy time McCarthyism had of it in Canada.

Dismissed: Nathan Popkin, a political scientist who came from a Louisiana Jewish populist background, if you can picture that. Nathan was rather nervous when outside a classroom and seemed like a pushover for college purifiers. "Our Clarence Darrow," smirked Jerry Sperling, with a mixture of snideness and accuracy. Popkin lambasted the administration during his dismissal hearings in a senatorial style which resurrected all the classic arguments for academic freedom. He gave the purgers a run for their money. He talked where he could and hired a lawyer to fight through a year long series of hearings. It was rumored that it had cost the university something like a hundred thousand dollars in legal fees and administrative salaries to make

Popkin's dismissal stick. But they succeeded. After all, what is public money when a principle is at the stake.

Prudence Wheeldon, a sociologist from Rhodesia, was also dismissed. But she had been promised a tenure-track position on joining the department. So Wheeldon got her own lawyer and carried her case beyond the university's Academic Appointments and Tenure Committee and into the courts. They ruled that university tenure in British Columbia was in no way a contractual obligation and was "merely a moral commitment" by a university. Well, so much for that. She moved to the Gulf Islands and gave up trying to teach in BC.

There were two or three others who quit the department in disgust after the purge. Some had seen the handwriting on the wall and had left to take teaching positions elsewhere. I landed a tenured associate professorship at the University of Toronto. Had I remained at Simon Fraser I probably wouldn't have come up to the "new standards of academic excellence" which the administration invoked.

The most eminent victim of the purge was Kathleen Gough Aberle. During the 1960s she was one of the leading anthropologists in North America. This stemmed from her reintroduction of the economic-political context of traditional anthropological topics, be they ethnographies of South Indian peasant society or the intricacies of kinship. One didn't have to agree with the specifics of Aberle's work in order to appreciate that she was an anthropologist with an indisputable international reputation. Only at Simon Fraser University could one have found boobs with the effrontery to dismiss Aberle for lack of academic credentials.

There was not a social scientist on the committee to determine Aberle's qualifications for tenure. A scratch crew of commerce scholars, chemistry wallopers and literarians were to decide whether Kathleen Aberle was up to their academic standards. Tenure was denied. Aberle had published in journals such as *Monthly Review*, which was specifically mentioned as an indication of her "questionable scholarship". Given the nature of her appointment this meant that she would no longer be rehired. (Tom Bottomore, though nominally a member of the university, had long since removed himself to England. He supported the denial of tenure decision without ever leaving the Sussex fens.) Shortly after, Aberle was fired outright for "dereliction of duty", meaning that she refused to cross a picket line challenging the collective dismissals. That was when the writ hit the fan.

"An act of sheer intellectual vandalism," wrote Marvin Harris from Columbia University in a widely circulated open letter. "It demonstrates the contempt of the Simon Fraser administration for scholarship and academic reputation," wrote Eric Wolf in a similar letter. There were comparable responses in academic journals and from senior social science faculties around North America. The Simon Fraser administrators were somewhat taken aback by all this and had some of their boyos find out who this Kathleen Aberle was. They only then realized that they had just sacked a scholar with an international reputation. Time for some quick, but principled, backpeddling.

The administration suggested to Aberle that if she separated her case from the other dismissed faculty, the university would reopen her tenure hearings with a good prospect of a different decision. But she wouldn't. And a few years later it was all forgotten, water under the bridge. Kathleen stayed in Vancouver with her family and never taught at a university in BC again. Simon Fraser University rebuilt its social science departments with safe and sane retreads, and the occasional tubthumper to add a little colour.

Another half dozen faculty in other departments either quit or were not rehired during the following year, a spin-off of the purge. I don't know what happened to most of them — except Leonard Minsky, a former English professor. He presided over the establishment of Northwest College in Terrace during the short-lived New Democrat government, only to be ousted when the Socreds regained power. Minsky finally decided that enough was enough and left BC for good.

The purged faculty had shown a certain gullibility which became evident in the actions of those who they themselves had hired. Of the PSA members who accepted the purge and carried on teaching through the strike, a number were individuals who had been hired by the now dismissed faculty. As is almost inevitable in such conflicts, many in the rump department became the most vociferous opponents of the purgees. Regardless of their academic paper or lack thereof, the defenders of the purge quickly received tenure.

Far be it from me to suggest that anything like a blacklist of faculty purged by Simon Fraser University operated in British Columbia. We've surely all been warned often enough about conspiracy myths in a pluralistic society such as ours. But it is passing strange that academics with sound qualifications and reputations before the purge could never afterward find teaching positions in even the scruffiest colleges in this province. Strange too that those who left the province did well in their academic or allied careers, but that all those who remained in or returned to British Columbia never worked in their field again.

In the years immediately after the purge Simon Fraser University's degree-granting stock fell and its student enrollment declined as denunciations rolled in from both Canadian and American professors. The Canadian Association of University Teachers censured the university, until it assured the Association of its commitment to academic freedom. Stung by such criticism, the Simon Fraser faculty joined the administration in defense of their reputations and launched into a campaign of writing letters, rounding up allies and going on "informational" tours. To the accompaniment of copious crocodile tears and indignation it was revealed that they, the supporters of the political purge, were the victims of "left McCarthyism".

By 1973 Simon Fraser University had more or less turned Canadian academic opinion around so that the victims were now looked upon as the guilty party. What was the convincing argument the university used? The ability to offer teaching positions which for a while were among the most highly paid in Canada. Academic freedom is one thing but money is money after all. Simon Fraser had no difficulty in rounding up all the talent it wanted. The university and the local press hyped "the return of academic excellence".

There was soon more academic excellence capering about than you could shake a stick at. Simon Fraser University established a Criminology Department which it promoted as the "first complete penology program in Canada". It set out to train and provide a scientific basis for prison guards, public and private police, parole officers, aspirant wardens and others in the growing security industry. It was the New Social Science in action, and "professionalism" was the watchword. The man picked to head the Criminology department was an Egyptian by the name of Ezzat Fattah.

When he first arrived in BC, Chairman Fattah opined that because of the province's resource industries and migratory workers a subculture of disregard for the law had evolved here. That comment was supposed to show how Modern Criminology understood the role that culture played in crime. That was too much even for jaded union leaders, who usually dismissed Simon Fraser University as just a Socred gas house. A flurry of condemnation threatened to mar the university's new image. Today that kind of talk about "the dangerous lower classes" would be right in line with the new scholarship, but it was still too blatant then, and Fattah had to keep his claptrap for internal consumption. (He reemerged a decade later as a hoofer on the anti-terrorist conference circuit in Canada.) But his department was wildly successful. Within a short time, Criminology had more students than all the rest of the social sciences combined.

The Political Science, Sociology and Anthropology department was broken up into three separate units. The new Political Science department was handed over to one Edward McWhinney, a senior import from Thatcherland, "Sanders of the River" arriving to patrol the Fraser. Initially touted as an authority on security operations, he was given the task of straightening out the social sciences. Those recently concerned with defending scholarship from politicization saw nothing incongruous or hypocritical in the fact that a few years later McWhinney made a run for a federal Conservative Party nomination while teaching at Simon Fraser University. His candidacy was vetoed by party leader Joe Clark so McWhinney returned to keeping his files and was trotted out from time to time whenever the Vancouver press required the opinions of a Constitutional Expert.

New recruitment filled the positions in what remained of the Sociology and Anthropology department. A coterie of retreads were gathered up from Britain and America, scholars still engaged in shuffling off the coils of serpents already slain many times over in the academic salons of the 1950s. Listening to them was like entering a time warp. It really didn't make much difference because student enrollment in the social sciences plummeted and the department was relegated to the back burner.

The biggest winner in the purge was the Archaeology section, which had consisted of two professors. The senior man was from Arizona State University while the other was his former student there. It's strange how academic excellence always seems to run in such close circles. When the PSA department was placed under administrative trusteeship, Archaeology was split off and later made into a separate department. The two archaeologists walked away with a large slice of the budget and developed an unsuspected talent for media hype and grant getting — a talent which became the hallmark of scholarship at Simon Fraser University.

The Archaeology department acquired its own yacht/research vessel to cruise the coast in summer expeditions. That was as good for press copy on slow days as filler about mission boats had once been.

For a while archaeology became a growth industry on the hill. The department hired new faculty and teaching assistants and acquired its own lab complex where students got to walk around in white lab coats being scientific. Droves of students came flocking to them, students who had always been deeply concerned with preserving the "archaeological prehistory of this province" and who thought that "establishing a scientific typology of ground slate artifacts" was the grandest of intellectual enterprises, came tumbling out of the woodwork.

President Ken Strand, the most visible figure connected with the purge, was put out to pasture in the economics and business department after a suitable period. The senior administrators decided to find a new figure to hold down the front office while they restored the reputation of the university. After a circumspect search they settled on hiring Pauline Jewett, a former Carleton University professor, an Honest-to-God Canadian, and a woman to boot.

Jewett told all who would listen that Simon Fraser University "must put its growing pains behind it." (Bring out the Sloan's liniment.) She stumped meetings of the Canadian Association of University Teachers demanding that it lift its censure of Simon Fraser University, and in general she oversaw the establishment of the reign of academic excellence. The university launched a host of daring new programs; a luxurious crop of tin-horn gurus, shell game *philosophes*, and academic slush hunters sniffing out whatever fashions were marketable mushroomed up. Intermixed in all of this were some actual scholars doing solid academic work. But they can tell their own story and a polemic such as this is not the place for a balanced overview.

The wildly philistine temper of developments at Simon Fraser University took on a Brechtian quality. They might comprise material for a book in its own right — if an author could be found who didn't feel that reality had already done the job better than any satire could.

The View from Middle Earth

High Tide

Jerry Sperling, a Toronto expatriate, used to say, "They like to think that Toronto is the Paris of the North, but what it really is is Canada's Cleveland." That's not fair. It's a city of clean streets, the first subway system in Canada, and has been voted one of the most livable cities in North America — by Americans. But there is a certain unintentional farce to a city which can collectively revel in its claim to urbanity by erecting a concrete pylon, the CN Tower, and anointing it as "the tallest man-made, free standing structure in the free world". It is as if Torontonians were intent on overtaking the builders of the Eiffel Tower.

The University of Toronto is located in the heart of the city, where all real universities should be. It had its share of academic careerists ogling wider vistas of influence and it wasn't immune to intellectual fads and political fashions, but the university was committed to and did make room for scholarship. Once you had tenure at the University of Toronto you could dispense with much of the *impedimenta* of college life and pursue your work, lead where it may (within reason). Nor were you required to continually promote yourself. That you were there, a member of the department, said all that was required as to your competence. It may not have been the best of all intellectual worlds but it was better than that which exists at many universities.

In a major university teaching does not entail finding ways to entice or dragoon students to learn. It is up to the students themselves to learn or not. The professor's role is to see to it that they are presented with salient material and ideas which extend and debate generally accepted truths. For this to work there has to be a core of students who do not require catechism lessons and who can bring their own critical faculties to bear on a topic. A body of such students is absolutely essential to a great university. They are as necessary as dedicated professors and a well-stocked library.

Many of the students in my graduate courses were more like junior colleagues than typical university students. Indeed, in one graduate course over a half of my students were themselves teaching part-time at some college or other. Some of their research papers were the equal of articles appearing in professional journals. In fact a few papers originally written for my courses ultimately did get published in revised form. It was one of the most rewarding teaching experiences I ever had.

Bill Dunning and Tom McFeat, two senior members of the department, had striven to recruit Canadian faculty in the hope of creating a center of Canadian research in anthropology: Stuart Philpott, Mike Levin, Gordon Inglis, myself, Claire Hoppen and a few others, were predominant in the social anthropology section.

Our group might have played a role in establishing some independent directions in Canadian anthropology had we acted together and stayed together. But we let it slip away from us. Although we got along well enough together we went our own ways and generally did not involve ourselves in the academic politicking which is a fundament of establishing directions in scholarly fields. We frittered away the potentials of the situation by simply pursuing our own work.

I taught graduate classes at the University of Toronto and undergraduate ones at Scarborough College, a car-commuter campus on the eastern outskirts of the city. Upon arriving at Scarborough College I got into the soup almost immediately by trying to drum up faculty support for the people who had just been dismissed at Simon Fraser University. Most of the faculty in the anthropology department signed a petition urging that the Simon Fraser administration rescind the dismissals and open negotiations with those they had sacked. But they were an exception.

I gave a talk on the matter to the Scarborough social science fac-

Carol behind our house in Scarborough, 1972.

ulty at the beginning of the term. The tone was set by a warning given by Dean Arthur Kruger, a political scientist and Cold War academic. He gave me five minutes to present my case to the assembled faculty, who heard me out in lip-curled silence and offended faces, some complaining that they objected to listening to "propaganda" in a meeting called to deal with academic matters. The most serious assault yet on academic freedom in Canada didn't fall within that realm. There was some support from my colleagues in the anthropology section but they were the exception.

Teaching at Scarborough College was not so much a job as a penance. The students combined high school know-nothingism with baseless pride. They were thoroughly jaded and bored with schooling before they ever came through the college doors. What with kindergarten and thirteen years of public school they had been in school for fifteen or sixteen years before they arrived at a second year college class. Most of them had stopped listening to anything which sounded even vaguely familiar. That was probably why novelty, no matter how ludicrous, was so prized in teaching.

For many of my students the test of whether a topic was significant, whether a viewpoint was valid or not, depended on how it was treated on television. Whenever a new television season's "social problem" hit the tube you could trace its presence in the next batch of student papers. I was constantly preparing and reworking lecture materials. Absolutely pointless. They squeezed more effort out of me than I'd given to any other classes but most of them remained loyal to their news media-derived views.

The students knew they were the "most important component of the academic community". It was they who brought in the cold cash. Underlying a complicated financing formula the Ontario government basically funded colleges according to the number of more or less live bodies each had enrolled: the more students, the more funds. A tremulous administration bent over backwards to see that any student who failed even the very watered-down exams was provided a reexamination to assure a pass. "Scarborough College is not a second rate institution" was a recurrent refrain of the administration and faculty. They were right — it definitely wasn't second-rate.

As a Scarborough faculty member you had the feeling of being a glorified hireling. You had to be prepared to defend any decision to fail someone through a series of appeals. Students who handed in papers which were verifiably plagiarized, others whose work showed a total absence of reading or knowledge of the topic, yet others who had gotten through on little more than burbling catechisms — if you failed them you were in for a long, messy fight. No student in the PSA department at Simon Fraser University, which had allegedly undercut academic standards, would have gotten away with what was common practice at Scarborough.

A sociologist by the name of John Lee did a simple but dumbfounding study of Scarborough's degree-granting record. It hit the metro newspapers and as a consequence he was shunned by many of his colleagues. What did he do? He discovered that in the six years during which the college had been ladling out degrees under aegis of the University of Toronto it had graduated some three to four thousand students but that less than a dozen students in total had ever been flunked because of failing grades. Virtually everyone graduated as long as they were still breathing and paid their fees. After pondering over an appropriate reply Scarborough College contended that this remarkable rate of matriculation was due to the level of excellence among its students and staff.

I was first frantic, then angry and finally developed a tired indifference to most Scarborough students. That may seem like a terrible admission for a teacher to make. But my task, as I saw it, was to present anthropology as cogently as possible. My job was not to cozen, plead with or otherwise beguile students to learn. That was the wrong outlook for Scarborough College. Of course there were some outstanding teachers and some fine students even there. There were individuals determined to learn and capable of doing so. It was a joy to have a few of them in a class; but they were swimming against the tide at Scarborough. The only enlivening moments came from the graduate courses I taught on at the downtown St. George campus.

I came to Toronto enthused but within a year I was in a funk which lasted until we left. It should have been different. I was a tenured professor at the University of Toronto, a prestigious position with a good salary. But they were among the most empty and unproductive years of my life. I spent a lot of time walking our two Saint Bernards along the deserted beaches below Scarborough Bluffs. I drank too much. I could hardly wait until the final exams were marked in spring; we'd pile dogs and camping gear into the car, lash the canoe to the top and head west. The trouble was that we always had to go back.

The Charge of the Beaver Brigade

It must have been during the fall of 1972 and the spring of 1973. A safe and sane Canadian nationalism was in fashion. On the CBC, Pierre Berton was communing with the spirit of John A . McDonald and the National Dream. It was that kind of year in Muggsborough.

A new arrival trundles into the anthropology department as an administrative assistant and wants everyone to understand that they aren't dealing with a mere secretary. Her desk is soon festooned with a poster proclaiming "Continentalism Is Treason — The Canadian Liberation League". It has a stars-and-stripes-festooned eagle hovering over a map of Canada with its talons touching Ontario. Operating on the presumption that all things have to be explained in monosyllabic simplicity, Ms. Westchester proceeds to do just that. The League saw itself as a nationalist movement which would harness the Canadian Conservative tradition to oppose American imperialism. Brilliant, eh?

After a winter of mobilizing the Canadian Liberation Leaguers hold a mass rally in one of their members' apartment and reveal that the Liberal government is the main agent of the continentalism sapping Canada's precious patriotic fluids. The last straw of Liberal perfidy was not the imposition of the War Measures Act to round up a half dozen kidnappers — patriots appreciate toughness above all else or even any especially gross demonstration that corporate capital runs the Liberal Party. The final "treachery" revolves around the fact that the budget of the Canadian Armed Forces is going to be cut back a few percent by the Trudeau gang. "Our Armed Forces are the first line of defense against American domination," proclaims one Canadian Liberation League flyer. Ah . . . you didn't know that?

The League's big effort, the spring offensive, is to mount a mass demonstration of like-minded patriots to descend upon Ottawa. The call goes out — "All to the National Defense Headquarters". A mass rally of about a hundred turns up to demonstrate their support for the Canadian Armed Forces. Following that the bulletin boards around the University of Toronto are plastered with announcements of meetings to study the lessons of their On to Ottawa Trek. Some time later it is decided that the Canadian Liberation League "has done the task it set for itself" and they disband. Possibly they should have allied themselves with the Brownies.

> Land of the silver birch, home of the beaver
> Where the mighty moose wanders free.
> High on a rocky ledge, I'll build my wigwam.
> Tum di di, Tum di di, dum, dum, dumb.

Ms. Westchester decides that it is more effective to work "inside the system" and she prepares to get a degree and then a teaching position. At about this time Feminism appears on the Toronto scene as a marketable item. Ms. Westchester and another graduate student set out to uncover the neglected history of women in the labour movement. That is, they are going to interview wives of union leaders to chronicle how these women were themselves sorely oppressed as a gender.

It so happened the daughter of Harvey Murphy, one of the historic figures of the Canadian labour movement, was a graduate student in the anthropology department. Against Mary's better judgment she introduced this liberation duo to her mother, but after an hour Isobel Murphy didn't want to have anything more to do with them. As it turned out that was the response they got from most of the "subjects" they approached. So they bewailed the "self-imposed passivity of women in the old left" and let it go at that.

But there's an epilogue. Sometime later a group of graduate students looking for fundable dissertation topics glommed on to the idea of doing a team study of a single-industry town from an anthropological perspective. They were going to study a Canadian working-class community but without any of "the usual romantic misconceptions". Ms. Westchester became part of the braintrust behind this project.

Like all other such studies ever floated, this one was going to be based on "new approaches"; their study was also going to be "relevant" (not "redolent"). After a stint of grant-getting labours, a drove of graduate students descend upon Sudbury to establish a "research base". They move their gear to Sudbury and begin delving into the customs of smelter workers and those of unsalaried reproduction workers (i.e., their wives). But the team isn't going to be like past anthropologists who just took information from the community. They are going to give something back in return. What? They are going to, and for a short while actually did . . . wait for it now . . . offer classes in Consciousness Raising!

> Cocaine Bill and Morphine Sue
> Were walking down Bloor Avenue.
> Honey take a whiff o' me, Honey take a snort o' me.

> They come to a drugstore painted green
> The sign outside said 'Free Morphine.'
> Honey take a whiff o' me, Honey take a snort o' me.

Leaving on the Ebb Tide

I remember exactly where we were when we heard of the September 11, 1973 military coup in Chile, driving back to Toronto from Vancouver, about eleven at night on a stretch of empty road north of Nipigon. Ten-second news flashes sandwiched between pop music on a late night

Visiting Carol's parents' farm, central Manitoba, 1973.

radio station, reports fragmentary enough to allow you to hope that the Popular Unity government might yet prevail. But by the time we got to Toronto it was clear who had won.

So many years later it is easy to forget the way in which Canadian notables spewed out apologetics for the coup. It is easy to gloss over the sickening clucking about how "the coup was lamentable but an expectable response to extremism". The main task came to centre on pressuring the Liberal government to open the doors to Chilean refugees literally fleeing for their lives. There was a great deal of antipathy even to that. The Canadian Association of University Teachers sat on its ass and refused to be drawn into this "controversial issue". The general response around the university confirmed my deepest pessimism.

A noon-time rally organized in support of Chilean refugees and the Popular Unity forces in Chile met with overwhelming indifference and considerable outright hostility among the students at Scarborough College. Scarborough's principal, Ralph Campbell, delivered himself of a rambling reminder about "the limits of democracy" to naive faculty members like myself. But at least he signed a petition, however grudgingly, in support of an emergency policy toward Chilean refugees. Hardly two dozen of the faculty at Scarborough would even go that far.

Equally depressing was the student left in Toronto which, individually or in cacophonous concert, largely dissolved into sanctimonious posturing and sectarian phrase-mongering. Whatever effective pressure was put on the Canadian government to modify its refugee policy came from unions, church groups and anyone but students and academics.

During my upcoming sabbatical year Carol and I decamped for the Gulf Islands in BC. I worked on the ground crew at the Vancouver airport during the following spring and summer but returned to teach at Toronto for a final year.

During the two years I had been away, the intellectual climate around the university had become noticeably more mean-spirited. A battalion of entrenched academics whom I had written off as the residue of the earlier Cold War era were beginning to reemerge into the limelight. A few years later they and squads of newly minted like-minded scholars began to dominate the intellectual climate of the Toronto intelligentsia.

In addition to the Babbittry of the suburban campuses, the University of Toronto had spawned a number of right-wing student groups. What I had never before seen in Canada was organized Jewish chauvinism. A strand of that was a widely circulated student journal of Herut persuasion. One of its typical themes was that all Palestine was Jewish land and that Palestinians were merely the cast-off litter of Arab countries who had filtered into the region only after the Zionists had arrived there. Anyone who challenged that view or who opposed Israeli crimes was "morally co-responsible for Auschwitz," etc. In the intervening decades such statements have become commonplace, but at the time it was shocking.

Another of the new right-wing student groups at the University of Toronto was the Edmund Burke Society, co-founded by Paul Fromm. Fromm went on to distinguish himself when his society, re-named the Western Guard tried a take-over of the Ontario Social Credit Party. This was even too much for Real Caouette, then leader of this far-right federal fringe party. Later, during the 1980s, Fromm attempted a similar breach of the walls of the Tory Big Blue Machine, and eventually settled into a life-long career as a radio talk show host.

There were also students of a similar ilk engaged in a "watch operation" which involved monitoring the courses of suspect teachers to gather information on subversive teaching. One student in my Scarborough classes who was always asking about Marxist interpretations of topics in the most incongruous contexts turned out to be one of these monitors. A course on cultural ecology is an unlikely place to look, but witch sniffers can find anti-semitism or subversion in Gold-ilocks and the Three Bears.

In 1977 I returned to put in a final year of teaching at the University of Toronto. Carol had remained in Vancouver and I was staying at the old Wellesley Hotel on the corner of Spadina and College. Milton Acorn lived on the floor above me and was near his apogee as the "people's poet" of Canada. Since I wasn't a poet he didn't bother to shade meanings with me and we had some lively two-way monologues down in the Silver Dollar Bar or upstairs over a bottle of Bushmill's.

The Spadina district was probably the closest you could get to the Lower East Side in Canada. It had been a Jewish working-class neighbourhood for almost a half century and during the previous generation streams of Hungarian, Portuguese and other European immigrants had put their stamp on the district. It was what a city core should be. Had Carol and I moved there initially, Toronto might have been more bearable. It was a measure of my despondency that we never had made that move.

During the year I became involved in trying to write Harvey Murphy's life history; his daughter talked me into that. Harvey was in bad health and it proved impossible to obtain a coherent account from him. But his fragmentary reminiscences of his young manhood around the Spadina district as a left-wing union organizer during the 1920s and 1930s were fascinating. The streets, street corners and buildings which I passed on weekend rambles shed their contemporary guise and one visualized a quite different Toronto from that which now exists.

I couldn't take any more. I quit the University of Toronto with the understanding that I'd never again get as senior a teaching position as this. I left with a feeling of relief but also of sadness for all the wasted years and sacrifices made in getting to that position. I was returning to British Columbia with the intent of writing the kinds of books I felt were important and with the determination to reach a working-class audience. I had no job prospects or pension plan whatsoever.

FIFTEEN

Hard Passage Home

On the Job Again

I've always been sort of intimidated by machinery, operating machinery to close tolerances under pressure is something I've usually shied away from. But that was what working on the Air Canada ground crew at Vancouver International Airport entailed. I found it challenging.

We worked in five-man teams and during a shift each team would bring in and unload, service and reload seven or eight aircraft. Each member of the team had a roster of tasks to perform and each week we rotated positions. It sounds regimented but in fact it was quite the opposite. It made sense and it worked well.

There were a half dozen types of aircraft, each with its own complement of hatches and service panels and its own pattern of work. There are usually a number of planes being worked in or out at the same time and the scene looks quite chaotic. Tractor trains are racing past each other, service vans and trucks are burbling around the tarmac, mobile conveyors and automatic loaders and an array of other equipment is shuttling about to no apparent purpose. But it is a finely tuned operation, each team doing its own job and using well established procedures of co-operation.

We'd bring the aircraft into its dock; ground wires on, wheel shocks in place, ground power cables attached, the boarding bridge swung into position and the aircraft doors sprung open. At the same time the two men operating the automatic unloader or driving the tractor train are waiting for the "engines off" lights on the belly of the aircraft to come on so they can race to the cargo hold doors to get the luggage out.

Operating the automatic loaders which extract or insert two-tonne cargo containers into the holds of larger aircraft is a tricky business. You stand on a raised bridge and work a bank of controls; there are about a dozen movements which have to be made in the correct sequence to get the containers joggling out of the hold, turned, bumping out on to the bridge and down the elevator, then sideways off the loader on to one of a string of trailers being pulled alongside. It's team work, you're dealing with tolerances of an inch or less and you have to be fast. I found it quite satisfying.

Loading was a trifle more relaxed. On the smaller planes, cargo was loaded by hand. You'd crawl inside the belly and manhandle the luggage, mail, air express, cases of frozen fish and even coffins with their occupants. The minutiae of how to stow the cargo were different for almost every flight. One would be an easy flight to load while another would have mountains of freight and no place to stow it. Maybe some snarl-up in servicing the plane developed or some piece of ground equipment you were using would break down or run out of fuel at least once a shift and that would provide momentary panic. You'd race around trying to get a replacement machine, find that they were either all in use or tagged for repair and have to devise some alternate strategy.

When the plane was ready to depart we'd push it out of the loading dock and on to the tarmac where it could taxi on its own. You've locked and double checked the cargo doors, pulled back the bridge and disconnected the ground support systems. The tractor has been coupled to the towing bar and the lead hand is talking to the pilot through headphones. You're behind the wheel of the ten- or thirty-ton tractor positioned below the nose of the plane. On the signal you let the clutch out very smoothly and push the aircraft out of the dock, straight back, without any jolts. There may be anywhere from fifty to three hundred passengers on board and the least jolt sends a shudder through the plane. If it is a Lougheed 1011 its belly arches above you like the underside of a metal whale and you have to crane your neck to see where the nose is in relation to the dock. Any overcompensation in steering and the towbar twists the path of the plane into devilishly contrary directions.

When we worked we worked flat out. But when we had finished a flight and were waiting for the next one we weren't required to fill the time with busy work. It was one of the few jobs I've ever had where the shift was over before you expected it. I never had to force myself to go to work, as I've had to in other jobs.

Almost everyone on the ground crew was fine to work with. But listening to some of these same guys was gut wrenching. Their conversations were an endless debate about professional sports and consumerist fantasies. When not that it was a rehash of television plots. As for grasping toward some understanding of the world around them, forget it. A considerable number of the younger workers hated "frogs" and "Pakis", "Arabs" and "homos", "the Russians" and the man in the moon. But it was appalling.

Only a few of the ground crewmen hired by Air Canada each spring ultimately became permanent employees. Young workers were constantly being recruited to supplement the permanent core and then let go in fall. Of the circa two hundred people on the ground crew there was not one woman and only one non-Caucasian, a Chinese-Canadian employed as a cleaner. At forty years of age I was one of the oldest employees on the ramp — the "old guy". Although I was physically able to hold my own with any of them on the job I really began to feel that I was from another era.

Despite its reputation, the union then representing the Air Canada ground crew workers demonstrated how a certain kind of labour unionism can be a useful extension of the personnel office. All the squabbles about who had seniority on some job or explanations of why some days didn't constitute holidays, etc. were dealt with by the shop steward. However, when it came to going to bat for a union member or getting the members to stand together against the company for their own interests, it was another matter.

For instance, just before I started on the job one man who had worked on the ground crew for more than a dozen years took home a leftover roast from the galley of a terminating flight. He was supposed to throw all remaining food into the garbage regardless of whether it had been touched or not. But he took this roast and was caught by a supervisor, charged with "pilferage" and fired. This was one of the senior men on the ramp and someone who was well liked to boot.

Others on the ground crew grumbled about the decision and complained to the shop steward, who had been on the case with a union staffer. "You all know the rules about taking so much as a book of matches from a plane. It doesn't matter that it was going to be thrown out, he had no right to take the roast. We can't defend him because legally we don't have leg to stand on. We tried to talk the company into settling for a one-year suspension but they were determined to make an example of him . . . Let that be a lesson to everyone. It's not worth it."

That is what the union steward said, not the personnel manager. That was it. Not the slightest inkling that you shouldn't take decisions coming down from management as if they were the word of God. And sure enough, after a while others on the ground crew were repeating the company line about the guy who was fired and about how "it was his own fault".

After I returned from a final year of teaching at Toronto in the spring of 1977 I lazed around getting my book, *Stump Ranch Chronicles,* into print but finally got a job in the Vancouver Main Post Office. In applying for a job like that one naturally makes up a totally spurious work record since to admit to having been a university teacher would disqualify you immediately. To get that job of lugging bags and boxes around one had to go through a battery of intelligence and aptitude tests more extensive than those used for entry into graduate school. I suspect they merely served as a rationale for the arbitrary decisions of a hiring panel which screened each applicant.

I worked on the night shift loading and unloading trucks in the basement of the Vancouver Post Office along with some thirty to forty other guys. It entailed constant though not especially heavy physical work — enough so that by morning your body knew you'd put in a full shift. The worst was that it was mind-numbing work. Before half the shift was over you felt you'd already put in more than eight hours.

The night shift crew consisted of a few middle-aged alternate life-style loyalists, a few older men who had lost long-term jobs elsewhere, a number of university graduates and others with quite checkered job histories. The majority of my fellow workers were in their late twenties to mid thirties and had once had hopes of some modest success. Most were happy to have finally landed a secure job.

There is so much occupational training in Canada which leads nowhere. For example, one guy I worked with had studied auto mechanics in vocational high school and had then spent three more years training at the Vancouver Vocational Institute only to find himself stymied. He went as far afield as Churchill, Manitoba to find a garage which would apprentice him but it went broke before he had completed his program. Back in Vancouver he wound up working in an un-unionized steel warehouse where, by his account, they got two days work from you during each shift. He was a willing worker too. Although not at all politically conscious he could appreciate the difference which the presence of a strong union like Canadian Union of Postal Workers made. A good union creates a solidarity among workers on the job who may not otherwise have that much in common. When it came down to it all of us on the loading dock, with two exceptions, joined a brief wildcat strike over some issue I've now forgotten. That never could have happened among Air Canada ground crews.

While the pay was adequate the job at the Post Office was terrible. In addition to being unbearably boring it was the sort of job which thwarts everything else in your life. You have no other life. By the time I got home and had breakfast it was mid morning. I'd get a restless sleep until supper time, stagger around the house for a couple of hours and then go off to work again. I usually had to work on weekends and was hardly ever able to go out with my wife because one of the other of us was either working or sleeping. It was no way to live. So after six months I quit.

A few years later some two thousand job seekers lined up around the Vancouver Post Office, many of them for a night and a day, just to apply for fifty temporary jobs like this.

Biograph: Barleycorn Sagas

The Admiral Hotel in North Burnaby was once a working-class neighbourhood pub. I would drop in for a few beers and sit alone reading a newspaper, until Jens Johansen, a fisherman who lived near our place, introduced me to some of his cronies. From that I got to know a circle of regulars who I could join and reorder the affairs of the world with. One was Fred Mattersdorfer, a recently retired longshoreman who kept himself busy roving around the backlands of BC inspecting placer claims he'd once staked and in general giving the bush skills of his youth one last workout.

Fred had been born in Fernie and into the vortex of union militancy which once coursed through the mining communities of the Kootenays. His father had emigrated from Germany and had wound up in the coal mines of the Crowsnest Pass at about the turn of the century. As a strong union man his father was periodically laid off and rehired during the booms and busts until the mid 1920s when he was blacklisted and never worked in the mines again. The whole family scraped by on whatever odd jobs were available and by living off the land in a today difficult to visualize combination of gardening, hunting and fishing.

As well as being a mining and resource region, the Kootenays had been a refuge area for dissenters, war resisters and communitarian groups of all stripes. Layer upon layer of such emigrants were tucked away in those mountain valleys. In the single-industry mine towns arguments of assorted American and European left political movements were once part of everyday currency. It was not a typically Canadian region.

One of Fred's heroes as a young man was Harvey Murphy. It must have been in the early 1930s when Murphy was crisscrossing the coal towns and stump ranch hamlets of the region drumming up contributions and support for the long-drawn-out Blairmore strike in "the Crow". Fred dove right into mobilizing support then and again during the bitter Corbin strike.

Two years later Fred went to Spain as part of the International Brigades and appears in the footnotes of a book about the MacKenzie-Papineau Battalion. There is even a brief glimpse of him in the film documentary *The Good Fight*. His accounts of battles from Teruel to the retreats from the perspective of shifting dugouts were extended by chronicles of where some of his comrades had come from and what had happened to them. Fred's accounts of Spain and international events of the time were intimately interwoven with accounts of men who had ridden the rods, placer mined gold, etc., and who returned — if they survived — to work in every kind of industry in British Columbia over the next generation.

I don't know how often I tried to get Fred to sit down and record some of his memories of the Kootenays, its people and culture as he'd known them. But he wouldn't do it. It was just too different — readers wouldn't understand it and he wouldn't do his friends and the dead the disservice of presenting them piecemeal. He was enthusiastic about my books but recording his own accounts — that, no.

Two of Fred's drinking buddies were Charlie Brodrick and a guy I only remember as John. John had grown up on the outskirts of Dawson City. His father had come in on the tail end of the Yukon gold rush and had stayed on to become a horse packer. John's older brother emigrated south to BC where he also wound up as a horse packer working for the mines in the Zeballos region during the late 1930s and early 1940s. Could he possibly have been the packer at Musketeer Mine when I was a child? It seemed highly improbable, but that is the way things sometimes happen.

John came south later and finally became a longshoreman before retiring. If anything he was politically quite conservative. He seemed a strange drinking buddy of a guy like Mattersdorfer but they grooved on comparing hunting and bush techniques of an other era.

Charlie Brodrick was a quiet bachelor eking out his last years on an old-age pension in a rooming house nearby. He had been born in a small town in the West of Ireland, had immigrated to Canada in the 1920s and had worked as a farm hand on the Prairies and in southern Ontario for most of his adult life. While living in Saskatoon during the 1930s he had gotten to know and had briefly shared a room with Sam Scarlett.

Sam Scarlett is now forgotten but he was once an almost mythic figure in western Canada. He had emigrated from Britain to America at about the time the IWW was formed and quickly became one of its better known wandering agitators. He was arrested many times and was finally scooped up along with other IWW leaders in the police raids of President Woodrow Wilson's "New Freedom" which heralded America's entry into World War I. After serving part of a long jail sentence, Scarlett was deported to Britain but later managed to re-enter Canada. By the late 1920s he was familiar to Western Canadian resource workers and by the early 1930s Scarlett was a leader of the Workers Unity League.

"He wasn't so old really, maybe in his middle or late fifties then. But he'd had an awfully hard life," said a seventy-plus-year-old Charlie Brodrick. "Beaten up badly, too many times. Spent too many times sick and hungry. That last stretch in prison had broken his health. The judge — oh he was a dirty devil — he gave Scarlett a year and some in jail, just for speaking in support of the striking miners in towns around Estevan. The judge wanted to break his spirit. A year and more of hard time he did. He wasn't the same man I'd known after he came out.

"I was interested in everything Sam Scarlett had to say, me still being a young fellow then. And he was a likable man. But there wasn't anything I could do about conditions. Organizing farm workers, like you then found on the Prairies, was impossible it seemed to me."

"He'd still give talks and went out to support what union action there was. But there wasn't as much as you might figure around Saskatoon in those times. Sam wasn't basically against the CCF, which was coming on strong then, with the Regina Manifesto and all. But he felt it was just the last gasp of the kind of movement he'd seen fail when he was first in the US thirty years before. He didn't give it much chance of achieving the hopes that people put on it. I think he felt it was sort of hopeless. After all those years of battling and educating, people weren't any more advanced toward taking power here than when he first started. Maybe even slipped back some.

"I tried a number of times to get him to take some money for himself to live on. At the time I had a steady job and figured that he deserved all the help I or anyone else could give him for all he'd done. But he wouldn't take anything for himself. He died not many years after."

That was the gist of a reminiscence I jotted down. It wasn't the sort of thing which Charlie normally discussed. I intended to capture these fragments in the manner of Vilhelm Moberg's novels but apparently it's beyond me.

Jens Johansen was a generation younger and had grown up on a northern farm in wartime Norway. He had some quizzical things to say about how everybody in Norway became a "resistance worker" after the war was over, even the most reactionary farmer who thrived on sweated labour. He became fed up with being an underpaid and knocked about farmhand, and ran away at age fourteen to work at odd jobs until he became a seaman. In the course of a dozen years at sea he'd been to every port and coastal town I'd ever heard of and a hell of a lot more I hadn't.

Jens had a tremendous memory for detail; what a backstreet of an Ecuadorian river port had looked like and what had happened there on a given day, twenty years before. He seemed to have a bottomless fund of such plotless but fascinating accounts. His stories were rife with sardonic understatement, tales of the schemes of poor and the powerful alike. Jens was a jovial cynic and I enjoyed the irreverence of his accounts. Spoofs of anything from Hindu spirituality, Brazilian gaiety, British justice and the underside of the Third World as experienced by an astute seaman. He didn't make any allowances for traditional customs passed down from time immemorial. His accounts had a lot to recommend them over the apologetics and blind piety which passes for multicultural tolerance. They were honest and warmly human.

Jens had landed in Vancouver when the Downtown Eastside was a skid road rather than a "community". He'd stayed in the old camp worker hotels which were turning into flophouses and for the first year lived a desperate hand-to-mouth existence. Finally he managed to land a job in the first of a string of logging camps, setting chokers and manhandling haywire equipment for outfits running down the backside of obsolescence. Coming into town to blow his stake he wondered how long it would be before he copped it on one of those jobs. Luckily, he had managed to get into fishing when that was still possible. For the last dozen years Jens had run his own gillnetter, "a forty thousand dollar fishing license with a few old planks wrapped around it," and made a passable living at it.

There was a Yugoslav fisherman who hung around the Admiral whom others figured was "too crazy to mess with". He was, too. But he was also a repository of accounts about the internecine struggles which have simmered for so long in the Balkans. Murat was a squat powerful man then in his late forties. He had been born in a small town of the Dalmatian coast and had been not quite sixteen when the War ended. As a Yugoslav Moslem he had later managed to attend an Islamic seminary in Turkey and from there had gotten to Canada. He was now the part owner of a seine boat.

We got to talking about Ivo Andric's novels which Murat knew well and could provide a living geography and historical background for. He also talked matter-of-factly about his own father who had been an officer in a local militia allied to the Ustashi, someone who had executed partisans and their supporters and finally had been executed by them. Murat told of Byzantine alliances and bloody vendettas among a kaleidoscopic array of factions in wartime Yugoslavia in an indifferently callous way. It was chilling, but it was more interesting and thought-provoking than the usual beer parlour conversation.

There was no shortage of homegrown Canadians whose views fundamentally paralleled Murat's. There were those whose allegiances were limited to the narrowest of self interest and who were quite ready to let others "root hog or die". A few were vociferously reactionary as well as being racist. No one thought that they were "too crazy to mess with". It's a distorted sort of class solidarity which accepts people and attitudes like that.

By comparison, Jim Taylor was a paragon of Edwardian Tory civility. He was in his mid seventies and came in each afternoon for two beers and to read his newspaper. Jim had spent some twenty years as a supernumerary on deep sea freighters but none of his accounts of sailing into South Pacific ports during the 1940s and 1950s were interesting. What was of interest was his reading, because Jim was a lifelong devotee of British colonial history: voyages of discovery, biographies of obscure statesmen and one time great boyos of the Raj, especially the wrangles of political sachems in early British Columbia. While his interests were more antiquarian than historical I enjoyed them.

In the Rain and Wind

I always wanted to try commercial fishing but it was a couple of years before I had any leads. It was Howie White who put me in touch with one of his fishermen neighbours at Pender Harbour. Jim Warnock was in his late fifties and had fished almost everywhere along the coast over the past four decades. He was known as a crusty character even among other fishermen. "You're going out with Jimmy Warnock? I hope you like spuds and boiled cod," said one of his fellow fishermen. Nevertheless, Warnock was willing to give me a try and I was willing to put up with a lot in order to break into fishing.

We set off for the west coast of Vancouver Island to get in on the April 15 opening of the spring salmon season. The *Delwood Hills* was a forty-foot ferro-concrete West Coast troller, a boat with a deep hull and with a wide upswept stern to ride over following waves. It was Jim's real home and he kept her in top shape. After a two-day run we put into Ucluelet. I still haven't any idea of what I'm supposed to do as a deckhand.

Warnock slept in the wheelhouse and when he heard the first boat engine being fired up in the morning he'd roll out of the kip, stagger down the ladder and start the engine, cast off the moorings and be away up the channel in under five minutes. The first thing after leaving harbour was to lower the troll booms, tie off and throw in the stabilizers, aluminum devices which hang from the booms and keep the boat from bouncing around too much. I'm always rather uncoordinated first thing in the morning but I'd be on deck fumbling away at guy lines, leaning over the side of the boat to fasten the stabilizer shackles as we roll from side to side. If you don't do it in the proper order you can't get the stabilizers tied off and have to pull them back in and start over. It's simple enough, except when it's new to you and you are three-quarters asleep. I'd be out there mumbling away to myself, "Remember — booms down, then tie off the stabilizers before you throw them over the side."

Near the entrance to Ucluelet we roll past spines of jagged rock and partly exposed reefs with the seas breaking around them. Other trollers are dipping and surging out around you, their hulls white and gray, jade green or patchy red, lead orange and black. They skitter up and over the swells in the pre-dawn light. We're heading out to the Banks.

South Bank the closest in, Southeast Bank about ten miles straight out, and Big Bank some twenty-two miles to the southwest. "Here's an easy way of getting the heading for when you're coming out of Ucluelet. See that notch?" says Jim pointing to an indentation in the mountains behind the village. "Line that up with that low hill in front — that's called 'the Gunsight'. Keep that to your stern and you'll be headed straight out to Big Bank." Warnock liked to commemorate navigation such as that even though he had a thirty-thousand dollar automatic pilot.

Jim Warnock had begun fishing with his father when he was twelve. His family's history stretched back to the early years of commercial fishing in the province. His father's father had been a Gulf Island stump rancher who fished with oar and sail for the Fraser canneries before the turn of the century. Jim had crewed on seiners and on packers, had jigged for cod off Triangle Island and had long-lined for halibut around the Queen Charlottes. He'd skippered his own seine boat for years and had even gone chasing after tuna a hundred and fifty miles out in the Pacific when warm currents brought them this far north. Now he mainly trolled for salmon.

Jim could be pretty taciturn. He might not say twenty words in half a day and then burst out with a story, which often would be an account of some marine disaster or other, and which could be from one end of the coast or the other, from the previous season or of his father's time. Although he was not usually a demonstrative speaker when recounting a tale of sinkings and near escapes Jim would provide dramatic pauses, synoptic context, speculative asides, guessed at dialogue, and usually a moral to be drawn from the event. He knew the histories of boats and fishermen along the coast by the hundreds. There was hardly a locale along the coast which didn't have some sort of reminiscence attached to it for him.

There is only the skipper and one deckhand on a troller so the deck-hand gets to do a little of everything. I'd stand watch at the wheel, scrub things down, tighten this or loosen that and do the endless minor maintenance which a working boat requires. But my main job was butchering fish after they were landed. The salmon species taken by gillnetters and seiners are used for canned fish and all the gutting and cleaning is done at the canneries. But troll caught salmon are for the fresh fish market, which pays premium prices but requires that the fish be cleaned immediately after being caught, before the body fluids taint the flesh. Cleaning them properly is critical for getting the top price.

You catch a few fish throughout the day but mainly your catch comes in a few hours when the salmon decide to feed — if you are in the right place and your bait happens to approximate what the fish are feeding on. The catch depends partly on how fast you can haul up and clear the lines and get them down again. If the deckhand is experienced both he and the skipper may be working the gear. But my main task was to butcher the fish as Warnock hopped around, peered over the stern watching the lines come up, ran the gurdies, snapped the leaders on and off the main lines and flicked salmon on to the deck.

"Keep it clean. Always keep the deck around you clean. I don't know how many men have wound up slipping on the guts and winding up with a broken leg because they haven't kept the deck clean," sermon-ized Captain Warnock. You are constantly dipping up buckets of sea water to wash the deck and hatch with. The fish guts get tossed over the side as you are butchering. Seagulls are screeching and swooping around as they battle for gobs of guts before they sink.

There are six mainlines running from the two booms extended out from the side of the boat. Lead sinkers looking like cannonballs carry the lines down, let us say thirty-five fathoms. There are four leaders on each main line so you actually have twenty-four sets of gear out fish-ing. The leaders are attached to the mainlines by snaps and have to be removed and replaced one by one as you bring the line up to check for fish. These leaders carry the lures, plugs, flashers, hootchies and hooks which are the business end of the troll gear. Every trollerman has his own ideas about which combination of enticing doodads to hang on his lines under specific conditions, what depth and speed to troll at and so forth. It is part of the mystique and critical private knowledge of commercial trolling.

Shooting the gear over the stern and pulling it up to check for fish is

Burrard Inlet below our house in Burnaby, 1980.

easy. But doing it quickly and efficiently — and actually landing any fish that may be on the line — is another matter. Warnock seemed to be moving in slow motion when he cleared the lines but when I did it everything seemed to be running three times as fast. There was always something to keep an eye on.

The lines are pulled up by Simplex gurdies, old-fashioned but reliable power winches. There are tap lines from the boom running through a ring which keep the main lines away from the side of the boat. The outside line is attached to a "pig board", a kind of hollow fin which keeps that line separated from the others. That has to be pulled in, detached and reattached every time you bring an outside line up.

You've got the gurdy on and the mainline is coming up as you stand in the sternwell. The boat is rolling a bit, you're peering over the stern watching for the stoppers to appear. Each leader and set of gear has to be removed from the mainline before you can pull any more up. Maybe there is even a fish on one. Then all this has to be replaced, step by step, as you let the line down again. When the fish are biting it's hectic.

If it's blowing too hard you normally don't go out trolling. But the weather can come up quickly on the west coast of Vancouver Island and when you are out on the Banks the skipper has to decide whether it is just a passing squall or not. If it looks to be worsening you pull up the gear and head for port.

Those West Coast trollers are wonderfully seaworthy boats, but there were still a few twenty-six foot double enders around, like the *Valkyrie ll*, built long before the middle of the century to work the river mouths. It's scary even to watch them in bad weather, rolling around, ten miles off shore. There you are in the sternwell — at one moment a troller off the starboard rises on the top of a wave and its hull is level with your masthead. Then, ten or twenty seconds later, it's down in a trough and all you can see of it is the top of its mast.

But I got to trust the *Delwood Hills*. In a blow, the seas might slosh across the deck at its waist but the upward curve of the stern kept the working area out of the wash. A wave comes rolling down on you, looking quite horrendous as you sit in a trough looking up at it — even though you know the boat is going to rise on it. Up she goes, first slowly and then faster, slewing around a bit with her stern to the weather. We are in the stern pulling up the gear. ("Oh Jeez . . . This one is going to break over us," I think.) But at the last moment the boat picks herself up, twists to the side a little, rides up over the crest and slides down the other side with no more than a fringe of spray thrown in your face. I let go of my last-minute hammerlock on a nearby stanchion.

Rolling back to port with streamers of sun lighting the headlands around Ucluelet and black storm clouds above us, white-capped green swells work the boat so that at times she is almost lying on her side. I knew then that that was what I should have been doing instead of teaching. But my trolling only lasted about a month. Warnock was pissed off at our poor catch and decided to go back to Pender Harbour and wait for the main season. He also decided he wanted an experienced deckhand for that.

After a taste of trolling I bent every effort to get on another boat. The end of May saw me beating the bushes of the Sunshine Coast for fish-boat owners who might be talked into taking me on as a crewman. Finally I was directed to Lew DeBroca, a character known throughout the district for hiring all sorts of oddballs to work on his museum-piece seiner. DeBroca offered to take me on when the seine season opened in July.

There are Brocas and DeBrocas fishing all over the southern coast. Lew's father had established a thriving fish buying station near the entrance to Seymour Inlet sometime before World War I which remained an important depot until the late 1940s. The family had run a couple of seiners but the operation seems to have come apart when the old man retired. Lew's mother, a woman then in her seventies, still ran a bait herring operation from the old depot. I think she was actually the brains behind what remained of the family business, parlaying land and gravel holdings into the income which sustained the peripatetic fishing ventures of her two sons.

Lew had started out well enough. He'd been one of the youngest seine boat skippers fishing for Nelson Brothers. He'd bought his seiner from them some twenty-five years earlier and had done quite well for a while. But things had gone backward. The boat was now in plain decrepitude. Lew was easy to work with and skilled at a hundred and one things. He was certainly knowledgeable about fishing, about the coast and how to handle his boat. He probably would have been a good fellow crewman. But he was no skipper. The ship's log contained the names of all the guys who had crewed for him over the last twenty years — some one hundred and thirteen men to date. The summer I worked for him all three of us on the crew were completely green and had never worked on a seiner before. That is unheard of. Besides, there should have been a crew of four.

The *Silversides* was a year older than me and had remained much as originally built. She'd been built for the Nelson Brothers fleet in 1935, I'm not sure where but possibly down in the Sterling Shipyard near where I grew up. She was a very small seiner by today's standards, a classic wood-planked boat which had been only recently modified by the addition of a seine drum. DeBroca had the dubious distinction of being among the last fishermen on the coast to table seine with her. That is the type of fishing depicted on the old Canadian five dollar bill, where the seine net is hauled in and folded on a table-like deck on the stern, a slow and laborious process.

The net drum which Lew had finally installed was, characteristically, second-hand and too heavy for the boat. It made her unstable and we had to unwind half the net and stow it in the hold whenever we moved through rough water. The fresh water tanks had rusted out years before and in their place were a collection of jerry cans which we filled by rowing ashore to creek mouths. The deck machinery was indescribable. Little had been added to the original and nothing was kept in a decent state of repair.

Getting an old wooden boat into shape for the fishing season entails some occasional challenges but mainly it involves a lot of tedious hard work. Scraping and caulking and painting, tightening and replacing links and bolts and cable, getting the propeller blades straightened and the heat exchanger reattached. I lived on the boat, helping with those repairs on an unpaid basis. Lew wasn't as simple as he sometimes acted. The United Fishermen and Allied Workers Union was dead set against scams like that. But fishing is still a nineteenth century industry in many ways and if you are trying to break into it you may put up with things you otherwise wouldn't accept.

I spent a month at DeBroca's place helping him get the boat in shape for the seine season and in the process met a number of the people scattered around this once isolated fishing hamlet then being transformed into a resort area. Although Lew emphasized his Portuguese ancestry he and many of his relatives were part of the loose network of non-status Indian fishermen along the coast. His kids were a varied lot, both in how they looked and how they acted. Their eldest daughter was a withdrawn young woman who attended the Native Survival school which had been established by the Sechelt band at the head of Seymour inlet. In contrast, his younger daughter was a socially adroit thirteen-year-old who was very bright to boot. She beat me often enough at chess to prove it. The eleven-year-old son was a brash and pushy kid, the apple of Lew's eye, who everyone predicted would become "one hell of a skipper". That is not as unalloyed a compliment as it may seem. The youngest son was a delightful kid who you might worry about as a parent, because he would walk into the side of a shed while ambling along examining a leaf. They were a reminder of how variable humans can be even within a single family, let alone within a larger group.

The seine season normally starts on the first of July but we didn't get away until the beginning of August. The fishing is only open for a couple of days a week and only lasts till mid fall. But finally we are off. It's a glorious summer day with just enough breeze to kick up a light chop as we head up Malaspina Channel and head for Lund, that beer parlour hamlet I remembered from my first job on the *Gulf Wing*. We make the traditional first-night fuel stop.

Next day, by the time we reach Yuculta Rapids the tide is running too fast for us to get through so we anchor in a bay and wait. At the end of a couple of hours Lew decides to bypass the rapids by going through a very shallow side passage. "Hey Lew, we've waited this long, let's wait till the tide slacks off." No reply. ("Oh Christ, he's going to ground her right here. That will be the end of the fishing season. After all that work.") But no, he picks his way through this gut — you could see the rocks sticking up from the bottom — and some minutes later we come out above Yuculta Rapids.

We make our way up the Inner Passage and enter Johnson Straight in the late afternoon. Beams of sun leak though a sky quilted with black rain clouds. The *Silversides* beats through a heavy chop as we run along the empty inner coast of Vancouver Island. The bow rises and crashes down rather than riding over the chop and this opens up the improperly caulked seams in the foredeck so that a steady drizzle of sea water sprays the fo'c'sle where we sleep and where our gear is stowed. I'm trying to cook a roast during all of this. It's breathtaking and miserable at the same time.

Late that night we come through Blackfish Sound, cross the shallows off the southern tip of Cormorant Island and approach Alert Bay. I'm at the wheel and Lew has been refueling again. I'm not going to take the boat into a narrow moorage nor am I going to let either of my two teenage fellow crew members try it either. "Can you take her in Lew?" ("Let it be on his head.") Although he's well pickled he works the *Silversides* around piers, down lanes of fishboats moored two deep — a surge of power here, a quick reverse — and drops her into an inner berth as neatly as you please. We tie up and Lew steams up to the Nimpkish Hotel to get a couple of rounds before they close.

Established as a Nimpkish mission village, Alert Bay had become the regional centre of fishing companies and Indian commercial fishermen by the turn of the century. Franz Boas, Edward Curtis and sundry other anthropologists had put into town in their time. Complementing them were calls by cruise boats which delivered well-heeled tourists who had helped sustain traditional carving as an industry. By the second decade of the twentieth century Alert Bay had become an important center of Native Indian entrepreneurship and from the mid 1930s on it became the locus of the Native Brotherhood of BC. It is the major regional fishing port and the home base for a number of Indian fishing fleet owners.

Alert Bay is a beautiful locale, the settlement strung along a sandy shore and looking out across a wide straight to Vancouver Island. But it has approximately equal numbers of Indian and non-Indian inhabitants and there was a good deal of free-floating racial hostility. There is also a hidden history of many-faceted politics emanating from critical class differences within the Native Indian population. That is normally obscured by the pervasive ethnic nationalism, while it is an important topic most anthropologists and others have avoided like the plague. However, I only saw the community through the eyes of a crewman on a seiner.

Alert Bay was DeBroca's home base during most of the seine season. He was actually waiting for the districts around Thompson Sound and the entrance to Knight Inlet to be opened, where he made his main catches. In the meantime we made weekly forays to channels and bays along Johnson Straight. Seining is highly restricted as to place and duration of openings. It depends on the timing and size of the runs and on the Fisheries Department estimations of how many salmon in a particular run have been taken and how many have to be saved for spawning. There is a ouija board quality to the openings, in fishermen's eyes. We could have used Luke Mettaweshkum and his scapulamancy shamanism to locate where the Department of Fisheries would permit the next seine opening. When it is announced the boats rush to that locale, swirl around setting or waiting to set and work as long as physically possible while the area is open for fishing.

Basically, the idea is to set a net some 1,300 feet long and about 130 deep in a circle — preferably around some salmon. You close the purse by hauling in the purse lines and then reel the net in on the drum until you have a small enclosure beside the boat. The fish in it are brailed into the hold. Then you scoot around to find a likely place to make another set.

A set begins as the skiff drops astern and jettisons a buoy attached to the net on the drum. The skiff man rows like hell in one direction while the seiner roars away in the other to make a circle. The skiff acts as a sort of sea anchor dragging the net off the drum. The drum operator (me in this case) slacks off or brakes to give an even feed. The net just whips off the drum and if it catches you it's goodbye Charlie. Every so often the net would get hung up on the lip of the drum well because DeBroca was carrying far too much net. I'd have to brake the drum and flip the net off by hand without getting hung up.

The crux of the set is to bring the purse lines on board after the circle is made and to close the purse as quickly as possible. Seining is very much a team effort. Normally there are four crewmen plus the skipper working together. We were one man short. You have the drum to worry about, the winch is running and the purse line is coming in over a confined deck. There are plenty of ways for an accident to happen under the best of conditions. But nothing on the *Silversides* worked the way it was supposed to. If there was some haywire way of doing things that was the way we did them. I worked over a temperamental old deck winch, feeding in the purse lines and watching that I didn't get my leg caught in one of the coils. I constantly worried that somebody, maybe me, was going to get hurt.

To make things worse, the two youngsters who were my fellow crewmen were sure that they had mastered the job after the first week. Ignorance and overconfidence are a dangerous mix in seining. Sure enough, the tie-up man got himself balled up while throwing out the buoy in an open set. He sees the rope uncoiling around his feet and falls overboard. Just pure luck that he wasn't caught in the net rope and pulled under. There were other near accidents too.

While you can usually work with anyone on a task in front of you it is when holed up in port that strains among crew members emerge. We would be tied up in Alert Bay for three and four days a week. Even with doing regular repairs and maintenance there wasn't much to keep busy at. There is a lot of lounging about and going for walks along the shore. You may even cast a line in the doggerel fishery.

In any case, after the fourth week of fishing, when we were back in Alert Bay, I got into an argument with one of the other crewmen. DeBroca, who had had a few drinks, tells me that I had better learn to get on with them if I wanted to stay aboard. One word led to another and he wound up firing me. The next morning, after he'd sobered up and I'm packing my bag, Lew says, "Ah well, I guess I'll give you another chance." But I'm thinking, "Who knows what other stunts he'll pull after this."

I was so disgusted that I didn't pursue the possibility of landing a job on one of the other fishboats around. Following on everything else I was totally demoralized. That was how I went back to driving cab in Vancouver.

When I was younger and the industry was still buoyant I could have made a living at fishing, been happier and still have done some writing. But in retrospect, it is now clear that there was no real prospect of my breaking into the fishing industry in 1979. Men twenty years younger and more adept than me, individuals who already had long experience in fishing, gradually found it impossible to get berths and ultimately had to find jobs elsewhere.

SIXTEEN

Gorky In Terminal City

Babbitt's Revenge

It's pointless to say much about driving taxi. It was still unusual to find a former university professor behind the wheel of a cab in 1980 but whatever background I brought to it didn't lead me to experience driving taxi much differently than others have. One phony aspect in some accounts is the cabbie who recounts the innermost thoughts revealed by passengers. The job usually doesn't work that way.

I drove for four years, four days a week on average, ten to eleven hours a day. Typically, I made some twenty-odd trips a day, and I figure that I hauled some fifteen thousand people around Vancouver. I had a real conversation with perhaps two or three dozen passengers but haven't the vaguest notion of what the majority of my fares thought. It might have been better if I could have treated driving as a kind of anthropological field work. But I wasn't driving cab to learn anything, I just couldn't find any other work.

You could always get a job with MacLure's then. The company had fallen upon hard times since I had driven for them twenty-five years earlier. MacLure's were amenable to people working anywhere from one to seven days a week as long as they brought in their quota of cash. Drivers were constantly being hired and fired. Or they quit. That's the way the company liked it. The first and last attempt to unionize the company a decade previously had foundered on that turnover. Real wages were worse in 1980 than they had been in 1959 and over the next three years the take home pay got less and the hours spent driving longer.

MacLure's, like all cab companies, operated on a straight commission basis. They avoided paying any benefits to the drivers who weren't on the full-time list. The majority of us, who only drove forty to fifty hours a week, were "part-time". Repairs, gassing up, filling out tally sheets, waiting around for a cab was done on your own time. Any charge to a company account which for some reason was rejected came out of the driver's pocket. I don't know how many times I wound up paying for the charge vouchers of billion-dollar outfits like BC Telephone. You never knew what your pay packet would be with one deduction or another. If you didn't like the accounting MacLure's tendered, you could quit.

Have you ever seen that 1920s business sermonette entitled "The Customer is Always Right"? In a loose paraphrase, it informs you that "The customer pays your wages and puts food on your table. He is the finest person you know, the customer is the wisest person you know, etc., etc. The customer is always right." It is a catechism of abject servility. MacLure's actually had an enlarged copy of that hanging in the dispatch office for all to ponder. It wasn't supposed to be taken as a joke. It was as if they had schemed to make the job as degrading as possible.

At first I worked the night shift. Ten hours driving at night was my limit but some drove from late afternoon till the next morning. I'd stagger home, collapse into bed and come out of drugged sleep a couple of hours before I was due back at the cab lot again. My days off were spent getting some badly needed sleep. For that I earned fifty, sometimes sixty, dollars a shift. On the day shift it was less, more like a hundred sixty bucks a week.

I'd hang around the airport to catch the evening flights until about 10 p.m. but after that one had to work the tourist hotels, disco joints and bars of fun city for trips. I never realized how many petty thugs, degenerates and loonies there were wandering around Vancouver at night — intermixed with boozed-up high rollers out on a spree. Some of the side streets in the West End looked like a TV crime melodrama, with flashy pimps, male and female hookers, and cruising cars filled with punks looking for trouble.

The prostitutes themselves were alright. They were civil. They gave you the address, paid their fares at the end of the run without any hassle and didn't have *pronunciamentos* they needed to bandy about.

Although I have no idea of what they were like as individuals, as passengers the hookers were far preferable to the junior executive swingers and lumpen we packed around.

The consistently most offensive fares were the air crews of Air Canada. They were so bad that many drivers didn't want to take them even though it meant a trip out to the airport. Air Canada crews were the most gratuitously insulting, the most vociferously reactionary fares one encountered. It must be a company subculture because I never once witnessed people from any other airline act the way the Air Canada crews did constantly.

It never varied. They thought that they were *pukka sahibs* and that we had better treat them that way. Pilots, co-pilots and pursers regaled themselves with horror stories of Trudeau and his "French government". They opined that President Reagan had taught the US air controllers a lesson. They maundered about "Arab terrorists" or "the drag of the underclass" and reveled in the wisdom transmitted by *US News and World Report* or comparable journals. The flight attendants were just as bad. Where did Air Canada find these people?

I made a point of never talking with them if it could be avoided. No matter how insulting Air Canada crews were, if you dared to answer them back they would have their director phone up the manager of MacLure's and demand to have you disciplined. I have a transcript of an interchange with one Air Canada crew which I was going to take to the Labour Relations Board or to court if I was fired. I intended to reproduce part of that transcript here just for the record. But there is no way of conveying just how odious this lot was without making it sound like a caricature.

Most cab drivers develop a thick skin, which doesn't really help much. It would have been best to be completely indifferent to what anyone said providing they didn't actually touch you and as long as they paid their fares. There were occasional dodgy situations. Some crazy would get into the cab and sit in the back seat, just behind you, as you drove through the dark streets. Sometimes I would be both scared but also angry enough to fight — a bad combination. I can now understand what happens to police who deal with these situations constantly. By the end of three months I was becoming very bitter about everything.

"If that's the way this is going to affect you you'd better quit the job right now, because it's not worth it," said Carol. But shortly after that I was transferred to the day shift, which at least got me away from the violence.

Every day is similar yet always a bit different. You may get a call from the Marpole stand to pick up a tug boat crew waiting at a Fraser River dock and take them to New Westminster. Alternately the fare may be only a two-minute trip from a beauty salon to some Kerrisdale dowager's lair. Maybe you get a fare from the airport to a downtown office tower, then a trip from the Four Seasons Hotel to a Twong Pouch Studies Conference at the University of BC, and next an elderly woman going to a doctor's appointment. Myself, I always liked to get a trip from the docks because it usually meant you would be hauling foreign seamen around, people you could conceivably talk to.

It's the rare person who sticks in your mind. One of the more memorable fares I had was a young woman going from the Saskatchewan Wheat Pool in North Vancouver to South Granville. It was only on the longer trips that you had the opportunity to get into a real conversation with a passenger. It was a sunny fall day and we got to talking while coming across Second Narrows bridge. I pointed out where, as a kid, I had clambered over log booms to fish for crabs, now all industrial shoreline. She said she'd done the same while living with an aunt on a North Shore reserve but could never eat the catch because she was allergic to shell fish.

She was from an old Squamish mission family and had gotten a scholarship to attend a small Catholic college in Montreal in the early 1970s. There she became involved in Native youth conferences and was recruited by Walter Currie, one of the leading impresarios of Native Studies, to join his Native Teachers program at Trent University. She'd taken courses at Trent with Ron Vastokas, a fellow student of mine at Columbia, and from Chris Huxley, one of the former graduate students I'd known at Simon Fraser University. After getting her degree she'd steamed off to a teaching post on an isolated Yukon reserve.

The way she described it, it was a classic case of culture shock. The students in this Yukon reserve school wouldn't listen to or accept her any more than they would any other outsider. It didn't matter that they were "her own people". She couldn't stand it and had to leave before the school year was over.

Back in Vancouver she had met a Greek ship's officer. A whirlwind romance, marriage and emigration to live in his family home on a Greek island in the Aegean. That was where she had just come from. "It sounds great. Sun, sea and tranquility," I ventured, sensing that it obviously wasn't all that great.

"Well yes, but . . ." It would take some time till she got used to living in Greece. Although her parents-in-law spoke English she was having a lot of trouble learning Greek. What was worse was that women there were expected to confine themselves to raising children and keeping house. No, it wasn't just her family or the class that they were members of, it was a general expectation on this island.

She had just flown back to visit her husband on his ship. Vancouver somehow seemed a great deal better now than it had previously. At that point we rolled up to the optometrist she was going to and I never got to hear the rest of her story.

Come to think of it, there was an even more memorable fare I had. On a dark January morning two passengers from the plush Four Seasons Hotel get into the cab for a trip to the airport. I listen to them talking to each other. What the hell — they're speaking Yoruba! We're going down the dark, empty street leading to the airport when, after rummaging through my memory for an appropriate phrase, I say, *"Ki lon' shay Ibadan?"* ("What's doing, Ibadan?") That elicits a startled response from my passengers. "Whaa . . .?" they say in unison.

It turns out they are both Nigerian businessmen, one the owner of an insurance company and the other a marketing executive of an allied Nigerian firm. They are looking over investment opportunities in North America and have never been in Vancouver before. Although it was only a wild guess on my part they both are from Ibadan. I swap a few reminiscences of places around Ibadan a quarter century earlier with the insurance baron. We had both bought *akara* ball snacks from a woman peddler who stationed herself in front of the Paradise Club. "The Paradise Club — that is gone now, a long time ago," he says on parting.

But driving cab is not as interesting as you can make it sound. At the end of four years hardly any of the drivers I had started with were left at MacLure's. No wonder. Despite working forty to fifty hours a week I could barely have supported myself, let alone a wife, on what I earned. And my take fell within the average, otherwise I would have been fired. It was a full-time job with less than half pay. It was basically Carol's pay which supported us. It was demeaning.

One of my last trips came off the cab stand across from the Sunrise Hotel at the corner of Hastings and Columbia. Three guys and a girl get in. A drag queen promoting a petty drug deal is doing the talking. "Now cabbie, don't you worry your head about getting your fare. I'm Safire, honey. And I get a hundred a hit . . . a hundred dollars. Hee hee." His sidekick is an affable young thug who jokes about having recently gotten out of stir after serving time on an aggravated assault charge and already being out on bail awaiting sentencing on a new burglary charge. The wide-eyed girl beside him, who looked like a wholesome Daisy Mae, was their shill. They had latched on to a university student who was trying to unload a batch of pills he'd acquired somehow.

The student is totally out of his depth and is taking this lot to his girlfriend's place where the drugs are hidden. The three guys go into the apartment, come out soon after and begin to argue on the sidewalk. Their mark is frightened and apologetic. The Sunrise Hotel denizens get back in the cab and I take them back to where I picked them up. On the way back they work out how they are going to snatch the pills now that they know where they are. All this is mixed with violent posturings and haggling over the fare.

Although I'd had much worse trips than that, that was the last straw. I quit not long after.

I'd intended to drive cab only until I'd figured out what to do next. By digging into research for another book I put off making any practical decision. During the four years I drove cab I also put close to forty hours a week into the research and writing of an annotated bibliography of left-wing literature. It was absurd.

From the Button Moulder's Crucible

Although books have always been important to me I had never contemplated becoming a writer. I had turned to writing as I became disaffected with the university teaching. While I wanted to reach working people as readers my rationale was not so different from why I'd gone into anthropology. That is clearer to me now than it was at the time. I set about to raise the dead and to snatch memories from the button moulder's crucible.

My first book in this vein was *A Very Ordinary Life*, a life history of my mother and her times. It was a matter of embarrassed silence among most of my colleagues at the University of Toronto. But I was determined to get that book out, as a testimony if nothing else. At least it would be on the record. That was in 1973.

Anyone who believes that writing a life history is simply a matter of asking a few questions and turning on a tape recorder is quite mistaken. There is so much in a life. There is always so much which has to remain unsaid which you can merely allude to and which you cannot provide the context for. The context is really a slice of the world during the span of a lifetime. You strive to present an honest portrayal of experiences and reactions. Doing a life history is a moving and frustrating endeavour even when there are no personal emotions involved.

Of the twenty-seven North American publishers I approached with an outline of *A Very Ordinary Life*, none were interested. James Lorimer & Company informed me that they only published "books of social importance". Monthly Review Press said much the same. When I committed *A Very Ordinary Life* to New Star Books, which was then run by Barb Coward and Steve Garrod, who set out to publish books by and about working people in Canada, and who succeeded better than anyone could have reasonably expected. They had no experience in book publishing but they did have a lot of élan.

Part of New Star's success was due to a stream of enthusiasts who carried copies of the first titles into their own circles. Jack Scott's, Helen Potrebenko's, my own books were initially passed from hand to hand and only slowly filtered into bookstores. For a couple of years I made selling trips around BC for New Star Books on a volunteer basis. While many independent bookstore managers were sympathetic, titles by unknown authors from an unknown press and about working people's lives didn't seem saleable to them.

A Very Ordinary Life, while it is first and foremost a life history, with all the disparate threads which a life entails, by its very essence it conveys some views which are anathema to the purveyors of Canadian social patriotism. It challenges the institutionalized anti-German racism which had reigned uncontested in this country for more than sixty years. It includes a bittersweet reminiscence of the socialist working-class culture of Berlin during and before the Weimar era. Mainly the account is about the multitudinous experiences of anonymous working people from various national backgrounds in Canada over a half century. But it suggests that the forces of reaction and class oppression were as evident in Canada as they had been in Germany. That in itself constitutes a horrendous blasphemy to some.

One lady literarian writing for *Quilt & Quire*, the book trade journal, did pick up the gauntlet. Canada was the greatest country on earth and Canadian school maxims were the measure of historical truth and morality. *A Very Ordinary Life* exemplified a grey, unreflective, "all too ordinary" life, she held, and went on to berate my mother for "not standing up to Nazism". This from a young academic ensconced in a rural Ontario college who had obviously never experienced oppression or faced any hardship in her life. The self-righteous arrogance and willful ignorance about what is entailed in real lives and actual historical situations outside her own charmed circle was unshakeable.

Although the book met with this sort of hostility in certain quarters it also was warmly received by many other readers at the time. That pleased and surprised me. Today, with the resurrection of World War II chauvinism, I expect that *A Very Ordinary Life* would become a target of organized hate mongers. But my mother is beyond their grasp now.

In the end, *A Very Ordinary Life* went through three printings and sold some eight thousand copies. Small potatoes for a major publisher but rather successful for a tiny, completely unknown press. Ironically, the book wound up as assigned reading in more than thirty college courses across Canada. However, working people invariably proved to be its most appreciative and insightful readers.

I next compiled the accounts of two immigrant stump ranchers and migratory workers. *Stump Ranch Chronicles* includes some classic descriptions of homesteading but also of work in the camps and industries of the resource frontier from the pre-World War I era to the 1960s. They do pay tribute to friends and neighbours and the joys wrung from that world but the jobs and conditions portrayed by these two men are hardly nostalgic. Still, if anything deals with homesteading or is a first-hand account of the frontier industrial era in Western Canada it is invariably pegged as nostalgia.

"Nostalgia" or "anecdotal" is what commentators say when they don't like what is being recounted in oral histories but don't want to say why. That charge suggests that an account is untrue or simplistic, without specifying how and why that is so. But then, little if anything in the lives of working people is worthy of consideration by some mental giants.

At least *Stump Ranch Chronicles* was enjoyable to write. Both Arnt Arntzen and Ebe Koeppen told their own stories with verve and passion. As distinct from my other books, where so much is left unsaid, *Stump Ranch Chronicles* had a feeling of completeness to me, maybe because it is so patently fragmentary and episodic. For a number of years afterward I occasionally heard individuals say about it, "You know, something almost exactly like that happened to us when we were at ... etc., etc."

I suppose that wanting one's books to be reviewed honestly and favourably is simple vanity. But one comes to accept that many reviewers simply cannot comprehend anything much different from what they are used to hearing. Anything other than the catechism lessons of the age just doesn't register with them. The mere mention of certain topics, for instance "Native Indian history" or "Japanese-Canadian fishermen", triggers a reflex response largely unrelated to what is actually said in a book. With unintended humour, some commentators will point out that the author has failed to repeat the usual dogma and to that extent is uninformed or biased.

It's impossible to convey the amount of work which went into compiling *Indians At Work*, a history of Native Indian labour in British Columbia from *circa* 1860 to 1930. In a sense I'd been collecting information for it for over a decade. I wrote it in a decidedly unacademic style and laced it with occasional sarcastic digs at the pieties which usually accompany the subject. However, the documentation for the text is backed with some eight hundred citations drawn from almost three hundred published and unpublished sources.

The book demonstrates that whatever else they were, Native Indian people also were workers in most of the major industries of BC for over a century. The text details what some of that work was and something of the industries and conditions which prevailed. It suggests that wage labour had important consequences for Native Indians, some of which were not necessarily for the worse.

Homer Stevens told me that he had a copy of *Indians At Work* during the first year he went back fishing after thirty years as a union official and that in between work he'd go below decks to read a few more pages. Bill Wilson, then head of the United Native Nations, declared that he knew of all the particulars mentioned but sent a number of copies around the province to others he thought should read the book.

Since *Indians At Work* was one of the only extant accounts of Native labour history I half expected that it would stir up debate and possibly even initiate a some historical reevaluation. Dead silence! No Canadian history journal ever reviewed it. Even historians engaged in unearthing uncharted social history preferred to sidestep the topic. It didn't exist as far as most Canadian scholars were concerned.

After four years and sales of two and a half thousand copies, *Indians At Work* went out of print. Stage door Johnnies continued their routines about "pre-industrial value systems", "spiritually directed societies" and similar old favourites. Reincarnations of Grey Owl disseminated updated versions of *Kibbo Kift the Woodland Kindred* to the acclaim of all. So be it. I should have expanded on my implications to the effect that romanticism not only blinds people to the actual history of Native Indians but also is frequently a vehicle for reactionary and anti-working class biases. You might as well be hung for a sheep as for a lamb.

An earlier book was titled *A Man of Our Times: The Life History of a Japanese-Canadian Fisherman*. *A Man of Our Times* is a brief account by Ryuichi Yoshida, an eighty-nine-year-old Issei fisherman, union organizer and sometimes newspaper editor who describes some of his life and doings in his own words. It was based on interviews by Maya Koizumi, a Japanese woman who not only was fluent in the language but who knew more about the specifics of the Issei world than did most of her contemporaries. I participated in the interviews only in a secondary capacity but did the editing and wrote the appendix on Japanese-Canadian labour history. I did that not merely as an editor but as someone who had grown up in conditions comparable to those which Yoshida described from his own perspective.

One of the failings commentators found in the book was that it did not appreciate "the unique culture from which it sprang". Ah, the wisdom of introductory anthropology classes. *A Man of Our Times* was also dogmatic because it suggested that there were critical similarities in the lives of working people in BC regardless of which backgrounds they sprang from. Yoshida's story furthermore offended those loathe to see accounts of class struggle within the Japanese-Canadian community brought to light even fifty years later. It may have seemed too close to the bone for those who try to picture all conflicts as inter-ethnic ones and the ethnic bourgeoisie as the only legitimate spokespersons of "their community".

A Man of Our Times became a target a decade after its initial publication when a right-wing demagogue masquerading as a sociologist at the University of BC got on the case. One Werner Cohn charged that the internment of the Japanese-Canadians during World War II was due to the racial hostility and Marxist ideology of the long defunct Federal Fishermen's Union. As evidence Cohn reproduced one paragraph of one article in one issue of the union bulletin written some forty-five years ago.

Mainly, Cohn was out to smear the present-day United Fishermen and Allied Workers Union but he prominently cited *A Man of Our Times* for "falsification of history" since it failed to mention his own fantasy plot. That his charges flew in the face of any sane view of the political realities of the time was neither here nor there. Cohn had apparently not even read *A Man of Our Times*, which only touches on the white fishermens' unions in a footnote and deals almost exclusively with Japanese-Canadian fishermen and other workers within the Japanese-Canadian community itself.

As a clincher to his exposé, Cohn "revealed" that Angus McInnis, a veteran CCF leader and the man who indisputably had done more than anyone to try to defend the rights of Japanese-Canadians at the time, was "really" a collaborator in the internment. Cohn closed with the call for an "Old Testament prophet" to deal with these matters, tacitly offering himself for the job: the Prophet from Brooklyn Heights.

This may seem like low farce but Cohn made the rounds of the hotline radio shows in Vancouver and was given air time to disseminate his vitriol. That Canadian universities and supposedly scholarly journals such as *BC Studies* would facilitate such slanderous ravings suggests that we have almost come full circle to the standards of the McCarthy era.

Along the No. 20 Line was the last of the books I published with New Star Books. It is a set of reminiscences of the Vancouver industrial waterfront in the mid to late 1940s. It should really be read aloud since it attempts to resurrect the sounds and sights of that urban environment. It also provides a collection of accounts of the people, work and attitudes which then prevailed. I like it very much. For me, the book does recapture some of that world. But the only readers who were enthused about it were older men and women who had known Vancouver East at that time. Apparently *Along the No. 20 Line* had the honour of being one of the two most regularly stolen books from the Carnegie Centre library, but it was only a modest success on the market.

"Stop! Wait just a minute now. This is all too negative. There must have been some positive responses to these books or some joy and feelings of accomplishment that you derived from them. Otherwise it seems unlikely that you'd have gone on writing them."

Well, yes that's true. Writing them seemed important and was vastly more fulfilling than teaching ever was. I never found writing to be the lonely endeavor which others have. When I wrote I was often surrounded with voices and images at least as alive as everyday life. There was also the feeling of having saved something of value which otherwise would have been lost — that gave me a sense of accomplishment. But it wasn't a realistic estimation.

Over the course of seven years I put out six books with New Star Books. Carol and I did much of the typesetting and layout on them ourselves. When everyone was contributing their time on a volunteer basis the absence of any royalty payments didn't bother me. But as the press became established and began to get operating grants, the new manager hired an assistant editor and paid typesetters and assorted freelancers to do the kind of work which Carol and I did on a volunteer basis. In a straightforward business arrangement one would never allow oneself to be treated that way.

One should know when to quit. But instead of giving up writing I set up Draegerman Books to publish *Traces of Magma*, a bibliographic survey of left-wing novels from around the world. "Draegerman" is a term which was once part of the vocabulary of every mining community in Canada. It refers to the miners' rescue teams which went underground to bring out the living and the dead after mine disasters. It's rather presumptuous to use the term for the name for a press but it approximated how I felt about these books. It's indicative that the term itself had been totally forgotten and fantastic suggestions were made about what "Draegerman" allegedly meant.

Traces contains annotated references to three thousand books by some fifteen hundred authors from ninety countries. It was clearly an impossible task but once started the thing wouldn't let go. There was always one more area or period or group of writers to investigate. I'd always known that they must exist but to unearth their names and their work and something of their lives — that was the hook which kept me at it. *Traces of Magma* is the kind of survey which I would have liked to have had in my hands twenty years earlier. Although it contains a few errors and has a number of lacunae it is a source book which one should be proud of. But no one wanted it.

There's no need to recapitulate the absurdities of one-man publishing ventures where anything you do is inevitably dismissed and you lose money as well. After three years of work I put together the materials and printed some five hundred copies of *Traces*. That is ridiculous enough in itself but it took endless mailings to sell even that number. Most of the left in Vancouver, those who even heard of it, thought that *Traces* was frivolous. They were too engaged in serious matters to waste their time reading novels. Working people, even those who read my earlier books, naturally didn't want a bibliography.

With that I should have finally learned my lesson but over the following twenty years I went on to write six more books, three of them published and three not. That did give me a sense of completion.

SEVENTEEN

Coming In At the End

Makar Potrebenko is dead now so I may as well end with him. "You two will probably hit it off together," his daughter opined. "He's a man's man." That constitutes a damning insult in Irene's lexicon.

Since Makar had been enthusiastic about *A Very Ordinary Life* I figured that we would have something to say to each other. But I had no idea that he would turn out to be a reaffirmation of all those immigrant camp workers and adoptive uncles I'd grown up with. Making allowances for a Ukrainian accent, his gusto and unfashionable insights reminded me of so many people I'd once known. I had been beginning to wonder if I hadn't dramatized them in memory. But there they were again.

"Ah, so it's you Pat. After all these years we meet again," I said to myself, recognizing an old Irish railway worker long since gone. Instead of black tea and games of cribbage it was vodka and talk.

Makar had been born in a small peasant village near the western reaches of the Russian Empire under a Tsarist regime which was already tottering but which still seemed eternal from the perspective of a village square. Almost completely self-educated, Makar was well read and immensely knowledgeable about the world, past and present. He had used his eyes and ears and mind during seventy years of living.

I've listened to some good chroniclers but Makar was probably the best of them. He had an epic view of things but also an appreciation for detail. As called for, he could reproduce long passages of dialogue, or some facsimile thereof, by a secondary character in Gogol or Furmanov, or a bantering debate between an anonymous Doukhobor farmer and a migrant railway worker in the Kootenays fifty years earlier. He might slip back and forth between accounts of the struggle against Batista and that against Machado, not so much confusing them as seeing them as stages of the same struggle. It sometimes came as a shock, that here was a person who had lived through and kept track of so many of the major and minor events of our era as they were happening.

We sat around the kitchen table, looking out over a huge vegetable garden and brush-tangled lot, dipping into a bowl of borscht during a rambling two- or three-hour discussion on a rainy February afternoon. It might begin with the current happenings in Thatcherland or Argentina, consider the most recent crusades of hot-line radio kleagles, loop back into reminiscences of the Ukraine during Makar's youth. We might detour through *The Gadfly* and how that turn-of-the-century novel, set in mid nineteenth century Italy, touched the feelings of his own generation. I might enter my own accounts about the ruins of Berlin or reminiscences of my fellow workers in construction camps thirty years earlier. That might move us to a Jack London story or an account of how Max Hoelz met his end. Makar was the only person I ever met, other than my father, who had even heard of Hoelz. That was the breadth and quality of concerns which, in measure, once existed among at least the bards of the immigrant working class of western Canada. It's hard to believe, I know.

Makar would interweave reminiscences of petty but bitter quarrels in impoverished homestead districts of the Peace River and the trajectories of individuals who crossed paths in coastal logging camps and camp worker districts of Vancouver. I'd throw in my share of stories, disagreements with history and arraignments of the Great at the bench of posterity; both of us presuming that the foreseeable future would probably be dominated by approximately the same degree of truth and justice as prevails in the present.

Maybe it's somewhat unusual, a forty-year-old and a seventy-five-year-old man sharing views, comparing notes, attuned to each other's allusions. It made his children feel uneasy. They wondered why anyone my age — their age — who was not a relative, would be interested in talking to Makar. They wondered what I wanted from their father.

"Come in, come in. Thanks for your visit. You are still driving the taxi?" says Makar, going down to the basement to tap his supply of homemade plum vodka.

"Still at it — but not every day. If you don't earn anything for your work you might as well do as little as possible. I'm broke whether I drive five days or three days, no matter."

"So ... Somehow I didn't think you would stick at it so long. Now you have to pay for learning too much. Well, never mind. Here, help yourself. *Nasdrovya!*"

"*Salud.*"

"What you think is going to happen in Poland with this Solidarność? I see where the new Pope says he is going to fly into his country if the government don't give in to Walesa ... Being the Pope maybe he don't even need no airplane, he can just order the Holy Ghost to put him down there. Pretty soon God is going to be talking like a Polish Pan. Even when I was a boy it was so. There was more miracles in Poland than bathtubs. You couldn't dump a load of cowshit from the barn without looking first to see if not a miracle happened on that spot at some time. A cross that cried, a fire that wouldn't burn up some saint, a place where some kids a few hundred years before said they saw Christ's old lady."

That's the way Makar would talk at times. Compared to the obligatory pieties in vogue it was immensely refreshing. Reminiscing about his own childhood during the First World War and the illusions which permeated that world he might say,

" 'We', Mighty Russia, was the biggest country in the world. Not the Tsar sitting in St. Petersburg but Russia with its lands and peoples stretching from Siberia to Poland was just going to 'toss its cap' on its enemies. Everybody in the village talked like that, people who didn't have even cabbage and potatoes to eat through the last winter. Sure. Nine years old, sure I repeated all that even if my mother could beat me and my father didn't have two rubles to rub together."

A year later Makar and his family had become refugees and were sent as farm labourers to the Central Ukraine.

"We arrive in the Ukraine and everybody is split up. So many are sent to this village, so many to that estate, and are put up in whatever barns or sheds are available. Since most of the men are in the army there is work for all of us on the big estates. My mother, my two sisters and me all worked in the fields just to earn our bread.

"In the winter I went to school in the nearby village — part of the year for three years. Till the Revolution reached us. That was my schooling. So you see, I'm well educated to give directions on how the world should run. That's why I can make comments on fellows like Pushkin and such."

Or there might be a more bitter reminiscence of his youth back in his home village in the by then Polish-occupied Ukraine.

"There always were Poles in our district and we got along alright. You met Walter, who comes to visit me here. He was born in the next village from ours and he was a Pole. So, fine. But after the First War Poland took over and a new kind came in. They held the whip. Each one became a landlord or a policeman or a boss of some kind over us. From what I know myself, from what our village and our district suffered after they conquered us. Terror? After those Piłsudski officers were finished with you, you would agree to anything. They acted like Nazis towards us. Just once I would like to hear the newspapers talk about that. But no, never."

"But Makar, what about internationalism, that ordinary working people, whatever their nationality have interests different from what their rulers plan for them. Didn't you believe in that as a Bolshevik?"

"Yes, certainly. We believed that. There was going to be, even in our own times, an end to this business of one was Russian or Tartar or Pole and so forth. That communism would replace all those tribal loyalties. But has that happened anywhere — even in the Soviet Union? Not so far as I see. Just the opposite. It's not so simple — not now, not sixty years ago. Besides, I'm no Christian. Not even when I was a boy and had to go to church. If somebody slaps me on one cheek I'm going to slap him even harder on his cheek, if I can."

"That's no answer."

"Ho, ho. Don't come to me for answers. Like your mother said, as you put it in that book, 'We knew a lot of things and most of them didn't turn out like we expected.'"

No! That's not it! That's not the way our conversations went, now that I see what I've written. It's too compressed. It lacks the asides and the allusions of the spoken word. I still can't get a handle on them it seems.

Over the years Makar had developed a cheerful pessimism which cloaked a tolerance of human failings and weaknesses. This was mixed with an unapologetic, self-satirical gusto which sustained him. I can't think of many people whose accounts were as sagacious. Maybe it was in the telling. Possibly it stemmed from Makar's unflinching honesty and an outlook that didn't bow to respectability or the fashions of the day, not even to those of the contemporary left.

Part of what made that particular class culture so powerful was its sense of continuity with the past. Historical consciousness is considered more of a burden than a source of strength by most North Americans. People talk about events of a generation and less ago as if they happened in some never-never land, as something unrelated to themselves or the present. They are proud about "not looking back".

But to Makar the lives and struggles of people a century or two before were quite alive. He could hear the voices of Pugachev's peasant levies as others once heard the indictments of survivors of the Thirty Years War. It may be that some sections of the European working class has retained that quality, though I doubt it. It is quite an inheritance. It links the living and the dead in a kinship of mutual obligation and support which can be stronger than allegiance to any particular nation or political cause. It can survive repeated defeats and overcome isolation.

"The fight to throw down Tsarism was going on for two hundred years before the Bolsheviks finally did it," says Makar in a loose paraphrase. He might launch into an apocryphal tale of Tsar Alexander's reason for finally freeing the serfs, to the effect that there had been recurrent outbreaks of armed rebellion and two massive peasant risings over the previous century, and that serfdom must go if Tsarism was to remain. Makar would throw in a quizzical remembrance of the Decembrists, possibly with a fragment of a Pushkin poem which he had learned by word of mouth as a boy in his peasant village. Somewhere in all of this would be a whole tangle of *narodniki* and bemused but dedicated teachers and agitators of the last quarter of the nineteenth century. There would be accounts of Social Revolutionaries like Maria Spirodonova, who overlapped with his own life: what she had done and why, what had happened to her and how that had struck a responsive chord among the Russian working class and peasantry in the first decade of the twentieth century.

There might be a reminiscence of the Polish-Ukrainian writer Ivan Franko whose life touched on much of the revolutionary ferment of the generation before 1917 and who died in a small Galician town in the middle of the First World War. This might evoke a thumbnail sketch

Makar Potrebenko at home in his northeast Burnaby garden, 1987.

of one of Franko's novels which Makar had first read in the backlands of the Peace River. That led to reminiscences of a fractious immigrant homestead world in northern Alberta or events around coastal logging camps in BC during the 1940s and in the post-war years. None of the people or situations were reduced to schematics and they were all part of a larger picture. Characters from fiction, individuals from history and people Makar had known personally rubbed shoulders in this mural.

Makar, like his stories, was an amalgam of *narodnik* anarchist, internationalist, Russian nationalist and working-class anti-authoritarian. His children would vehemently deny the latter. He himself knew the contradictions involved in all of this.

There is so much more to be said, but Makar wouldn't want that all dredged up again. I wanted to write his life history but he wouldn't have it. "When I leave this earth I don't want to leave any trace of my life on it behind." But he did anyway.

Makar was part of a generation in which the best and the most daring believed that the world would, finally, rise on new foundations, and that they were going to be a part of helping it to happen. It wasn't only they themselves but all those generations standing behind them who were going to witness a world where, for the first time in human history, there would be justice. That vision transformed people, sometimes only briefly but other times so that they transcended the boundaries of normal possibilities.

Makar had mellowed and had modified his expectations and outlook over the years. Yes, there had been far too much bloodshed entailed in throwing off the yoke and much which was plainly antithetical to the hope for human liberation had been reinstituted. Yes, the forces of oppression seemed to have a Lazarus-like ability to resurrect themselves both in old and in new forms. No, a classless society had not emerged anywhere and it seemed that we were further than ever away from that end. But that vision could still strike fire, even in old age.

Future chroniclers may look upon those who came of age during the last quarter of the nineteenth to the first third of the twentieth centuries as witnesses to an extraordinary millennial period in human history, one which only emerges once every few centuries. We won't meet their kind again in our lifetimes.